Forged in Battle?

Life in South Africa's 32 Battalion, 1975–1993

Will Gordon

Helion & Company

Helion & Company Limited
Unit 8 Amherst Business Centre
Budbrooke Road
Warwick
CV34 5WE
England
Tel. 01926 499619
Email: info@helion.co.uk
Website: www.helion.co.uk
X (formerly Twitter): @Helionbooks
Facebook: @HelionBooks
Visit our blog at helionbooks.wordpress.com

Published by Helion & Company 2025
Designed and typeset by Mach 3 Solutions Ltd (www.mach3solutions.co.uk)
Cover designed by Paul Hewitt, Battlefield Design (www.battlefield-design.co.uk)

ISBN 978-1-804516-67-6

British Library Cataloguing-in-Publication Data.

A catalogue record for this book is available from the British Library.

For details of other military history titles published by Helion & Company Limited, contact the above address, or visit our website: http://www.helion.co.uk

We always welcome receiving book proposals from prospective authors.

To Sonia, Louis and Cupe Habig, who always believed in me

Contents

List of tables and maps

Maps

Tables

List of Abbreviations

AA	Anti-aircraft
ACP	Angolan Communist Party (*Partido Comunista Angolano*)
ANC	African National Congress
AWOL	Absent Without Leave
AZT	Azidothymidine
BC	Black Consciousness
Bn	Battalion
BP	Bophuthatswana Police
CDF	Ciskei Defence Force
CIA	Central Intelligence Agency
COIN	Counterinsurgency
ComOps	Communication Operations
Codesa	Convention for a Democratic South Africa
DODDC	Department of Defence Documentation Centre
DRC	Dutch Reformed Church
ECC	End Conscription Campaign
ELNA	Army for the National Liberation of Angola (*Exército de Libertação Nacional de Angola*)
FALA	Armed Forces of the Liberation of Angola (*Forças Armadas de Libertação de Angola*)
FAPLA	People's Armed Forces of Liberation of Angola (*Forças Armadas Populares de Libertação de Angola*)
FES	Field Engineer Squadron
FNLA	National Front for the Liberation of Angola (*Frente Nacional de Libertação de Angola*)
FRELIMO	Front for the Liberation of Mozambique (*Frente de Libertação de Moçambique*)
GDP	Gross Domestic Product
GOC	General Officer Commanding
HQ	Headquarters
MA	Military Area

MFA	Movement of the Armed Forces [Portuguese] (*Movimento das Forças Armadas*)
MG	*Militêre Gebied* (Military Area)
MID	Military Intelligence Division
MO	Medical Officer
MOAU	Memorandum of Agreement and Understanding
MPLA	Popular Movement for the Liberation of Angola (*Movimento Popular de Libertação de Angola*)
NATO	North Atlantic Treaty Organisation
NCO	Non-Commissioned Officer
NGK	*Nederduitse Gereformeerde Kerk* (Dutch Reformed Church)
NP	National Party
NSM	National Serviceman / National Servicemen
NUSAS	National Union of South African Students
OC	Officer Commanding
PAC	Pan-Africanist Congress
PAIA	Promotion of Access to Information Act [Act 2 of 2000]
PAIGC	African Party for the Independence of Guinea and Cape Verde (*Partido Africano da Independência da Guiné e Cabo Verde)*
PF	Permanent Force
PCP	Portuguese Communist Party (*Partido Comunista Português*)
PLAN	People's Liberation Army of Namibia
PLUA	Party for the United Struggle of the Angolan Africans (*Partido da Luta Unida dos Africanos de Angola*)
RPG	Rocket-propelled Grenade
RSM	Regimental Sergeant Major
SAAF	South African Air Force
SAAO	South African Army Order
SADF	South African Defence Force
SADFI	South African Defence Force Institute
SAI	South Africa Infantry Battalion
SAMC	South African Medical Corps
SAMS	South African Medical Service
SAP	South African Police
SAW	*Suid-Afrikaanse Weermag* (South African Defence Force)
SMG	Submachinegun
SO1	Staff Officer, 1st Class
SSO	Senior Staff Officer
STD	Sexually Transmitted Disease
SWA	South West Africa
SWAPO	South West Africa People's Organisation
SWATF	South West Africa Territorial Force
TB	Tuberculosis / Temporary Base

TDF	Transkei Defence Force
TEIN	*Teeninsurgensie* (Counterinsurgency)
TF	Task Force
UDF	Union Defence Force / United Democratic Front
UNIP	United National Independence Party [Zambia]
UNISA	University of South Africa
UNITA	National Union for the Total Independence of Angola (*União Nacional para a Independência Total de Angola*)
UPA	Union of the Peoples of Angola (*União das Populacoes de Angola*)
UPNA	Union of the Peoples of North Angola (*União das Populacoes do Norte de Angola*)
VD	Venereal Disease
VIB	Volkskas Insurance Brokers
WP	Warsaw Pact
ZANU-PF	Zimbabwe African National Union – Patriotic Front

Ammo	Ammunition
Camo	Camouflage
Recce	Reconnaissance Commando / Regiment
Recce Wing	Reconnaissance Wing
Std	Standard

AK47	7.62mm WP Assault Rifle
FN FAL	7.62mm NATO Belgian assault rifle
FN MAG	7.62mm NATO Belgian general-purpose machinegun
Galil	5.56mm NATO Israeli assault rifle
PKM	7.62mm WP General-purpose machinegun
PPSh	7.62mm WP submachinegun
R1	FN FAL, built under licence in South Africa
RPD	7.62mm WP Light machinegun
Sten	9mm British submachinegun

South African Military Ranks

Gen	General
Lt Gen	Lieutenant General
Maj Gen	Major General
Brig	Brigadier
Col	Colonel
Lt Col	Lieutenant Colonel
Cmdt	Commandant (equivalent to Lieutenant Colonel)
Maj	Major
Capt	Captain

Lt	Lieutenant
2Lt	Second Lieutenant
WO1	Warrant Officer, 1st Class
WO2	Warrant Officer, 2nd Class
SSgt	Staff Sergeant
Sgt	Sergeant
Cpl	Corporal
LCpl	Lance Corporal
Cpln	Chaplain

Acknowledgements

Forged in Battle? is based on the dissertation that I wrote for a PhD at Stellenbosch University. First and foremost, I would like to acknowledge the contribution of my PhD supervisor, Ian van der Waag, now at Rabdan Academy, who possesses a rare ability to extract the best efforts from his students. He knows intuitively when to encourage, cajole, admonish, reprimand, compliment, sympathise, advise or critique. The book is much richer because of his comments and suggestions, and his guidance played a central role in the research process.

The dissertation was completed in the History Department of the Faculty of Arts and Social Sciences at Stellenbosch University. Albert Grundlingh, Sandra Swart, Anton Ehlers and Leschelle Morkel, all from this department, deserve acknowledgement for providing financial and administrative assistance throughout the research project. Carol Kat and Gert van Deventer, of Stellenbosch University's Copyright and Trade Marks Department, assisted with permission to publish the dissertation.

The examiners of the original dissertation made several suggestions that ultimately enriched the book. A particular word of thanks in this regard to André Wessels and Fankie Monama, for constructive, unbiased and fair critique.

Many of the following acknowledgements stem from the research and work for the original dissertation. I could not have completed the dissertation, or the book in its current form, without the invaluable aid of several people who deserve not only acknowledgement, but also my sincere thanks:

For a first time author, the advice, guidance and encouragement of Duncan Rogers, owner and Managing Director at Helion & Co., made for a streamlined publication process. A word of thanks, too, to Antonio Garcia for putting us in touch and encouraging me to pursue the publication of *Forged in Battle?* Antonio's advice was always sound and his support meant much.

Many friends, colleagues and relatives deserve a mention for their support over the past few years. Their contributions have covered the range of moral, financial, academic and physical support. William and Glenda Gordon (sadly, neither saw the completion of the book), Johan von Willich, Gys Loubser, Jana Hattingh, Marit Kleynhans, Carel Kriek, Hannes and Tanya Verhoef, Liz Vincent, Dave Humphris, Tara Lyle, Jeremy and Carien Punt, Gerhardt and Stienie van Greuning, Sas and Helena Otto and Lennart Bolliger all contributed in one way or another.

The staff at the South African Department of Defence Documentation Centre was always friendly and eager to help. The former director, Louise Jooste, was unstinting in providing a wealth of knowledge to help guide my research in the right direction. WO1 Riaan Blaauw processed my applications for access to classified documents through the Promotion of Access to Information Act expeditiously and also gave sound advice on which documents to list on the application, and which to ignore. Steve de Agrela and Gerald Prinsloo will, I think, be relieved by the decrease in 32 Battalion-related enquiries coming their way. Evert Kleynhans, now at Stellenbosch University, was instrumental in facilitating quick and efficient access to vital documents. He also helped to draw the maps used in the book. We had a lot of fun and became firm friends through our research.

The influence of librarians and archivists is often underestimated. Gabriele Mohale at the Historical Papers archive, Ashley Rode at the Dag Hammarskjöld Library, Reinet Faasen at Stellenbosch University's JS Gericke Library, Mary-Lynn Suttie at the University of South Africa's Library and Anna Clarke at *The Guardian* newspaper were all very helpful in facilitating research at their respective institutions.

The men and women associated with 32 Battalion who agreed to be interviewed – nameless here for evermore, in the words of Edgar Allan Poe – made this book richer and deeper through their contributions.

Finally, I would like to thank my wife, Christien, for her unhesitating and unstinting support. *Forged in Battle?* was researched, written and published over the course of several years. Christien never lost faith in the project (even when I occasionally did), never complained about setbacks or late nights and was always ready to celebrate milestones, big and small. Thank you, my Dear.

Preface

Forged in Battle started as research towards a PhD at Stellenbosch University, which was successfully completed in 2019. As such, Stellenbosch University owns the copyright of the original dissertation. The university, as well as the History Department and my PhD supervisor, have kindly given permission for this, a slightly revised and reworked version, to be published by Helion & Co. Their contributions are indicated in the acknowledgements. It should also be noted that sections of the original dissertation have previously been published as academic works in various forms. While the publications differ from the dissertation, which differs from this book, readers who follow Border War literature closely may notice some overlap.

Since the research in *Forged in Battle* is underpinned by archival sources from the South African Department of Defence Documentation Centre (DODDC), a brief discussion of the archive is necessary to understand the value and limitations of the book. Records in the DODDC generally fall into two distinct categories – classified and declassified material. All records in the DODDC relating to military operations and administrative matters, created up to and including 31 December 1969, are deemed open and declassified, and are thus automatically available to researchers. This includes all archives related to the establishment of the Union Defence Force (UDF), both world wars, and the Korean War. A further exception is made for all correspondence files classified as restricted, which were created up to and including 31 December 1975. All archival documents falling outside these periods, regardless of their original security classification, are thus classified and, in theory, inaccessible.

Only the first four, largely uneventful, years of the Border War fall into the declassified period. The remainder is covered by three laws governing access to classified documentation. It does not take a great legal mind to deduce that there is bound to be a certain degree of discrepancy in such a case. The first and, theoretically, foremost is the Constitution of the Republic of South Africa, 1996. According to Section 32, 'Everyone had the right of access to … any information held by the state…' The Department of Defence Act (Act 42 of 2002) cautions that, subject to the Promotion of Access to Information Act (PAIA), no document may be made available to the public before a period of 20 years has elapsed since its creation. However, PAIA (Act 2 of 2000) states that, inter alia, 'The information officer of a public body may refuse a request for access to a record of the body if its disclosure … could reasonably be expected to cause prejudice to … the defence of the Republic; the security of the Republic; or … the international relations of the Republic…' or would reveal potentially embarrassing information about agreements between the state and other parties. Additional provisions are made to deny access to documents that would provide information of weapons, tactics, equipment or the organisation of the South African National Defence Force.

This legal quagmire complicates researchers' access to information immensely, and a fairly complicated, and very time-consuming, process has to be followed to gain access to documents about the Border War and other post–1970 topics. Anyone wishing to research these topics has to apply for access to such identified archival documents through the Promotion of Access to Information Act. The traditional weapon in the armoury of the historian – the systematic trawling of archives – is thereby negated and the methodology of post–1970 historical research differs significantly from commonly accepted practices. Archival finding aids, the only access route to classified information in the DODDC, offer only the briefest descriptions of the content of files, and researchers need almost esoteric intuition to identify documents that are even remotely relevant to their research. Additionally, the process can take several months to complete. There is also no single complete list of all previously declassified material at the DODDC, and very little indication of the language in which a document is written. Researchers could thus potentially apply for a document to be declassified, when such a document is already deemed open, as there are no appropriate measures in place to indicate whether a document is declassified or not. A researcher is thus left at the complete mercy of the reading room staff, who may or may not draw the relevant boxes to check whether a document is declassified or not. Additionally, researchers face the prospect of applying for the declassification of a document, paying the declassification fee, waiting however long the process might take, only to find that the document in question contains no relevant information at all.[1]

Two aspects of researching post–1970 military topics at the DODDC are particularly relevant to this, and any other archival-based, study. Firstly, and perhaps most significantly, it is virtually impossible to follow up on 'leads' uncovered during the research process, as this would not only entail a subsequent PAIA application, but would carry no guarantee of success. While pre-1970 topics can be approached with the mind-set that, if enough time and effort is spent at the DODDC, the necessary information will be found, this is simply not the case for post-1970 topics. The second aspect is that any research into the post-1970 era will, necessarily, be incomplete. No researcher can claim that he / she accessed all of the relevant documents on any topic during that time period.[2] Even the most exhaustive dissection of the finding aids will still leave certain documents undiscovered and, therefore, classified. Anyone with experience of archival

1 E. Kleynhans & W. Gordon, 'Legislative disconnect or institutional gatekeeping? The DOD archive, classified military information, and contemporary military historical research in South Africa' in *Scientia Militaria, Vol. 48 (1)*, 2020.

2 Cf. L. Scholtz, *The SADF and Cuito Cuanavale: A tactical and strategic analysis*. Johannesburg: Delta, 2020, p.224.

research will be aware that information is sometimes found in the most unexpected places; this is much less likely to happen when conducting research using classified documents. *Forged in Battle?* therefore does not claim to be the final word on 32 Battalion; it cannot. However, with access to around 15,000 newly declassified documents (a small percentage of which proved useful; cf. explanation above), it makes the best possible use of documents currently declassified, but it is perfectly possible that future projects, with their own access to newly declassified material, could provide additional insights.

Most documents about the Border War at the DODDC are in Afrikaans, which was something of a *lingua franca* of apartheid South Africa. All translations from Afrikaans to English – from primary and secondary sources – were done by the author, keeping as close to the tone, meaning and vocabulary as possible while maintaining a level of intelligibility. The original Afrikaans text, where applicable, is provided in the footnotes, at the end of the reference. Stellenbosch University's policies and procedures were followed regarding ethical clearance for, and issues surrounding, interviews. All photographs in *Forged in Battle?* are from the DODDC.

Introduction

From 1966 to 1989, during the so-called 'Border War', security forces of South Africa were engaged in a low intensity war against the People's Liberation Army of Namibia (PLAN)[1] as well as the People's Armed Forces for the Liberation of Angola (FAPLA), who was providing support and secure bases of operation to the South West Africa People's Organisation (SWAPO).[2] This conflict formed part of the South African government's policy of a Total National Strategy[3] to combat the perceived 'multi-dimensional threat'[4] to South Africa by liberation movements in other parts of southern Africa. A large part of the actual fighting during the war was done by what eventually became known as 32 Battalion of the South African Army. This Battalion was made up, initially, of a white South African officer corps with black troops and non-commissioned officers (NCOs); during the latter part of the war, some of the black NCOs were also commissioned. Most of these troops were Angolan or Namibian – due to the way in which national borders were drawn up by colonial powers, the same ethnic group might live in two different countries – who were already engaged in fighting FAPLA as part of the National Front for the Liberation of Angola (FNLA), even though some of them had been trained in the USSR when their leader, Daniel Chipenda, was still with the Popular Movement for the Liberation of Angola (MPLA).[5] Since the unit operated far more in the Owamboland region of South West Africa and Angola than any other area, it should be noted that the majority of the inhabitants of Owamboland were sympathetic to SWAPO.[6]

1 PLAN was the military wing of the SWAPO. However, in most sources SWAPO and PLAN are used interchangeably when referring to PLAN, as are FAPLA and MPLA.
2 S. Nujoma, as quoted by V. Shubin, *The Hot 'Cold War': The USSR in Southern Africa*. London: Pluto, 2008, pp.201-202.
3 J. R. Dutton, 'The military aspects of national security' in M. H. H. Louw (ed.), *National Security: A Modern Approach*. Pretoria: Institue for Strategic Studies, 1978, pp.104–106.
4 C. Alden, *Apartheid's Last Stand: The Rise and Fall of the South African Security State*. London: MacMillan, 1999, p.68.
5 Shubin, *The hot 'Cold War'*, p.278.
6 P. Stiff, *The Covert War: Koevoet Operations in Namibia 1979–1989*. Alberton: Galago, 2004, p.16.

Although the clash between forces of the South African Police (SAP) and the PLAN at Ongulumbashe on 26 August 1966 is generally accepted as the commencement of the Border War, the period between 1966 and 1975 saw few other engagements between security forces from South Africa and those forces that were to become their adversaries during and after the Angolan independence process. Leopold Scholtz identifies only four other events, two in the Caprivi and two in Angola (although he alludes to at least two more), between Ongulumbashe in 1966 and the start of Operation Savannah in October 1975: In the Caprivi, two groups of SWAPO insurgents attempted an infiltration in 1968 – all the participants were either killed, captured or fled to Zambia – and a larger infiltration in June 1974, where all but six of the insurgents were killed by the SAP.[7] In addition, elements of the SADF were involved in a clandestine operation against SWAPO in southern Angola during May and June 1974 – during which the SADF suffered its first casualty of the war – and there was Operation Sausage in August and September 1975, a series of cross-border operations north of Owamboland and the Caprivi. Twenty-six SWAPO and MPLA soldiers were killed during Operation Sausage.[8] FJ du Toit Spies describes what are, judging by their dates, probably the two engagements alluded to by Scholtz: on 27 March 1973 a SAP base at Singalamwe in the eastern Caprivi was attacked by SWAPO, wounding seven policemen, and 'a month later' five black South African policemen were killed in a SWAPO ambush in the Caprivi.[9] SWAPO also claims to have killed 37 of a 39 man patrol in April 1973.[10]

In establishing the parameters of the forge from which 32 Battalion emerged, this book considers the relative sparsity of military activity on the part of South African Defence Force leading up to 1975, as well as the significant Cold War developments during the same time, indicative of the premise that the Border War only started in earnest in 1975 and examines the global political climate up to this date and lays the philosophical and theoretical framework of the remainder of the book.

32 Battalion was engaged almost continuously in the war and for its entire duration, as indeed the Roll of Honour attests. No other unit in the South African Army had as many contacts, 'kills' or casualties. Since success in guerrilla and counterinsurgency war cannot be measured by means of territory captured from the enemy, it had become customary since the Vietnam War to measure success in these types of conflicts by way of body counts and kill-ratios.[11] While this may seem unnecessarily cruel and inhumane, it was (and, to a certain extent, still is) used as a measure in counterinsurgency operations. With this in mind, it can reasonably be argued that, once the soldiers of 32

7 L. Scholtz, *Die SAW in die Grensoorlog: 1966–1989*. Cape Town: Tafelberg, 2013, p.11.
8 Scholtz, *Die SAW in die Grensoorlog*, p.14.
9 F. J. du T. Spies, *Die Angolese Burgeroorlog*. Pretoria: Militêre Informasieburo, 1980, p.202. Afrikaans: *'n maand later*.
10 G. Arnold, *Wars in the Third World since 1945*. London: Cassell Publishers Ltd., 1991, p.48.
11 Cf. G. Parker (ed.), *Cambridge Illustrated History: Warfare*. Cambridge: Cambridge University Press, 1995, p.353; the SADF seems to have had higher regard for these factors than for the prevalent consideration in Vietnam, 'battalion days in action'.

Battalion changed their allegiances from whatever these may have been previously to the Battalion itself, they became not only the workhorses of the South African Army (to which the majority of troops had no obligations as South African citizens may have been deemed to have had), but also one of its major successes. Of course, this did not come as a complete surprise. The battalion's first commander, Colonel Jan Breytenbach, recognised from the outset that the troops he had under his command had nowhere else to turn and nowhere to return to. He states that

> My Angolan troops and their families had lost their country ... there was nothing left to fight over, except for primitive survival in the face of a cruel destiny that had turned its back on my FNLA troops...[12]

Breytenbach therefore cultivated a battalion along the lines of the French Foreign Legion's motto of *Legio Patria Nostra*[13] (the Legion is our country) and actively encouraged the troops, the NCOs and the officers of the Battalion to place loyalty to the unit above almost everything else. The troops, as mentioned, did not have much choice in the matter, but, by including the white officers in this strategy, Breytenbach started a culture, which was to remain a key part of the unit, where '...the men and women, black and white, officers, NCOs and riflemen, had only this one overriding loyalty [to the unit] ingrained in their very psyches.'[14]

A significant difference between 32 Battalion and the conventional battalions of the South African Defence Force (SADF) is the fact that the majority of the members of 32 Battalion did not report for duty by themselves, but they arrived with their entire families in tow.[15] The most significant reason for this is that the majority of the troops of 32 Battalion were either ex-FNLA troops or refugees from Angola. This necessarily meant that it was impossible for them to leave their families behind (effectively in enemy territory) while they waged South Africa's war. As a result, in time, a base was established for the families of the soldiers, near the base of the unit itself.

This brought a greater deal of social interaction between members of the unit and their families, and also between the SADF (in the form of various commanding officers, officers and senior NCOs of the unit) and the families of the soldiers. For example, national servicemen were posted to staff the school that was set up in Kimbo (the area where relatives and off duty soldiers lived) and national service medical staff was sent to assist with the medical welfare of the families.[16]

12 J. Breytenbach, *The Tempered Sword: Forged in Battle Revisited; Operation Savannah and the birth of 32 Bn*. Bushwarrior.com, 2011, pp.279–280.
13 Breytenbach, *The Tempered Sword*, p.282.
14 Breytenbach, *The Tempered Sword*, p.289.
15 J. Breytenbach, *The Buffalo Soldiers: The Story of South Africa's 32-Battalion 1975–1993*. Alberton: Galago, 2002, p.130.
16 P. Nortje, *32 Battalion: The inside story of South Africa's elite fighting unit*. Cape Town: Zebra, 2003, p.186.

In 1989, with the end of the Border War, 32 Battalion was moved from bases in South West Africa and Angola and was re-established at Pomfret in the North West province of South Africa.[17] They went there willingly, with the assurance from several high-ranking military officers and politicians that they need not worry about their post-war future.[18] The soldiers of 32 Battalion became South African citizens in due course, to legalise their presence in Pomfret.

In 1993, however, the unit was disbanded. This put virtually all of the soldiers of the unit and their families (John Daniel puts this figure as high as 9,000 troops,[19] although this figure is almost certainly incorrect and is not the only uncorroborated, exaggerated statement in his article) many thousands of miles from their original homeland, in a country foreign to them in climate and language (many only spoke Portuguese) with little or no chance of making a successful living in the harsh conditions of Pomfret, which is an abandoned asbestos mine with little done to make it safe for habitation.[20] It has to be kept in mind that these soldiers had given their absolute allegiance to the unit; for them, this situation was akin to losing their country, their military and political leaders and livelihood all at once.

The situation illustrated is not unique to the South African armed forces. The American Special Forces also have a history of training and utilising local populations in conflicts outside the borders of the USA (notably in Vietnam[21] and, more recently, in Iraq and Afghanistan) as does the British Special Air Service. In most cases, however, these local forces can be seen as true partisan forces, since they engage purely in unconventional warfare in the areas where they are located at the time (i.e. their homelands). This was not strictly true for 32 Battalion, as by the end of the war, they were a mechanised, conventional force complete with artillery, armoured personnel carriers and an air support capability. They were, in effect, rather a surrogate force, although all of the soldiers of the unit drew SADF pay and benefits. Furthermore, 32 Battalion was never used in situ, that is as a force operating clandestinely from their hometowns or villages. However, significant parallels can still be seen between 32 Battalion and partisan and other surrogate armies. An even closer parallel could perhaps be found in Germany's use of African troops, or *askaris*, in German East Africa during the First World War.[22] Myron Echenberg also reveals parallels between the Senegalese Rifles (*Tirailleurs Senegalais*) and 32 Battalion, not least the racially hierarchical command structure of

17 Breytenbach, *The Buffalo Soldiers*, p.327.
18 Breytenbach, *The Buffalo Soldiers*, p.328.
19 J. Daniel, 'Racism, the Cold War and South Africa's regional security strategies 1948–1990' in S. Onslow (ed.), *Cold War in Southern Africa: white power, black liberation*. London: Routledge, 2009, p.43.
20 Breytenbach, *The Buffalo Soldiers*, p.327.
21 J. Breytenbach, *They Live by the Sword*. Alberton: Lemur, 1990, p.12.
22 Cf. M. R. Moyd, *Violent Intermediaries: African Soldiers, Conquest, and Everyday Colonialism in German East Africa*. Athens, Ohio: University Press, 2014.

both units.[23] Additionally, although the Senegalese Rifles did so for a much longer period, and in multiple conflicts, both units also fought to promote and protect the interests of a country to which they did not owe any allegiance: France in the case of the Senegalese Rifles and apartheid South Africa in the case of 32 Battalion.

The fact that the history of 32 Battalion exhibits these parallels with other unconventional forces, coupled with the unique social dynamic of the unit, makes it an ideal case to study when evaluating the effectiveness of surrogate forces, relative to the social impact on these forces. For this reason, this historical study of 32 Battalion will reflect not only on the military successes and failures of the unit, but on the social aspects involved in waging a continuous war for 14 years. Furthermore, because of the many similarities that exist between 32 Battalion and surrogate armies elsewhere in the world, the value of a study of the history of 32 Battalion extends beyond southern African boundaries. It is therefore hoped that this book will aid in the understanding of the complexity of the use of surrogate forces, making it clear that the decision to use such forces extends beyond the scope of military operations and considerations. It is hoped that this book will contribute meaningfully to the existing literature on such military matters.

Terminology

Three terms that are used frequently throughout this book require some clarification. The first relates to the conflict that took place from 1966 to 1989, between South African security forces and armed forces from Namibia, Angola, Cuba and South African liberation groups, popularly known as the 'Border War'. Gary Baines correctly advocates problemitising the term, and identifies 'Bush War', 'Apartheid Wars', 'Thirty Years' War' and 'National Liberation Struggle' as possible alternatives, though he, again correctly, explains that each of these are just as problematic as 'Border War.'[24] In *Forged in Battle?* the term is not used in a political context, as the – quite deliberate – aim is to focus on the plight of the men, women and children of 32 Battalion, rather than to highlight the achievements of a particular participant in the war. For this reason, and because the conflict has to be referred to in some way, the term Border War is used, without Baines's scare quotes. The reader has to be cognisant, however, that the term is problematic, and the author recognises that different terms might be equally legitimate.

Secondly, the nature of a study of a unit like 32 Battalion dictates that racial identification – as opposed to categorisation or, even worse, stereotyping – will be necessary. There is simply no other way to refer to, e.g., white officers, black NCOs or Portuguese soldiers. As with the choice of the term Border War, politics does not play a role in the

23 M. Echenberg, *Colonial Conscripts: The 'Tirailleurs Senegalais' in French West Africa, 1857–1960*. Portsmouth, New Hampshire: Heinemann, 1991.

24 G. Baines, *South Africa's 'Border War': Contested narratives and conflicting memories*. London: Bloomsbury, 2014, pp.1–3.

identification of different racial groups. Referring to black soldiers does not, in any way, imply a form of categorisation of hierarchy; it merely identifies the group of people that are discussed. The terms black, white, and so on, are used – non-politically – throughout the book. The term 'non-white' is used only where it would be inaccurate to use the word 'black', or where it is necessitated by a direct translation.

Finally, based on the same reasoning as in the first two cases, the country between South Africa and Angola is referred to as 'Namibia' throughout the book. Through the course of the Border War, the name changed from South West Africa (SWA) to SWA/ Namibia and finally to Namibia. While it is, of course, possible to use these terms in their historical context, it makes for a decidedly clumsy sentence when two, or even three, different names are used to refer to the same geographic location. Again, the choice of name does not indicate a particular political choice, but is rather an attempt to streamline the narrative.

Approach

For much of the nineteenth and twentieth centuries, before common access to the Internet and the attendant rise of social media and instant access to news from around the globe, military historiography followed a fairly set pattern. Journalists would be the first to write about conflicts, but their accounts would not necessarily reflect the image that military and political powers wanted to project. Therefore, journalism would soon be followed by official histories, commissioned by the relevant authorities, that reflected a more politically acceptable stance. This stance, however, would invariably not be acceptable to all the units involved in the conflict, and unit histories, or regimental histories, would soon follow, highlighting the role of particular units in combat. In a trickle-down process, where units may feel slighted in official histories, leading to the writing of their own accounts, the fourth wave of historiography stems from individuals feeling left out of unit histories, and publishing their own accounts, or memoirs. The final phase of military historiography is then written, largely by academics, 'after-the-fact', drawing on the first four variants and, hopefully, combining this with archival material. These authors will, however, 'have to contend with those who argue that lack of personal experience is a disqualification per se.'[25] Existing literature on 32 Battalion fall into the first four broad categories: Journalism,[26] official histories,[27] regimental histories, [28] and a plethora of personal recollections and memoirs.[29] The first three categories, and academic works

25 R. Holmes, *Acts of War: The behaviour of men in battle.* New York: Free Press, 1985, pp.8–9.

26 Cf. W. L. Steenkamp, *South Africa's Border War, 1966–1989.* Gibraltar: Ashanti, 1989.

27 Cf. F. J. du T. Spies, *Operasie Savannah: Angola 1975–1989.* Pretoria: SADF, 1989; S du Preez, *Avontuur in Angola.* Pretoria: Van Schaik, 1989.

28 Cf. P. Nortje, *The Terrible Ones: A complete history of 32 Battalion.* Cape Town: Zebra, 2012.

29 Cf. L. J. Bothma, *Die Buffel Struikel: 'n Storie van 32 Bataljon en sy mense.* Bloemfontein: LJ Bothma, 2007; M. Scheepers, *Striking Inside Angola with 32 Battalion.* Solihull: Helion and

that have been produced, however, invariably deal with the Border War as a whole – or even broader topics – and individual units receive scant attention.[30] Literature that focusses specifically on 32 Battalion is largely written as memoirs, necessitating a critical study of these sources to increase their academic usefulness. Such works have proliferated throughout the last decade or so. A large number of books, mostly autobiographical or quasi-autobiographical in nature, have been written by various personnel that served within 32 Battalion, including Jan Breytenbach, Louis Bothma, Piet Nortje, and other members of the South African Defence Force.[31] James Ngculu, Oswin Namakalu, and Vladimir Shubin, inter alia, offer something of a view 'from the other side'.[32]

Despite this proliferation, the fifth category of military historiography, 'after-the-fact', academic studies, has been limited, particularly in the case of 32 Battalion. This absence can further be subdivided into three voids in current literature on the SADF's involvement in Namibia and Angola, again in particular relating to 32 Battalion. The first is the fact that few or none of the existing works have been written from an academic point of view that attempts to incorporate as many sources from as many different angles as possible. Even though many of the current studies on 32 Battalion make use of academic scaffolding (such as footnotes and some form of referencing), an apologetic undertone is still unmistakable. With the exception of the examples illustrated above, this is also largely true for studies of the greater conflict in which 32 Battalion took part, the Border War.[33] As Arthur Marwick cautions, 'as citizens we are entitled to our own deeply held political and religious beliefs, but such beliefs have no place in … the pursuit of knowledge.'[34] Memoirs, as many of the existing books can be viewed, are necessarily personal and tend to focus on beliefs and experiences. Additionally, the issue of how war affects the social fabric of surrogate forces and their opponents are neglected in favour

Pinetown: 30° South, 2012; J. Taylor, *A Whisper in the Reeds: 'The Terrible Ones': South Africa's 32 Battalion at war.* Solihull: Helion & Rugby: GG Books, 2013; N. van der Walt, *Bos toe!: 'n Storie oor die laaste fase van die Grensoorlog soos beleef deur 'n junior offisier van 32-Bataljon.* Swartkops: N. van der Walt, 2007.

30 Cf. Scholtz, *Die SAW in die Grensoorlog*; I. van der Waag, *A military history of modern South Africa.* Cape Town: Jonathan Ball, 2015; I. Liebenberg, J. Risquet & V. Shubin (eds), *A Far-Away War: Angola 1975–1989.* Stellenbosch: SUN MeDIA, 2015.

31 Cf. M. A. de M. Malan, *My Life With the SA Defence Force.* Pretoria: Protea, 2006; J. Geldenhuys, *A General's Story: From an era of war and peace.* Johannesburg: Jonathan Ball, 1995; F. W. de Klerk, *The Last Trek – a new beginning: The Autobiography.* London: MacMillan, 1999.

32 J. Ngculu, *The honour to serve: Recollections of an Umkhonto soldier.* Cape Town: Philip, 2009; O.O. Namakalu, *Armed Liberation Struggle:* Shubin, *The Hot 'Cold War'.*

33 Cf. A. Feinstein, *Battle Scarred: Hidden costs of the Border War.* Cape Town: Tafelberg, 2011; C. Blake, *From soldier to civvy: Reflections on National Service.* Cape Town: Zebra, 2010; J. H. Thompson, *An Unpopular War: From Afkak to Bosbefok: Voices of South African National Servicemen.* Cape Town: Zebra, 2006.

34 A. Marwick, *The New Nature of History: Knowledge, Evidence, Language.* Basingstoke: Palgrave, 2001, p.267.

of examining their military value. A greater understanding of this nature could lead to greater sensitivity for the needs of local populations in future conflicts.

Jeremy Black, although writing about military history in Europe and the US, might just as well have been thinking about southern Africa when he wrote:

> … the mass readership of the last quarter of the twentieth century and into the 2000s was particularly interested in the experience of individuals; this led to the extensive use of oral evidence, both in books and on television. Indeed, war memoirs constitute an important part of military history publishing, overlapping with (fictional) war literature, which … helped to mould what was expected from memoirs…[35]

Black's rather bleak view of memoirs might be something of an exaggeration, but highlights a very real problem that military history, as an academic discipline, faces: due to the prevalence of non-academic works of military history, anyone with military experience can, potentially, consider themselves 'military historians'. In South Africa, which had a policy of conscription or National Service (for white men) for a significant part of the latter half of the twentieth century, this has resulted in a particularly large pool of potential 'experts', many of whom did, indeed, publish their memoirs about their military experiences. Furthermore, in a relatively young democratic South Africa, any interaction between black and white during the apartheid years almost guarantees a bestselling book. A history of 32 Battalion, then, has to surmount the combined challenge presented by these two factors. An examination of currently available literature is the logical starting point in explaining why yet another 32 Battalion history is needed.

Forged in Battle takes the form of a narrative history and adopts a qualitative approach, although some statistics, where possible, are used to make quantitative deduction. Compiling statistics from primary sources, though, was hampered by the difficulties encountered in gaining access to these documents, as explained below. The book draws heavily on previously classified documents from the South African Department of Defence Documentation Centre. Amid the myriad of personal accounts that have been published recently, a conscious decision was taken to emphasise the role of archival material, largely neglected in these accounts, in favour of interviews, in this book. The decision to ground the book on archival sources was informed, inter alia, by the thoughts of Paul Ricoeur[36] and Mark Woodruff.[37] The latter's view, written from a military history perspective, is particularly valuable and is characterised by contentions, accepted by this author, like 'The individual American fighting man in Vietnam had a very limited, very narrow, very personal view of the war. Even though one might expect him to have

35 J. Black, *Rethinking Military History*. London: Routledge, 2004, p.42. Parenthesis original.

36 P. Ricoeur, *Memory, History, Forgetting*, translated by K. Blamey & D. Pellauer, Chicago: University Press, 2004.

37 M. W. Woodruff, *Unheralded Victory: The defeat of the Viet Cong and the North Vietnamese Army 1961–1973*. Arlington: Vandamere, 1999.

the most accurate view of the war, in fact, his view was often flawed by this limited perspective.'[38] He also quoted Joseph Galloway as saying that he '... often finds individuals who were actual combat soldiers themselves 'retelling latrine rumours about actions they never saw as if they were the gospel truth.''[39]

Woodruff's contentions clearly indicate the problems inherent to relying on oral recollections. The archival foundations of this book are, therefore, vital to underpin the memoirist accounts that flood the market. In light of the philosophical approach to the book, then, few interviews were conducted to gain yet more personal recollections. That is not to say that interviews and oral recollections do not have value in themselves, but rather that they require a different approach and philosophy. Tim Keegan indicates how oral history can contribute to historiography, particularly for a book such as this, while also emphasising the need for a thorough archival base:

> ... we should not lose sight of the human individuals whose communal history we are trying to document. The richness and variety of the past should not be reduced to abstraction, for then it loses its human dimensions... But it is also true that rarely can oral testimony stand by itself as a source of evidence on the past, and it has to serve as a supplement to other, more formal, written sources of evidence...[40]

That said, historiography should not, indeed cannot, be exclusive and, for this reason, interviews were sought and are used in this book. Participants were given the option of remaining anonymous. Since the overwhelming majority chose to accept this offer, the decision was taken to treat all interviews as anonymous and to assign pseudonyms to interviewees. This served to assuage the fear of exposure that most respondents had, and it encouraged participants to have more freedom in their responses and expressions. The fact that they could remain anonymous was also a deciding factor in many interviewees' decision to share the contact information of their former comrades-in-arms. This snowballing effect was useful in gaining access to more interviewees, deepening the contribution of the interviews. All the interviewees were either soldiers in 32 Battalion, or civilians associated with the unit. In some cases, they were children of former soldiers. The interviewees' link to 32 Battalion is indicated in the relevant footnote.

While interviews were conducted, something of a pattern emerged: the former soldiers were much more comfortable, articulate and eager to share their recollections about fighting than about day-to-day life. Dependents, who did not take part in combat, shared their recollections about life in 32 Battalion, but were less knowledgeable about the military structure of the unit and how that influenced socio-military interaction.

38 Woodruff, *Unheralded Victory*, p.249.
39 Woodruff, *Unheralded Victory*, p.255.
40 T. J. Keegan, *Facing the Storm: Portraits of Black Lives in Rural South Africa*. Cape Town: Philip, 1988, pp.160–161.

The result is that interviews were used more frequently in the chapters about combat and social aspects, since this is what interviewees were most comfortable talking about.

In addition to personal and telephonic interviews, a collection of interviews, housed in the Historical Papers Archive, at the University of the Witwatersrand, in their Missing Voices Oral History Project, was consulted. Some interviews are also quoted from secondary sources. The pitfalls of relying on interviews have been well documented, none more so than by Ricoeur, who distinguishes between 'memorisation' and remembering, hence the emphasis on primary sources:

> With remembering, the emphasis is placed on the return to awakened consciousness of an event recognised as having occurred before the moment when consciousness declares having experienced, perceived, learned it. The temporal mark of the before thus constitutes the distinctive feature of remembering, under the double form of simple evocation and of the recognition that concludes the process of recall. Memorisation, on the other hand, consists in the ways of learning relating to forms of knowledge, know how, capacities marked from a phenomenological point of view by a feeling of facility, ease, spontaneity, in such a way that these are fixed and remain available for activation.[41]

Accepting Ricoeur's distinction between 'remembering', an act that happens largely spontaneously, and 'memorisation', which is a deliberate attempt, using particular techniques, at ingraining knowledge with the purpose of accessing it at a later stage, researchers of the Border War have to recognise that the oral accounts that exist are, for the most part, based on 'remembering'. This, for Ricoeur, is a much less reliable source of information and knowledge. The only viable alternative to relying on personal accounts, then, is to make use of archival material, complemented by oral recollections. While historians can never attempt to reach an absolute conclusion, the symbiotic use of a strong archival base and oral-historical sources can indicate consensual trajectories, as well as encourage debate and reinterpretation, 'the responsibility of every student of history.'[42]

41 P. Ricoeur, *Memory, History, Forgetting*, p.58.
42 S. Morillo & M. F. Pavkovic, *What is Military History?* Cambridge: Polity, 2013, p.67.

1

'The Forge': Southern Africa and the Cold War

The period following the Second World War was one of turmoil in Africa and the colonised world, with many countries striving for, and achieving, independence from their erstwhile colonial masters. However, these transitions from colonial-rule to self-rule seldom went smoothly, with factions in soon-to-be independent or newly-independent states vying for control of the government. These power struggles resulted frequently in protracted armed conflicts, often with the colonial powers also in the mix, trying to cling to power or to facilitate a peaceful transition.

This process of decolonisation took place against a Cold War landscape, marked by ideological competition between North Atlantic Treaty Organisation (NATO) states and East Bloc countries for spheres of influence in newly-independent regions. This tussle between East and West made southern Africa 'one of the cauldrons of the Cold War struggle'[1], through the use of surrogate and/or proxy forces.[2] To this end, the Soviet Union supplied aid and armaments overtly to a number of African liberation movements, while the USA was more covert in her support, although this was by no means absent.[3] Odd Arne Westad summarises the situation succinctly:

> It was the Marxist orientation of many Southern African liberation movements that made both Moscow and Washington take note of their significance to the United States, they threatened radical, Soviet-orientated regimes taking power in the Third World; to the Soviet Union, they hailed the beginning of a new stage of

1 S. Onslow, 'Introduction' in S. Onslow (ed.), *Cold War in Southern Africa: white power, black liberation*. London: Routledge, 2009, p.1.

2 J. Daniel, 'Racism, the Cold War and South Africa's regional security strategies 1948–1990' in S. Onslow (ed.), *Cold War in Southern Africa: white power, black liberation*. London: Routledge, 2009, p.43.

3 V. Shubin, *The hot 'Cold War': The USSR in Southern Africa*. London: Pluto, 2008, pp.2–3. It should be noted that Shubin, as a former Soviet officer, writes from and Eastern perspective. However, as most of the documentation available in South Africa are pro-West (or at least anti-East), Shubin provides a useful counterpoint and should not be disregarded.

> Third World social development, on which African leaders acknowledge the superiority of 'scientific Marxism'.[4]

After the departure of Portugal from Africa and the ending of Portuguese rule in Angola in 1975, three factions waged what essentially amounted to a civil war, with the purpose of being the first rulers of independent Angola. These forces were the MPLA – whose military wing was known as FAPLA – the FNLA, and the National Union for the Total Liberation of Angola (UNITA). At the same time, SWAPO strove to achieve independence in what was then called South West Africa (now Namibia), which was being administered by South Africa as a 'fifth province'.[5]

Because both the MPLA and SWAPO received extensive support from the East Bloc[6] (mostly the USSR, the German Democratic Republic, Czechoslovakia, Romania, Poland, Hungary[7] and, later, Cuba) and because SWAPO was engaged in a terror campaign in South West Africa[8], the South African government decided that intervention was necessary, both to halt the perceived southwards advance of communism and to protect the peoples of South West Africa (at that time primarily the white farmers of the mandated territory). They were supported in this thinking by the USA which, keen to strike a blow at communism, was also covertly supporting the FNLA and UNITA, from as early as 1960, before the FNLA had merged with the Democratic Party of Angola and was still known as the Union of the Peoples of Angola (UPA) under the leadership of Holden Roberto.[9]

Cold War theory

Surrogate / Proxy / Mercenary Forces

Sue Onslow presents a useful distinction between the terms 'proxy' and 'surrogate' forces. In calling Cuba a *proxy* of the USSR, but at the same time strongly denying that Cuba acted as a Russian *surrogate*,[10] she illustrates that a proxy acts in the interest of the 'parent', but does not necessarily do so at the behest of that parent. In addition, a proxy does not necessarily embrace the ideologies of the parent. Onslow illustrates this by contending that the gradual decline of Soviet involvement in Africa towards the end of

4 O. A. Westad, *The global Cold War: Third World interventions and the making of our times.* Cambridge: Cambridge University Press, 2005, p.207. Quotation marks original.

5 Shubin, *The Hot 'Cold War'*, p.205.

6 W. S. van der Waals, *Portugal's war in Angola 1961–1974.* Pretoria: Protea, 2011, p.167.

7 Shubin, *The Hot 'Cold War'*, p.15.

8 As quoted by Shubin, *The hot 'Cold War'*, p.204.

9 Shubin, *The Hot 'Cold War'*, p.8.

10 S. Onslow, 'The Cold War in Southern Africa: White power, black nationalism and external intervention' in S. Onslow (ed.), *Cold War in Southern Africa: white power, black liberation.* London: Routledge, 2009, pp.25–28.

the 1980s was directly challenged by Cuban 'activism and sense of internationalist duty,' indicating not only differing political ideologies between the USSR and Cuba, but also independent Cuban action. The link between proxy and parent remains intact, though, as Onslow admits that 'the extraordinary defence of Angola in 1987–1988 would not have been possible without sustained Soviet logistical support.'[11] Following this train of thought, UNITA would have been a South African proxy, as the actions that they undertook that were advantageous to Pretoria were, invariably, primarily also in the best interest of UNITA. Indeed, authors such as Jan Breytenbach would argue that Pretoria's aid to, and utilisation of, UNITA were frequently detrimental to the South African cause.[12] In contrast, a surrogate would, according to Onslow's theory, at least have to act in accordance with the wishes of the parent and Onslow implies that the surrogate's ideologies should, ideally, also stroke with that of the parent.[13] Perhaps due to the difficulties in examining the ideologies of various groups, especially in southern Africa during the Cold War, Onslow refrains from giving examples of surrogate forces. However, it could be argued that PLAN – and even *Umkhonto we Sizwe* – acted as FAPLA surrogates at various stages of the Border War, as their ideologies, as least as far as their thoughts on independence and the necessity to take up arms in order to establish and / or maintain positions of government, were essentially the same.

In the case of the former FNLA soldiers of 32 Battalion, neither category provides a neat fit. While these soldiers certainly acted at the behest of the SADF and to the advantage of South Africa's military position in Angola, they did not gain any advantage from these actions for themselves, as in the case of the Cuba/USSR or UNITA/SADF relationships. This disqualifies them from being a proxy. At the same time, though, it is unfathomable that the black troops of 32 Battalion shared Pretoria's apartheid ideology. For this reason, they cannot be viewed as a South African surrogate force either. The next logical deduction would, therefore, be that 32 Battalion was a mercenary force. However, two key considerations detract significantly from the mercenary argument. Firstly, and most importantly, a mercenary force wages war for monetary gain. The fact that the black soldiers of 32 Battalion were not paid at all for their deployment during Operation Savannah and, when they started receiving salaries from the SADF in March 1976, received far less than their white counterparts,[14] negates this crucial element of a mercenary force. Secondly, 32 Battalion was formally recognised as part of the military structures of the South West Africa Territorial Force (SWATF) in May 1976,[15] less than a year after their first contact with SADF delegates. This means that, if 32 Battalion is viewed as a mercenary force, the black Angolan troops went to bed one evening as mercenaries and woke up the next morning as SADF soldiers. Such a contention is,

11 Onslow, 'The Cold War in Southern Africa', p.28.
12 Cf. J. Breytenbach, *The Tempered Sword: Forged in Battle Revisited; Operation Savannah and the birth of 32 Bn*. Bushwarrior.com, 2011, pp.409–431.
13 Onslow, 'The Cold War in Southern Africa', pp.25–28.
14 P. Nortje, *The Terrible Ones: A complete history of 32 Battalion*. Cape Town: Zebra, 2012, p.161.
15 DODDC, 32 Bn, Box 14, G/OPS/3/3, Bevelsdirektiewe, Bevelsdirektief No.15/76 Ops 34.

obviously, untenable. The reality of the situation is that, for 17 years of their 18-year existence, 32 Battalion was as much of a formal SADF unit as any other. The circumstances that drove them to become part of the SADF structures in the first place is, to a large extent, unique in the context of the surrogate / proxy / mercenary force debate and defies fitting neatly into a definition.

Revolutionary War vs Insurgency

Revolution and insurgency / counterinsurgency are, in many aspects, two sides of the same coin. The aim of an insurgency being, by definition, the overthrow of a government or power, as opposed to a revolution which, depending on the stage it is in, can potentially be non-violent in nature.[16] The differentiation between these terms often becomes tenuous in the literature, with authors, depending on personal preference and, no doubt, political ideology, opting for either or both. An example of this can be seen in Enterline, Stull and Magagnoli's study of counterinsurgency (COIN) warfare, where they claim that what they call the 'classical COIN model ... draws in part on the precepts of Mao Tse-Tung's theory of revolutionary warfare.'[17] The implication that an understanding of revolutionary warfare is a precursor to developing a COIN strategy clearly illustrates the intertwined nature of the authors' understanding of the two phrases. Along similar vein, in reviewing the SADF's COIN strategies, Anita Gossmann refers to both the 'Insurgency in Namibia' and the 'South African insurgency'.[18] The conflicts in South Africa and Namibia differed not only in intensity and bloodshed, but in their very nature, with Namibian insurgents never able to establish bases in the country that they were attempting to 'revolutionise' by force, while South Africans insurgents always had a certain degree of internal support, despite a relative absence of violence. Therefore, a strong case could be made for calling the South African conflict 'revolutionary', while the Namibian conflict undeniably falls into the category of 'insurgency'. Enterline et al blur the differentiation further by their choice of conflicts to include in their study. To mention only the southern African conflicts among the 66 conflicts that they identify in the twentieth century, they include the Second Boer War (1899–1902), the Herero and Namaqua Wars (1904–1908), the Mozambican Civil War (1964–1975), the Namibian War of Independence (1966–1990), and the Angolan Civil War (1975–1990).[19] These conflicts differ significantly in intensity, intention, and strategy, especially when it is taken into account that Cuba is identified as the foreign power involved in the Angolan

16 Cf. J. P. Cann, *Counterinsurgency in Africa: The Portuguese Way of War, 1931–1974.* Westport: Greenwood, 1997, p.48.

17 A. J. Enterline, E. Stull & J. Magagnoli, 'Reversal of Fortune? Strategy Change and Counterinsurgency Success by Foreign Powers in the Twentieth Century' in *International Studies Perspectives 14,* 2013, p.180.

18 A. M. Gossmann, 'Lost in Transition: The South African military and counterinsurgency' in *Small Wars and Insurgencies 19 (4),* 2008, p.545.

19 Enterline et al, Reversal of Fortune?, pp.185–186. All names and dates of conflicts are quoted from the original.

Civil War. In addition, South Africa fails to receive a mention in the study, because of the fact that there was no foreign involvement in the COIN phase of the struggle. This analysis of Enterline et al's study is not intended as a critique – in fact, their attempts at creating a quantifiable model according to which COIN operations can be judged is laudable – but serves to illustrate the extent to which revolutionary war and COIN warfare is intertwined. For this reason, *Forged in Battle?* will view the two terms, as used in the literature, in a similar light, unless there is explicit evidence to suggest an author's different intention.

Counterinsurgency

As the colonial power, and the country most involved with Angola before independence in 1975, Portugal's approach to insurgency and counterinsurgency leading up to 1975 is insightful. Additionally, Portugal's doctrine was based on experiences drawn from British, French and, to a lesser extent, American sources[20] and was closely aligned with the doctrine South Africa would follow during the early years of the Border War. South Africa's doctrine was, in turn, largely based on the writings of French general André Beaufre, further illustrating the continuity of the counterinsurgency approaches of Portugal pre-1975 and South Africa post-1975. Beaufre based his thoughts on the French experiences in Algeria and Indochina.[21] Both these countries were part of the Third World, and both conflicts were similar in nature to the conflict in Namibia and Angola. Significantly for 32 Battalion, Beaufre was also interested in 'how to adapt conventional force structures and tactics to changing conditions of offensive and defensive warfare and military technology.'[22] The writings of Karl von Clausewitz, J. J. McCuen, Robert Thompson and Che Guevara also influenced South African COIN strategies, as well as case studies of the insurgencies in Malaysia, Kenya, Algeria, Cyprus, China and Vietnam.[23]

The Portuguese counterinsurgency doctrine, titled *O Exército na Guerra Subversiva* (The Army in Subversive War) was formulated by Lieutenant Colonel Nunes da Silva and drew from British experiences in Palestine, Malaya, Kenya and Cyprus between 1945 and 1960. As South African defence analysts would also come to realise from their own studies, four factors were identified as key to British success (or failure, in Palestine): Disorders were suppressed using minimum force, successful counterinsurgency depended on close cooperation between civil government and military operations (ideally under the command of a single individual), good intelligence and its collation under a single authority was vital, and decentralised, small-unit tactics was the most effective way of neutralising insurgents.[24] French doctrine agreed with British (although

20 I. F. W. Beckett, *Modern Insurgencies and Counterinsurgencies: Guerrillas and their opponents since 1750.* London: Routledge, 2001, p.136.
21 A. Beaufre, *Strategy of Action*, translated by R. H. Barry, London: Faber & Faber, 1967, p.20.
22 R. B. Foster, 'Foreword' in A. Beaufre, *Strategy for tomorrow.* London: Macdonald and Jane's, 1974, p.vii.
23 Daniel, 'Racism, the Cold War and South Africa's regional security strategies', p.38.
24 Cann, *Counterinsurgency in Africa*, p.43.

learnt more through failure than success), with the exception that the French did not identify the use of minimum force as a consideration[25] and, in fact, advocated a practice of *ratissage*, or 'raking over', of the local population.[26]

Significantly, in developing a counterinsurgency doctrine, Portugal departed from the traditional prescription for insurgency, laid out by Mao Tse-Tung in China and Vo Nguyen Giap in Vietnam. These two key theoreticians had identified five phases of insurgent warfare: the *preparatory* phase, preparation for subversion; the *agitation* phase, creating a subversive environment; the *terrorist and guerrilla action* phase, consolidating the subversive organisation; the *subversive state phase*, creating a government and armed forces; and the *final* phase, general insurrection and war. In countering this framework in *O Exército na Guerra Subversiva*, Portugal simplified its strategy by reducing their doctrine to only two stages; the pre-insurrection and insurrection phases. Pre-insurrection was seen as a combination of the preparatory and agitation phases, while everything that came thereafter was seen as the insurrection phase.[27]

The Portuguese reclassification is significant because of the tacit recognition that, once the insurrection phase had commenced, the counterinsurgency force was, by definition, initially reduced to a reactive role. During the pre-insurrection phase, pre-emptive measures could still be undertaken without military assistance or interference but, while social and political factors were still vital, once the insurrection phase had been reached military action was of paramount importance.

Although it has become more nuanced, the Portuguese way of thinking about COIN strategy continues to influence studies in this field. Enterline et al broadly distil writing about COIN to two strategies, 'enemy-centric' and 'population-centric'. The terms are self-explanatory, though very broad in scope. Enemy-centric strategies focus on the military destruction of insurgents, whereas population-centric strategies hold greater store by winning the political goodwill of the local population by providing them with security,[28] including socio-economic stability, reform or progress.

In what was to become a page in the South African counterinsurgency manual, Portuguese doctrine was explicit on the role of the military once the insurrection phase had been reached (and, indeed, during the pre-insurrection phase, should the military be utilised at that time). The individual soldier was seen as the primary point of contact between counterinsurgency forces and the local population. For this reason, the conduct of the soldiers played a vital part in the counterinsurgency strategy.[29] Breaking with the heavy-handed French approach in Algeria and the overwhelming American intervention

25 Cann, *Counterinsurgency in Africa*, p.44.
26 S. Robbins, 'Model Campaigns of Futility: The Portuguese in Africa, 1961–1974' in G. Fremont-Barnes, (ed.), *A History of Counterinsurgency, Volume 2: From Cyprus to Afghanistan, 1955 to the 21st Century*. Santa Barbara: Praeger, 2015, p.51.
27 Cann, *Counterinsurgency in Africa*, p.48.
28 Enterline et al, Reversal of Fortune?, p.180.
29 C. A. Fraser, *Revolutionary Warfare: basic principles of counter-insurgency (being a revision of 'Lessons learnt from past revolutionary wars')*. 4 Survey and Printing Regiment, pp.23–24.

in Korea, Portuguese doctrine encouraged the soldier to positively influence the local population towards the government.[30] Additionally, non-military actions were explicitly addressed in *O Exército na Guerra Subversiva*. Significant parallels are apparent between the socio-political aspects that were highlighted in Portuguese doctrine and those that later formed part of South African Communication Operations (ComOps)[31]: teaching and education, hygiene and health, public works and communications, agronomy and veterinary medicine, and industry and mining. It was envisaged that the military would assist civilian government with tasks as diverse as building schools and other civic institutions, teaching, providing healthcare and sanitation.[32] The final aspect addressed in *O Exército na Guerra Subversiva,* again exhibiting striking similarities with the future situation of South Africa, was that of logistic support. Although logistics do not play as large a role in counterinsurgency conflicts as they do in conventional warfare, because of its low intensity, even the modest logistical difficulties that are experienced in counterinsurgency are highlighted when such a conflict is enacted any distance away from regular sources of supply. Furthermore, in far-off counterinsurgency campaigns, Portugal saw additional benefits to a comprehensive logistic backup system: the morale of troops would be improved by regular and reliable logistics and this would, in turn, have a positive effect on the level and success of interaction between soldiers and civilians, aiding socio-political initiatives.[33]

Geopolitical and Strategic Framework

Although the developing world was the scene for many of the Cold War conflicts and influenced Cold War politics, the initial historiography predictably focused on the main protagonists, the leaders of the NATO and Warsaw Pact (WP) alliances. Almost 30 years after the fall of the Berlin Wall in 1989, though, the importance of and effect on developing regions in the Cold War is being recognised to an ever greater extent. Sue Onslow dubs southern Africa 'one of the cauldrons of the Cold War' and points out that 'a more complex picture is emerging of the dynamics of the Cold War and its corrupting effect on the transition to majority rule in Southern Africa ... the ideological contest between global economic systems, which intersected with the process of European decolonisation, intensified and prolonged the struggle between the remaining white minorities in power and black nationalist movements.'[34]

Chris Alden goes a long way towards illustrating this 'ideological contest'. Although significant historiographical strides have been made since his writing in 1996, the philosophic-theoretical foundation on which Alden based his arguments – that 'modernisation theory, rooted in classical liberalism, and Marxist-Leninist theory, rooted in a

30 Cann, *Counterinsurgency in Africa,* p.49.
31 Fraser, *Revolutionary Warfare,* p.49.
32 Cann, *Counterinsurgency in Africa,* pp.51–52.
33 Cann, *Counterinsurgency in Africa,* p.54.
34 Onslow, 'Introduction', p.1.

critique of classical liberalism, became the ideological pillars around which the debate on [and the struggle for] the Third World took place'[35] – still holds true.

Scholars in the Western World, of which South Africa was keen to be a part despite having her international standing decrease from being 'out of proportion to its relative power'[36] during the inter-war years to being ever more of a political pariah, 'identified socio-economic forces emerging out of the movement from traditional society to modernity as posing a challenge to the established political order in developing countries.'[37] To protect herself against this perceived threat, South Africa's governing National Party was quick to commit to 'support the West in any future war with communist powers.'[38] In contrast, Marxist-Leninist theory – espoused by much of newly-independent Africa – 'placed the process of modernization within the context of its cosmopolitan socio-economic theory, one which saw communist revolution as the ultimate (and inevitable) political expression of changing socio-economic conditions.'[39]

Robert McMahon, drawing on the writings of Westad, Scott and Colburn, adds another dimension to the philosophy behind global intervention in developing southern Africa:

> As recent scholarship suggests, the Cold War's ideological dimensions had at least as great an impact on the decolonising world as geopolitical trends ... In other words, not only did the superpowers (and certain lesser powers) materially and financially abet many of independent Africa's misguided development strategies and authoritarian policies, the rhetorically supercharged atmosphere of the Cold War era inspired those policies in the first place.[40]

This was especially true in Angola, where the MPLA, the FNLA and UNITA all played off the superpowers against one another. Agostinho Neto, leader of the MPLA, was an avowed Marxist and the MPLA received, by far, the greatest material support of any of the Angolan independence movements. The FNLA and UNITA were both, on the surface, pro-West and did, indeed, received Western support, but neither was averse to assistance from the East, notably China. By adapting and exploiting the 'rhetorically supercharged atmosphere', many other post-colonial governments and political movements were able to achieve similar results by embracing policies that would appease

35 C. Alden, *Apartheid's Last Stand: The Rise and Fall of the South African Security State*. London: MacMillan, 1996, p.2.
36 D. Geldenhuys, *Isolated States: A comparative analysis*. Johannesburg: Jonathan Ball, 1990, p.114.
37 Alden, *Apartheid's Last Stand*, p.2.
38 Geldenhuys, *Isolated States*, p.121.
39 Alden, *Apartheid's Last Stand*, pp.2–3. Parenthesis original.
40 J. J. Byrne, 'Africa's Cold War' in R. J. McMahon (ed.), *The Cold War in the Third World*. Oxford: Oxford University Press, 2013, p.107. Parenthesis original. Cf. Westad, *The global Cold War*, New Haven: Yale University Press, 1999; F. D. Colburn, *The vogue of revolution in poor countries*. Princeton: University Press, 1994.

either East, West or, ideally, both. However, this was not necessarily a lasting embrace. McMahon again illustrates:

> Yet, it is also true that the prevailing ideological currents manifested themselves most often through the widespread adoption of certain political *practices*, as opposed to *ideas*. A common sight throughout Africa in the 1960s and 1970s was the regime that publically [*sic*] distanced itself from either bloc's doctrine by pursuing a supposedly 'authentic' or nativist revolution that nevertheless relied on the substance of the Leninist and especially Bolshevik examples in a practical and operational sense.[41]

In this denial of the supremacy of the doctrine of either side, newly formed governments and independence movements were able to pay lip service to the superpowers and their allies that supported them, without completely alienating either the local electorate or the other superpower. However, by only adopting certain aspects of, especially, Marxist-Leninism, leaders in southern Africa were able to tailor their style of government to fit their needs and fulfil their wants. Agostinho Neto and the MPLA was the most aggressively and openly Marxist movement in Angola, but even their 'Subsequent FNLA historiography', as Fernando Guimarães notes, 'omits any reference to the PCP [Portuguese Communist Party]; and the role it played in establishing the MPLA as a political force, probably in the interests of appearing to be a broader political movement and thereby appealing to a wider range of internal and external support.'[42] The South African Military Intelligence Division (MID) certainly considered the MPLA firmly in the Soviet camp and identified Soviet plans to install a MPLA government in Luanda post-independence.[43] Holden Roberto's FNLA, on the other hand, was supported by the USA until the Tunney Amendment was accepted by the US Senate on 19 December 1975, effectively ending overt US support for the FNLA.[44] The South African MID confirmed aid from the US and added Italy, France, Zaire and China to the diverse list of FNLA contributors.[45] This did not prevent Roberto courting Soviet support, though. As late as 1974, the FNLA was still invited to the USSR's embassy in Lusaka for 'confidential' talks.[46] Lastly, UNITA, established by Jonas Savimbi at Muangai in eastern Angola on 13 March 1966, emphasised at their founding conference that 'independence, anticolonialism and anti-imperialism' would be central tenets of the

41 Byrne, 'Africa's Cold War', p.107. Emphasis and parenthesis original.
42 F. A. Guimarães, *The Origins of the Angolan Civil War: Foreign Intervention and Domestic Political Conflict*. Basingstoke: MacMillan, 1998, p.39.
43 DODDC, HS Ops Gp 1, Box 9, HS/11/3/14, Vol. 1, Waardering oor die moontlike gebruik / aanwending van Chipenda / FNLA tot voordeel van RSA.
44 P. W. Rodman, *More Precious than Peace: The Cold War and the Struggle for the Third World*. New York: Charles Scribner's Sons, 1994, p.173.
45 DODDC, HS Ops Gp 1, Box 9, HS/11/3/14, Vol. 1, Waardering oor die moontlike gebruik / aanwending van Chipenda / FNLA tot voordeel van RSA.
46 Westad, *The Global Cold War*, p.217.

organisation.[47] Though Eastern (notably Chinese Maoist)[48] influences are undeniable in the decisions taken at UNITA's Muangai Conference, only aid from the West, by way of American material and financial support and South African direct intervention, ensured that Savimbi continued to be a factor in the Angolan Civil War after 1975. At that time, the South African MID was, however, only aware of limited aid to UNITA from the white Angolan population and possibly Great Britain.[49]

This blurring of the Cold War frontlines in southern Africa, and the attempts of African governments at exploiting the situation, can be attributed to a series of misconceptions in both the USA and the USSR. During the political turmoil leading up to Angolan independence in 1975, despite American support to the anti-communist FNLA (or perhaps in defence of the cessation thereof) American Senator Dick Clark was of the opinion that 'The history of Soviet intervention in Africa … is one of almost total failure… If the MPLA wins [the post-independence elections], the Soviets will be lucky if they can hang on for a year or two.'[50] Henry Kissinger, the US Secretary of State, was more pragmatic when he argued before Congress: 'When one great power attempts to obtain special positions of influence based on military interventions, the other power is sooner or later bound to act to offset this advantage in some other place or manner.'[51] In the end, both Clark and Kissinger were proved wrong to a certain degree. Soviet influence in Angola certainly lasted for well more than 'a year or two' and, despite the dire prediction of Kissinger and although America did make attempts at combating Soviet influence in southern Africa, these were not particularly successful in undermining the Soviet presence in the region.

However, the American indecision and vacillation that led to Soviet domination of Angola was, in the opinion of Georgy Arbatov, not the politico-strategic advantage it appeared to be:

> As often happens in politics, when you get away with something and it looks as if you've been successful, you are practically doomed to repeat the policy. You do this until you blunder into a really serious mess. That is what happened in Angola… [leading up to 1976] Of course they [the USA] protested… But relations remained more or less intact and the fact that the Soviet Union became even more suspect and untrustworthy was hidden under the surface of what soon seemed to become business as usual. I began to worry that our government would remember only the success of the action and the absence of serious international complications… We were unable to resist further temptation to become involved in the complex internal

47 S. L. Weigert, *Angola: A Modern Military History, 1961–2002*. New York: Palgrave MacMillan, 2011, p.35.

48 Cf. P. Gleijeses, *Conflicting Missions: Havana, Washington, Pretoria*. Alberton: Galago, 2003, p.236 for an analysis of Savimbi's varying political lip service.

49 DODDC, HS Ops Gp 1, Box 9, HS/11/3/14, Vol. 1, Waardering oor die moontlike gebruik / aanwending van Chipenda / FNLA tot voordeel van RSA.

50 Rodman, *More Precious than Peace*, p.174.

51 Rodman, *More Precious than Peace*, p.179.

> affairs of other countries. After Angola, we went boldly down the path of intervention and expansion that we had beaten so assuredly. It led us through Ethiopia, Yemen, a series of African countries and, eventually, into Afghanistan.[52]

Without digressing to the impact that Soviet involvement in Afghanistan and the US reaction thereto has had on global politics to this day, it is clear that the Cold War superpowers had a vested interest in southern Africa – whether this was to exploit African resources, gather international support and/or allies or combat the global expansion of their adversaries – and that their choices in expressing these interests have had an impact far beyond the Cold War. It now remains to examine how this interest in Africa was expressed by the various protagonists. Because Africa '...was not simply a passive victim of outside interference, since its post-colonial elites exploited geopolitical tensions and fought the Cold War's ideological battles as ardently – and frequently more bloodily – as their peers elsewhere,'[53] southern African reactions to global intervention will also be examined more closely.

Events in southern Africa

The principal players in the Cold War in southern Africa are discussed in this section. Since the Soviet Union and the USA were the principal players in the Cold War, their involvement in southern Africa will not be discussed as separate subdivisions, although their influence permeates all the subtle layers of the Cold War in Africa. An emphasis is placed on three countries, inextricably linked with southern Africa, with established, recognised governments: Cuba, Portugal and South Africa. Although these governments, especially that of Portugal, were very much in a state of flux, none of these countries were involved in a civil war to establish governing legitimacy. Regarding the contest for Angolan government, three major politico-military organisations that contested the rule of Angola after independence: the FNLA, MPLA and UNITA are discussed. Namibia was then under South African administration, and remained so until the end of the Border War, and the main Namibian independence organisation, SWAPO, had close ties with the MPLA, which logically melds a discussion of SWAPO and the MPLA and negates the need to address Namibian involvement in the Cold War separately. The map on p. 38 indicates southern African countries that are discussed in this chapter (and the rest of the book) and some important cities and towns.

Although the role of Cuba in southern Africa only escalated to significant proportions after Angolan independence and therefore falls largely outside the scope of this chapter, a brief examination of the Cuban geopolitical philosophy leading up to 1975 is nonetheless important as background for future discussions about Cuba and southern Africa.

52 Arbatov as quoted by Rodman, *More Precious than Peace*, p.179.
53 Byrne, 'Africa's Cold War', p.117.

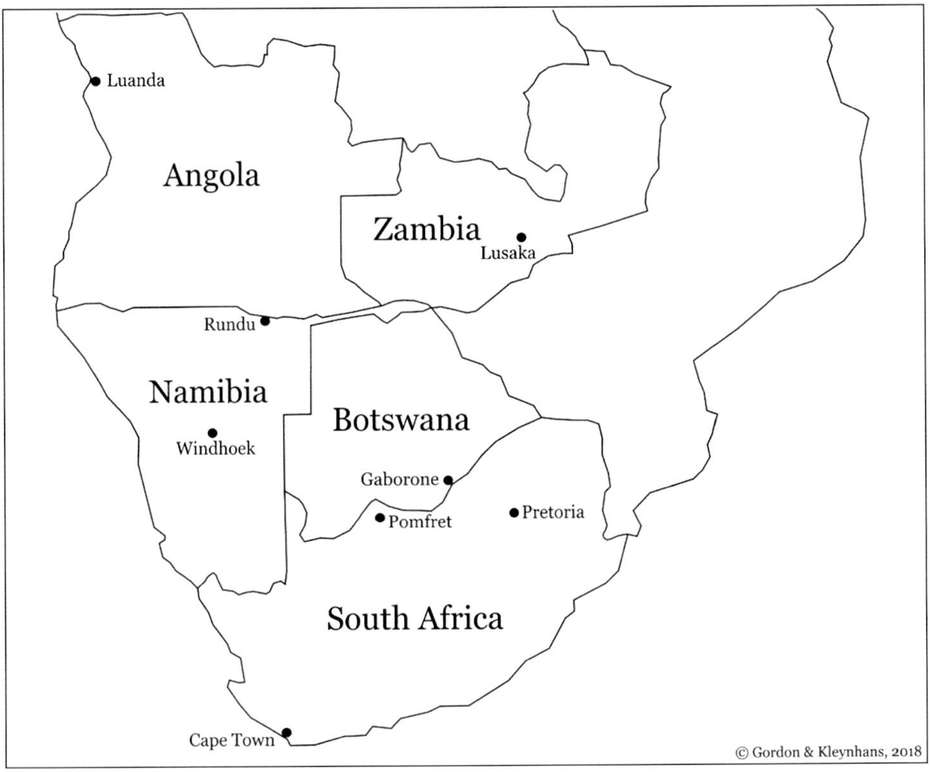

Countries and important cities / towns in south-western Africa.

From the start of Fidel Castro's rule in Cuba, the USA recognised that he would not be as easily manipulated as his predecessor, Fulgencio Batista. Piero Gleijeses contends that, from the outset, Castro dreamed of a Cuba that was free from US intervention and involvement.[54] Such a stance would naturally incline Castro, though not a committed Marxist, to look to the East for support for his impoverished country. The Soviet Union did, indeed, agree to provide Cuba with material support and Soviet aid began arriving in Cuba in 1960. Initially Soviet reasoning behind supplying Cuba was motivated by anti-West sentiments, but as it became ever clearer that the USA was not about to invade Cuba, as Fidel Castro had suspected,[55] Cuban-Soviet relations declined sharply, reaching a nadir during the USSR's 50th anniversary celebrations.[56] However, this was also the period during which Cuban involvement in Africa was on the increase.

54 Gleijeses, *Conflicting Missions*, p.12.
55 Hughes as quoted by Gleijeses, *Conflicting Missions,* p.19.
56 Gleijeses, *Conflicting Missions,* p.218.

Fidel Castro was a firm believer in the efficacy of irregular war. He believed that 'victory was always within the grasp of those who used the wiles of secrecy in their movements and surprise in their deployment of men and arms, terrain and tactics.'[57] These thoughts found successful employment in the Cuban Revolution, and Castro saw no reason why the same principles could not achieve success in Africa. Although the MPLA and Cuba had had contact in Brazzaville in 1963–1965, when Cuba had trained a small contingent of MPLA troops that were supposed to mount a guerrilla campaign against Portuguese colonial troops in Angola, this did not end satisfactorily for either party. The MPLA felt that the Cuban effort had been insufficient, whereas the Cubans came to consider the MPLA a disorganised movement with little political or military feasibility (while Portugal was still in power in Angola).[58] Nevertheless, a memorandum dated 22 November 1972, from MP Lozada, Vice-Minister of the Interior, to Raúl Castro, Minister of the Revolutionary Armed Forces, indicates a willingness on Cuba's part to re-establish closer links with the MPLA and send Cuban advisers to Angola to assess the revolutionary climate.[59] Following a Cuban delegation's visit to Angola in July 1974, Cuban opinion of the capabilities of the MPLA started to improve. The MPLA was now recognised as the most likely party to take over the government of Angola after Portugal departed.[60] Castro's vehement dislike of South Africa undoubtedly also played a role in Cuba's eagerness to share their meagre resources with African liberation movements. In addition, Castro's conviction that Pretoria and Washington had a much more formal and significant alliance than was actually the case,[61] led him to believe that, by striking at South Africa through the MPLA, he was effectively also attacking the US. However, a MPLA letter to the Cuban government, requesting military training, a transport ship, communication equipment, uniforms, air force personnel, political training and publications, military hardware, and financial assistance was largely ignored by Cuba until after Angolan independence. Some Cuban advisers, instructors and medical personnel were present in Angola in the lead up to independence, though.[62] Nonetheless, it fell to the USSR and Yugoslavia to put the MPLA in a position, from a military point of view, to successfully contest the 1975 elections,[63] as the large-scale deployment of Cuban troops to Angola, Operation Carlota, only commenced on 9 November, only two days prior to independence.[64]

In addition to Cuba, Portugal was another non-African country that had a significant impact on southern African geopolitics in the twentieth century. In order to understand

57 F. Castro, *My Life*, translated by A. Hurley, London: Penguin, 2007, p.205.
58 Gleijeses, *Conflicting Missions*, p.244.
59 Nortje, *The Terrible Ones, Vol. 1*, pp.41–42.
60 Gleijeses, *Conflicting Missions*, p.248.
61 Castro, *My Life*, pp.316–317.
62 DODDC, HS Ops Gp 1, Box 10, HS/11/3/14, Vol. 4, Interrogation of Cuban POWs at Silva Porto on 27–29 Nov 75.
63 Gleijeses, *Conflicting Missions*, p.250.
64 H. L. Blanch & I. Liebenberg, 'A view from Cuba: Internationalists against apartheid' in *Journal for Contemporary History 34 (1)*, 2009, p.93.

the role that Portugal played in southern Africa's Cold War, it is necessary to study the effects of Portugal's domestic, European politics as well as their independent actions in and regarding Africa. When Antonio de Oliviera Salazar became Prime Minister of Portugal in 1933, it ushered in the period of the *Estado Novo* (New State) in Portugal. As part of this New State, Salazar's Portugal, in contrast with the rest of colonial Europe, linked their overseas (*ultramar*) provinces inextricably with their European territory (*metropole*). Salazar's successor, Marcelo Caetano, expressed the philosophy behind the *Estado Novo* succinctly when he stated that 'Without Africa we would be a small nation; with Africa we are a big power.'[65] This meant that Portuguese domestic policy had a much larger influence on her colonies than that of other colonial powers, as Salazar, like Caetano, saw the possibility of increasing Portugal's stature among her European contemporaries through the effective administration of her colonies.[66] It also resulted in the process of *assimilicão*, in which Portugal tried to 'assimilate' the population of their colonies to Portuguese culture. In practice, this meant that a black colonial could attain Portuguese citizenship, provided that he could speak Portuguese, had a European lifestyle, wore European clothing, had a birth certificate and a certificate proving permanent residence and good health, could support his family, and was willing to make a declaration of loyalty to Portugal.[67]

Assimilicão did not prove as popular as Salazar had hoped, however. The downfall of Salazar's *Estado Novo* lay in its very success. After Portugal had invested a significant portion of her GDP in the *ultramar* provinces, the colonies became successful and capital started flowing back to the *metropole*.[68] This led to a realisation among Africans that their countries had a potential for generating wealth of which they were previously unaware. Despite the possibility of *assimilicão*, Angolans living under Portuguese rule were stimulated by the successful independence campaigns elsewhere in Africa, and it became apparent that Portugal would need to launch a counterinsurgency campaign in Angola following limited uprisings in 1961. Faced with the prospect of ever increasing demands on the manpower of the Portuguese Army – between 1961 and 1967 the percentage of the Portuguese Army deployed in Africa increased from around 5 percent to 75 percent[69] – Portugal's first military step was to include local soldiers in their Angolan armed forces. To this end, around 7,500 black soldiers were incorporated into the 50,000 strong Angolan contingent. Additionally, specialist, non-white units, among whom the *Flechas* that would become 31 Battalion of the SADF, were used as trackers and eventually became fully-fledged combat units.[70] Ian Beckett's contention that the 'number of Africans prepared to fight for Portugal far exceeded those fighting [against] them as

65 Robbins, 'Model Campaigns of Futility', p.50.
66 Cann, *Counterinsurgency in Africa*, p.16.
67 F. J. du T. Spies, *Die Angolese Burgeroorlog*. Pretoria: Militere Informasieburo, 1980, p.56.
68 Cann, *Counterinsurgency in Africa*, p.18.
69 Robbins, 'Model Campaigns in Futility', pp 52–53.
70 Spies, *Die Angolese Burgeroorlog*, p.107.

guerrillas'[71] is belied by the sheer number of Angolan political organisations motivated by the prospect of independence from Portugal[72] – if fewer Africans supported these movements, fewer movements would have existed – but nonetheless indicates the process of 'Africanisation' that Portugal was pursuing in her African *ultramar* provinces. South Africa would employ a similar strategy of 'Namibianisation' during the Border War.

In a move that was resented by a large part of the Angolan population and would be used as a rallying cry by liberation movements in future, Portugal relocated much of the rural Angolan population to protected villages (called *aldeamentos*) and coffee plantations (*fazendas*). In these protected areas, locals deemed loyal to the Portuguese cause were armed in order to protect themselves and their *aldeamentos* or *fazendas*. Initially, this move was successful and the insurgents from Zaire were denied an infiltration route to Angola,[73] but as the domestic situation in Portugal worsened, Portuguese efforts in Africa became increasingly ineffective. Additionally, some inhabitants of *aldeamentos* started viewing this step as a form of conscription by the Portuguese.[74]

Considering that Portugal was attempting to maintain a stable colonial environment in their *ultramar* provinces, circumstances in the *metropole* were far from ideal in the early 1970s. Salazar had suffered a stroke in 1968 and passed away in 1970. The policies of his successor, Marcello Caetano, had the exact opposite effect of those that Salazar's had had. Caetano changed the status of *ultramar* provinces to that of states and granted greater autonomy to these newly formed states, including voting rights for literates. Spies muses that, had Caetano's policies been given more time to take effect, the history of Angola might have looked very different.[75] *Metropole* Portugal, however, was moving in the opposite direction. Emigrants were flocking to other European countries and, in 1972, as much as 20 percent of young men called up to serve in Portuguese armed forces, mostly employed in their *ultramar* provinces, refused to do so.[76] Additionally, the Portuguese economy was effectively in ruins and inflation in Portugal was the highest in Europe[77], running just short of 20 percent in 1973 and 1974.[78] These factors inevitably permeated the Portuguese effectiveness in Angola, although the Portuguese armed forces in Angola were still superior to liberation forces.

On 22 February 1974, less than a year before Angola was destined to become independent, António de Spínola published, with the blessing of Portuguese Prime Minister

71 Beckett, *Modern Insurgencies and Counterinsurgencies*, p.136.
72 Cf., inter alia, R. Cornwell, 'The War for Independence' in J. Cilliers & C. Dietrich (eds), *Angola's war economy: the role of oil and diamonds*. Pretoria: Institute for Security Studies, 2000; Cann, *Counterinsurgency in Africa*; Robbins, 'Model Campaigns in Futility'; Guimarães, *The Origins of the Angolan Civil War*.
73 Spies, *Die Angolese Burgeroorlog*, p.109.
74 Weigert, *Angola*, p.23.
75 Spies, *Die Angolese Burgeroorlog*, p.144.
76 Cann, *Counterinsurgency in Africa*, p.89.
77 Spies, *Die Angolese Burgeroorlog*, p.145.
78 http://www.inflation.eu/inflation-rates/portugal/historic-inflation/cpi-inflation-portugal.aspx [Accessed 2018-07-06].

Marcello Caetano, *Portugal e o Futuro* (Portugal and the Future). Herein, he advocated for a greater degree of autonomy for Portuguese colonies, contrary to the *ultramar* concept and concluded that, with massive popular support for the various liberation movements, it would be impossible for Portugal to achieve a purely military victory in the *ultramar* provinces.[79] This emphasis on the political nature of war poured fuel on the already raging fire of discontent in Portugal and hastened the military coup that had already been planned by the Movement of the Armed Forces (MFA) which took place on 25 April 1974. Spínola was proclaimed the first president of the Republic of Portugal on 14 May 1974, but his authority was challenged by the power-hungry MFA, who still had effective control over the Portuguese military forces. After experiencing an increasing weakening of his political position, Spínola resigned on 30 September 1974.

Guimarães contends that 'In many respects, Portugal's colonies were intimately tied, on the one hand, to the collapse of authoritarianism in Lisbon and, on the other, to the collapse of the power struggle between moderates and radicals … the consequences of fighting the African wars had an overwhelming influence on the military officers that overthrew Caetano'[80] and illustrates three African factors that influenced the Portuguese military establishment leading up to the coup: Firstly, the immensely unpopular move of strengthening the Portuguese military forces in order to enforce colonial authority provided the very instrument that became the downfall of the Portuguese regime. Secondly, an attempt by the Caetano government to improve the public perception of conscription, giving conscripted officers the same career opportunities as volunteer officers, predictably proved unpopular with volunteers and strengthened the base of support of the MFA. Lastly and most significantly, Guimarães links the leftist orientation of the MFA officers to their exposure to the ideologies of anti-colonial movements in Africa, notably the MPLA and the African Party for the Independence of Guinea and Cape Verde (PAIGC).[81] The liberal ideas of these African movements found their way back to Portugal through the MFA officers, further increasing resistance to the last vestiges of Salazar and Caetano's more conservative *Estado Novo.*

Moving to Africa, the Angolan peoples' struggle for independence does not have as long a pre-independence history as that of some other countries, such as South Africa and even Namibia, having started on 4 February 1961 by MPLA attacks on Luanda.[82] This is offset, of course, by the length of the post-colonial struggle, which only effectively came to an end with the assassination of UNITA's Savimbi in 2002. However short the lead up to independence, the revolutionary soil in Angola sprouted forth a rich crop of liberation movements. Most of these were, however, short lived with three (MPLA, FNLA and UNITA) becoming the main political contenders after Portugal's departure.

79 Guimarães, *The Origins of the Angolan Civil War,* p.xiii.
80 Guimarães, *The Origins of the Angolan Civil War,* p.88.
81 Guimarães, *The Origins of the Angolan Civil War,* pp.88–89.
82 Robbins, 'Model Campaigns of Futility', p.52.

These three organisations were also, not coincidently, the ones that received the greatest amount of foreign aid and support.

Though Mário de Andrade, founder member of the *Movimento Anti-Colonialista*, and later contender for MPLA leadership, made the bold statement that 'There is no question of pledging our policy to either of the blocs dividing the world. The only promise we make to the two blocs is that we will honestly seek to exclude attempts at establishing a Cold War climate among the Angolan Nationalists and to prevent the implication of international intrigues in the Angola of tomorrow,'[83] on 24 May 1962, history would prove this a naive expectation. None of the three movements that were destined to become serious contenders for Angolan government after independence – the MPLA, FNLA and UNITA – were able to achieve much without external support and this support, in turn, was not forthcoming without at least lip service to a particular course. Although, as illustrated earlier, liberation movements were not averse to exploiting Cold War tensions to their advantage by playing off the West against the East, the broad bands of allegiance left the MPLA in the Soviet camp, UNITA mostly in the Western camp and the FNLA, the least significant of post-independence movements, also broadly aligned with the West. This arrangement suited the USSR well; from as early as 1900 Lenin, and his successors, had had an interest in southern Africa. The MPLA's apparent need of external aid provided an ideal excuse to establish a presence in the region.[84]

The MPLA's pro-East leaning is not surprising, considering that the movement was initially established as an amalgamation of the Party for the United Struggle of the Angolan Africans (PLUA) and the Angolan Communist Party (ACP) in 1956[85]. Contrary to the other main liberation movements in Angola, the fact that the MPLA incorporated the former ACP meant that it also included a relatively large number of whites in the organisation and therefore drew on the broader support of not only the black ethnic groups linked to the party – mainly from the Kimbundu ethnic group – but also a greater part of the non-African population than the FNLA and UNITA. From a very early stage of their anti-colonial efforts – possibly as early as 1961, when an MPLA delegation to Moscow made the request[86] – the MPLA was supplied by the Soviet Union.[87] The level of this support was to increase exponentially after Angolan independence – 'Moscow invested far greater hopes and resources in Angola, Mozambique and Ethiopia than it had done in Ghana, Guinea and Mali a decade or more earlier'[88] – to the point where the USSR became concerned about the potential return on their investment

83 Andrade as quoted by Guimarães, *The Origins of the Angolan Civil War*, p.xiii.
84 C. Andrew & V. Mitrokhin, *The world was going our way: The KGB and the battle for the Third World*. Perseus Books, 2005, p.423.
85 P. Stiff, *The Silent War: South African Recce Operations 1969–1994*. Alberton: Galago, 1999, p.96.
86 Shubin, *The Hot 'Cold War'*, p.8.
87 DODDC, HS Ops Gp 1, Box 9, HS/11/3/14, Vol. 1, Waardering oor die moontlike gebruik/aanwending van Chipenda/FNLA tot voordeel van die RSA, p.7; Stiff, *The Silent War*, p.96.
88 Andrew & Mitrokhin, *The world was going our way*, p.429.

in 1979, and issued an ultimatum to Angolan president José Eduardo dos Santos: the Angolan government needed to prove not only that they were capable of effective rule, but also that they could provide SWAPO with the support that they needed to maintain an effective armed campaign against South Africa. Failure to deliver on these demands carried the threat of the USSR withdrawing their support of the MPLA.[89]

The forerunner of the FNLA, the UPA, was established in 1958 from the remnants of the Union of the Peoples of North Angola (UPNA), which had existed since 1954. The UPA was the second movement to actively resist Portuguese rule, when they started a rural uprising in northern Angola on 15 March 1961. During this uprising, which lasted until May, UPA supporters killed a large number of civilians, indiscriminate of race.[90] As with the MPLA, the FNLA had strong tribal ties, drawing the majority of its support from the Bakongo ethnic group. Unlike the MPLA, however, non-African members were not welcome in the FNLA.[91] While this was not a deciding factor in the US policy towards the FNLA and although South Africa did initially provide some aid to the FNLA (not counting the assimilation of former FNLA troops into 32 Battalion), the anti-white policy of the FNLA no doubt contributed towards South Africa being more inclined to support UNITA after Angolan independence. Although the FNLA was theoretically 'anti-Portuguese, anti-communist and anti-MPLA'[92], the former seems to have been an insignificant consideration in international circles when considering aid to the FNLA. The USA certainly did not consider being anti-Portuguese – keeping in mind that Portugal was a NATO ally – a disqualifying factor for US support and assisted the FNLA with logistic support for their NATO weapon-systems, fuel and intelligence,[93] in addition to providing advisers and monetary support. Similarly, even apartheid South Africa considered the FNLA the lesser evil for a short while in the early 1970s.[94]

In 1964 Jonas Savimbi, then Secretary General of the FNLA, broke away with a mere 185 followers and formed the UNITA. Despite his humble start, charismatic Savimbi was soon able to expand his movement and drew the majority of his support from the Ovimbundu ethnic group in the south-east of Angola. Savimbi pursued many potential avenues of support for his organisation, visiting China, North Korea, Vietnam, the USSR, Czechoslovakia and Hungary in the first few months of the party's existence.[95] Ultimately, though, he was able to entice only Chinese support to their cause fairly soon after being established[96] and, after a South African evaluation that UNITA enjoyed the

89 DODDC, 32 Bn Gp 2, Box 260, 522/1, Vol. 1, Konferensies, Kongresse, Seminare, Simposiums en Vergaderings: Konferensies, Notule van Bevelvoerderskonferensie gehou te 32 Bataljon Hoofkwartier op 23 Feb 1980.
90 Robbins, 'Model Campaigns of Futility', p.52.
91 Stiff, *The Silent War*, p.96.
92 Stiff, *The Silent War*, p.96.
93 DODDC, HS Ops Gp 1, Box 9, HS/11/3/14, Vol. 3, Report no. 004/nov/75.
94 DODDC, HS Ops Gp 1, Box 9, HS/11/3/14, Vol. 1, Waardering oor die moontlike gebruik/aanwending van Chipenda/FNLA tot voordeel van die RSA.
95 Van der Waals, *Portugal's war in Angola 1961–1974*, pp.127–128.
96 Stiff, *The Silent War*, p.97.

support of the majority of Angola's white population, but lacked sufficient resources,[97] formed a loose but lasting alliance with South Africa as part of the latter's attempt at destabilising the MPLA government and their support for SWAPO.[98] Nonetheless, as late as 1974, South Africa – in an attempt to assist Western ally Portugal – made no distinction between MPLA, FNLA or UNITA when clandestine SADF troops managed to make contact with these troops in Angola.[99]

After significant intra-MPLA turmoil in 1974, Agostinho Neto emerged as the effective leader of the movement. He immediately formed a 'Soviet style Political Bureau'[100] and received recognition as MPLA president (over Daniel Chipenda and Mário de Andrade) from the East Bloc as well as Portugal. Nevertheless, Portugal seems to have realised that, despite their backing of Neto, no clear contender could be identified to govern Angola after 11 November 1975. For this reason, Lisbon suggested a coalition government between all the political movements in Angola. Although this was rejected by the three major players, the foundation had been laid for the Alvor agreement, whereby Portugal, the MPLA, FNLA, and UNITA would jointly govern Angola until independence. Thereafter, free and fair elections would be held to establish the post-Portuguese era government. Drawing on Fred Bridgland[101], Peter Stiff's summary of international support for the MPLA and FNLA, leading up to Alvor, indicates that neither of the liberation movements were genuinely interested in democratic elections and were hastily securing support for their military wings:

> Military aid to the MPLA was resumed by the Soviets in August [1974, after a brief hiatus] and they supplied US $6 million worth before the year ended. FNLA's principal source of military aid remained Roberto's brother-in-law, President Mobuto of Zaire, but the Red Chinese and Rumania also began supplying them, to offset the aid the Soviets and Cubans were extending to the MPLA. The CIA, too, had begun covertly channelling money to them in 1974, without telling the relevant working group of the US National Security Council.[102]

South Africa's involvement in the Border War was, like Cuba, not primarily aimed at protecting geographical sovereignty, but rather to oppose (in contrast to Cuba's support of) a government that Pretoria considered potentially hostile to South Africa gaining ascendancy in Namibia. South Africa's involvement in Angola and Namibia was largely

97 DODDC, HS Ops Gp 1, Box 9, HS/11/3/14, Vol. 1, Waardering oor die moontlike gebruik/aanwending van Chipenda/FNLA tot voordeel van die RSA, p.7.
98 J. W. Turner, *Continent Ablaze: The Insurgency Wars in Africa 1960 to the Present*. Johannesburg: Jonathan Ball, 1998, p.103.
99 Stiff, *The Silent War*, p.100.
100 Stiff, *The Silent War*, p.101.
101 F. Bridgland, *The war for Africa: twelve months that transformed a continent*. Gibraltar: Ashanti, 1990.
102 Stiff, *The Silent War*, p.101.

congruent with what French officer turned American academic David Galula described as the 'Hot Revolutionary War'. Galula identified three geographical areas in any insurgency-counterinsurgency conflict: red areas, where insurgents control the local population and carry out guerrilla warfare; pink areas, where insurgents attempt to expand their influence; and white areas, which are unaffected but under threat of insurgency.[103] Angola was, by 1976, a safe haven for insurgents who paid, at least, lip service to the MPLA, thus qualifying as Galula's red zone. The northern parts of Namibia could be seen as a pink zone, while central Namibia formed the white zone. Pretoria's war effort was, in large part, focused on maintaining and extending the white zone and diminishing the pink and red zones, even if the latter meant ignoring Angola's territorial sovereignty.

South African Prime Minister BJ Vorster's attempts to 'exploit cleavages on the African scene that cut across anti-apartheid sentiments and thereby gain limited forms of international acceptance'[104] gained South Africa some international traction, but she was still isolated, both geographically and ideologically, from the rest of the West. In an attempt to address this situation, and to combat the challenges that the African National Congress (ANC) issued to the South African government, Pretoria established a national security state to promote readiness. Chris Alden rightly puts the Cold War at the heart of the establishment of the national security state in South Africa and highlights three defining characteristics of this form of counter-revolutionary action:

> ...the governing authorities' acceptance of counter-revolutionary strategy, with its twin pillars of security and reform, as the foundation or basis of national policy; the implementation of the security and reformist measures contained within counter-revolutionary strategy by the state; and, at the policy-making level, the constant and evolving tension between security concerns and reform imperatives in response to the environment into which they were thrust.[105]

In contrast to the Cold War dynamics of Lusophone Africa and Cuba, South Africa was limited in its ability to agitate for external superpower aid because of the National Party's apartheid doctrine. Especially after the Sharpeville protests in 1960, during which the SAP killed 69 black protestors, international condemnation of apartheid increased significantly. The banning of black and seemingly subversive political organisations by South African Prime Minister, Hendrik Verwoerd, forced these organisations into exile. While they were compelled to continue their liberation efforts outside the borders of South Africa, the ANC in particular was able to effectively engage the international community and raise awareness of the political circumstances in South

103 D. Galula, *Counterinsurgency Warfare: Theory and Practice*. London: Pall Mall Press, 1964, p.70.
104 J. Miller, *An African Volk: The apartheid regime and its search for survival*. Oxford: Oxford University Press, 2016, p.62.
105 Alden, *Apartheid's Last Stand*, p.6; Miller, *An African Volk*, p.94.

Africa. Despite growing international pressure on South Africa's domestic policies, the country's internal situation, at least as far as the white electorate was concerned, was essentially positive. Following the banning of subversive organisations, the very public Rivonia trials where Nelson Mandela, Walter Sisulu, Govan Mbeki, and other prominent black political leaders were sentenced to imprisonment, and the election of John Vorster as Prime Minister after the assassination of Verwoerd in 1966, the South African economy boomed thanks largely to mining and agriculture – both propped up by cheap black labour – and political unrest was muted.[106]

In South Africa, where revolutionary and/or insurgent activity was negligible, compared to the rest of Africa, in the late 1960s and 1970s, the adoption of a national security state therefore seems excessive. However, international pressure on Pretoria about its apartheid policy had intimated that South Africa would be unlikely to receive assistance from the West – traditional South African allies – in the event of a communist-backed revolution. South Africa's establishment of a national security state was, therefore, pre-emptive more than reactionary and contributed to the fact that South Africa was the last southern African country to be governed by a political organisation with ties to the East, with the ANC only attaining the seats of power after the MPLA in Angola, the Front for the Liberation of Mozambique (FRELIMO) in Mozambique, the Zimbabwe African National Union – Patriotic Front (ZANU-PF) in Zimbabwe, SWAPO in Namibia, the United National Independence Party (UNIP) in Zambia. The merit or demerit of the longevity of minority rule in South Africa is not the point at issue, merely the contention that Pretoria's implementation of a national security state contributed towards that longevity.

Conclusion

A series of global historical events intersected in southern Africa during the middle of the twentieth century to provide the setting for the armed conflicts in the region. The end of the Second World War saw the rise of the two superpower blocs, NATO and WP. The opposition of these two forces permeated virtually the entire globe, with southern Africa being no exception. In addition, traditional European colonial countries were ever increasingly granting independence to colonies that had moved from enriching their colonial overlords to becoming liabilities. This was particularly the case with Portugal and her African colonies, especially Angola. White minority rule in South Africa and, to a lesser extent, Rhodesia, coincided with the rise of the Cold War and organically influenced the military thinking of these countries. The sum of all these parts amounted to extended conflicts in southern Africa, not only between white and

106 Cf. B. Ndaba & J. Smith, 'The Soweto massacre and the growth of a new Black Consciousness' in B. Ndaba, et al, *The Black Consciousness Reader*. Johannesburg: Jacana, 2017, p.153; Alden, *Apartheid's Last Stand*, pp.19–21.

black or pro-apartheid and anti-colonial, but also between various indigenous organisations vying for power in their respective countries. Both NATO and WP countries actively supported, if not encouraged, these conflicts to serve their own purposes. Faced with increasing political and economic isolation, South Africa mobilised her, already strong, economy and industry to become the leading power broker in southern Africa. The forge that would shape not only 32 Battalion, but much of southern African society during the second half of the twentieth century, although small by international standards, had an enormous impact on the inhabitants of the countries that were directly involved, South Africa, Angola, Namibia and Cuba.

2

'The Anvil': Joining the Battalion

Even the most casual student of the Border War is aware of the fact that, on the South African side, a number of units consisted of white officers and black soldiers. 32 Battalion was, originally, one such unit, with Koevoet, 31 Battalion and, to an extent, the 'ethnic battalions' of SWATF – 101 Battalion, 201 Battalion, 301 Battalion and so on – being other examples.[1]

Additionally, in the case of 32 Battalion, the white officers came from two resource pools: some were drawn from the SADF's Permanent Force (PF), while the rest were either national servicemen (NSM) or from the Citizen Force, where NSM were required to serve after their national service. These two groups did not necessarily share the same view of the war and South Africa's involvement in it, with the PF soldiers naturally being more pragmatic about the war than the conscripted NSM.[2] Nonetheless, Gary Baines contends that 'SADF veterans constitute a generation whose formative years were spent in the militarised environment of apartheid South Africa. As such, they shared certain lived experience that influenced their values and sense of collective identity.'[3]

While the generic grouping of all SADF veterans into a single 'generation' poses some difficulties – the formative years of *all* SADF veterans were certainly *not* spent in apartheid South Africa – the influence of military service on their identity and morals cannot be denied. This makes it sensible to examine the circumstances in which soldiers joined the SADF, and specifically 32 Battalion, in greater detail.

The black soldiers of 32 Battalion can also be divided into two broad categories: the ex-FNLA troops of Bravo Group that were the original 32 Battalion soldiers and then those that joined the unit at a later stage. The original members referred to themselves as *sete seis* (Portuguese for 76, the year in which they had become Bravo Group)[4] and were proud of the fact that they were the nucleus of 32 Battalion. Those joining later

1 Cf. L. Scholtz, *Die SAW in die Grensoorlog: 1966–1989.* Cape Town: Tafelberg, 2013, p.53.
2 G. Baines, *South Africa's 'Border War': Contested narratives and conflicting memories.* London: Bloomsbury, 2014, pp.18–19.
3 Baines, *South Africa's 'Border War',* p.171.
4 P. Nortje, *The Terrible Ones: A complete history of 32 Battalion.* Cape Town: Zebra, p.249.

were, initially, still from outside South Africa but, towards the end of the war and during deployments inside South Africa from 1989 to 1993, South Africans, both white and black, also joined the unit as riflemen. For this reason, it is just as inaccurate to refer to all the black soldiers of 32 Battalion by using the generic term 'Portuguese' as it was to refer to the soldiers of the Senegalese Rifles (*Tirailleurs Senegalais*) in French West Africa as all being Senegalese.[5] The make-up of 32 Battalion provides an ideal opportunity to study combat motivation; the reason why soldiers choose to go to war and join a specific unit.

Angola

Socio-Political Realities

Contrary to the largely comfortable lives that many of the South African conscripts – both those opposed to and supportive of the National Party (NP), SADF and their policies – had led before becoming involved in the war, Angola was in much more turmoil and the average standard of living was significantly worse than in white South Africa. Rialize Ferreira and Ian Liebenberg provide a succinct, if somewhat simplistic, version of the situation in Angola leading up to Operation Savannah in 1975. They point out that the country had been embroiled in war since 1961, with three nationalist guerrilla armies fighting the Portuguese. Holden Roberto's FNLA had the backing of Zaire, China and 'some Arab states' and contested the north of Angola. In the south of the country, self-proclaimed anti-communist Jonas Savimbi's UNITA opposed the Portuguese with aid from Zambia, South Africa and the US.[6] The third movement, Agostinho Neto's MPLA, was supported by the USSR and other WP countries.[7] The anti-colonial revolt by these three groups had begun in 1961. The Angolan economy was in recession due to the collapse of the coffee price (one of Angola's main exports at the time) as well as uncertainty and inefficiency in the cotton and fishing sectors. Portuguese authorities' failure to pay peasant cotton growers – a notoriously labour-intensive crop[8] – in their enforced growing scheme in 1961 was the catalyst for revolt.[9] Significantly, this occurred some 15 years before the SADF deployed to Angola, but the average Angolan was already experiencing hardship. The anti-colonial struggles that raged from 1961 to 1975 did nothing to alleviate pressure on the already lacklustre Angolan economy.

5 Cf. M. J. Echenberg, 'Paying the Blood Tax: Military Conscription in French West Africa, 1914–1929' in: *Canadian Journal of African Studies 9 (2)*, 1975, p.174.
6 R. Ferreira & I. Liebenberg, 'The impact of war on Angola and South Africa: Two southern African case studies'. In *Journal for Contemporary History 31 (3)*, 2006, p.45.
7 W. S. van der Waals, *Portugal's war in Angola 1961–1974*. Pretoria: Protea, 2011, pp.165–169; K. Maier, *Angola: Promises and lies*. Rivonia: William Waterman, 1996, pp.16–17; R. Ferreira & I. Liebenberg, 'The impact of war on Angola and South Africa', p.45.
8 M. de Andrade & M. Ollivier, *The War in Angola: a socio-economic study*. Dar es Salaam: Tanzania Publishing House, 1975, p.63.
9 R. Cornwell, 'The War for Independence' in J. Cilliers & C. Dietrich (eds), *Angola's War Economy; the role of oil and diamonds*. Pretoria: Institute for Security Studies, 2000, p.48.

After Lisbon announced the intention to abandon her Angolan colony, the war of independence that these three groups had waged against Portugal turned into a civil war for control of a soon-to-be-independent Angola. Despite the efforts of the SADF, including the deployment of the ex-FNLA troops that would become 32 Battalion, to secure as much of Angola as possible on behalf of UNITA before 11 November 1975, the date set for independence, the MPLA emerged as the victor in Luanda and assumed the mantle of government. However, as Zaire depended on the Benguela railway, that ran through Angola, to export its copper, President Mabutu Sese Seko could not afford to antagonise the MPLA. At the same time, the US and, particularly, South Africa were under increasing international and domestic pressure to cease or scale down their activities in Angola. The USSR, however, was under no such restrictions and continued to support the MPLA unabated.[10] Unsurprisingly, this resulted in the MPLA's armed wing, FAPLA, being significantly better supplied and provisioned than the armed forces of UNITA (the Armed Forces of the Liberation of Angola [FALA]) or the FNLA (the Army for the National Liberation of Angola [ELNA]). UNITA and parts of the FNLA were also geographically closer to the Angola-Namibia border, making them more likely to come in contact with, and be influenced by, South African forces. The MPLA, who had held sway in Luanda since the start of the struggle for post-independence power, drew its greatest support from urban Angolans, at least in part due to the fact that the MPLA propaganda machine was able to reach more people in the cities than in the country.[11] The rural population was much more inclined to support UNITA or even the FNLA. David Birmingham, illustrates how the people who had done the most to secure independence were now the ones that derived the least benefit from it, especially in an Angola that did not have much to offer her people in the first place:

> The heroes of the revolution had been the workers and the peasants. The workers in the capital had discovered that their expectations had been pitched too high and independence was not all golden. The peasants learned the same lesson even more bitterly. They had been painfully incorporated into the market economy by the colonial power in the 1960s. Now in the 1970s and 1980s they were even more painfully torn away from market opportunities. By the 1980s peasants in almost all areas of the country were disenchanted with their government and open to the suggestion that alternative political movements might offer them a better range of opportunities. The short-lived rebellion of the town was followed by the long-lasting rebellion of the countryside.[12]

10 H. De Beer & V. Gamba, 'The arms dilemma: resources for arms or arms for resources?' in J. Cilliers & C. Dietrich (eds), *Angola's War Economy; the role of oil and diamonds*. Pretoria: Institute for Security Studies, 2000, pp.71–73.

11 J. Pearce, *Political identity and conflict in central Angola, 1975–2002*. Cambridge: Cambridge University Press, 2015, p.34.

12 D. Birmingham, *Empire in Africa: Angola and its neighbors*. Athens: Ohio University Press, 2006, p.112.

This dichotomy between urban and rural revolt gives some perspective on the soldiers of 32 Battalion. For the most part, they came from more rural backgrounds, part of the group that Birmingham identifies as having a more long-term view of the struggle for independence and self-rule. While the city-based revolutionaries wanted a quicker solution, rural society was prepared to play more of a waiting game. This was both an advantage and disadvantage to the soldiers of 32 Battalion: their history would prove that their inherent patience would stand them in good stead, but a somewhat more aggressive approach might have succeeded in securing them a better future.

Although UNITA continued to oppose the ruling MPLA until the death of its founder, Jonas Savimbi, in 2002, neither UNITA nor the FNLA provided ordinary Angolans with a realistic opportunity to oppose the government in power. This left them with two choices: look for a better future elsewhere and abandon the hope of changing the Angolan political landscape for the better, or support an opposition group – UNITA emerging as the strongest contender – and endure the attendant hardship in the hope of a better Angola. The net result was that the Angolans who chose to look for a better future alongside the South Africans, because their own organisations could not adequately provide for them, were also those who were in the best geographical position to do so (cf. on p. 54). Therefore, very few members of FAPLA ever joined the SADF / SWATF, while troops from FALA or ELNA were much more likely to support the South Africans. Additionally, FAPLA had a much more active propaganda machine than either of the other two organisations, as illustrated by a flyer distributed to FALA troops in 1977, translated by the SADF, which claimed that:

> You are all suffering extraordinary [*sic*]. Savimbi and Unita are deceiving you. The FAPLA domain [*sic*: dominate] the whole of Angola and the enemy is only in the bush until our troops enter, then we destroy. You can all return to your families and live in peace, no [*sic*: now] Angola is free, without colonists nor South African racists. Anyone who can write can join the march to prevent Unita control in the bush. You will be accepted by FAPLA as a brother...[13]

It should be noted that support from FALA or ELNA was rarely given due to ideological or personal convictions, but rather in search of a better quality of life. In fact, a 1977 SADF analysis of the local population of the Omholo-region concluded, using the vernacular term 'terr', or terrorist, to refer to FAPLA, that 'the local population does not doubt that the terrorist will free them.'[14] An SADF intelligence summary for July 1977 echoes this sentiment with a case study of a black woman working in a bakery in Oshakati, claiming that the woman was very negative towards whites and very vocal

13 DODDC, 32 Bn, Box 7, G/INT/1/ALG, Algemeen, Soldados das FALA.

14 DODDC, 32 Bn, Box 7, G/OPS/3/3, Vol. 1, Insam, Insidentelys tot Insam 7/77. Afrikaans: *daar is ... geen twyfel oor die PB ... dat die terr hulle sal bevry nie.*

about it.[15] Nonetheless, the coincidental rejection of the USSR's communist policies by those that did seek greener pastures with the SADF created an environment more conducive to cooperation than would have been the case otherwise. Interviewed in 2005, former 32 Battalion officer, Kevin Fitzgerald, recalls his impression of the political alignment of the early, ex-FNLA troops: '...they hated communism ... more than they hated the Portuguese, they knew that they were educated, they knew what communism would do to their country. If the Americans had stuck with the FNLA ... Angola today would be successful.'[16]

David da Silva (pseudonym), a former soldier of 32 Battalion, echoes Fitzgerald's impression, recalling that the men of 32 Battalion 'hated FAPLA, and ... UNITA as well.'[17]

Some members of FALA and / or ELNA did, however, join the SADF as a result of hardships suffered at the hands of FAPLA. Despite the propaganda efforts and the perception in some areas that supporting FAPLA was the route to a better Angola, some FAPLA practices offended the local population and could only have encouraged them to join an organisation that resisted the MPLA, of which the SADF was, of course, one option. One such a practice, in the early days of the war, was for FAPLA to kill and slaughter the livestock of the local population to supplement their provisions. It was also not uncommon for FAPLA soldiers to take money and possessions of local villagers.[18] In an effort to deny UNITA the support of the local population in southern Angola, FAPLA launched a determined effort towards the end of 1976 to ensure that the civilians were not in a position to give any aid to UNITA. To this end, according to a SADF intelligence report, they robbed civilians of many of their possessions and livestock, and took 'any extra provisions' from the locals, so that it could not be passed on to UNITA.[19] While parallels can be drawn with successful 'scorched earth' policies elsewhere in history, notably during the Anglo-South African War of 1899–1902,[20] this intimidation and deprivation of the local population was sure to convince some of them that it would be better to support an organisation other than the MPLA, and South Africa was a viable alternative.

Several years into the existence of 32 Battalion, in 1982, the SADF investigated the possibility of establishing a 'political, cultural, social organisation of Angolans in SWA/ Namibia.' The aim of this organisation was to motivate Angolans in Namibia to support

15 DODDC, 32 Bn, Box 7, G/OPS/3/3, Vol. 1, Insam, Insidentelys tot Insam 6/77.
16 Historical Papers, Missing Voices, A3079-B1-11-001, Kevin Fitzgerald Tape 0/11, A3079/B.21.
17 Interview with David da Silva (pseudonym), former 32 Battalion soldier, Pretoria, 20-06-2019.
18 DODDC, 32 Bn, Box 7, G/OPS/3/3, Vol. 1, Insam, Message INL/213/FEB 77 from 2 MG to 101 TM.
19 DODDC, 32 Bn, Box 8, G/INT/5/1, Inligting samevatting, Message INL/341/OKT 76 from 101 TM to H Leer. Afrikaans: *enige ekstra lewensmiddele.*
20 Cf. F. Pretorius, *Life on Commando During the Anglo-Boer War, 1899–1902.* Cape Town: Human & Rousseau, 1999.

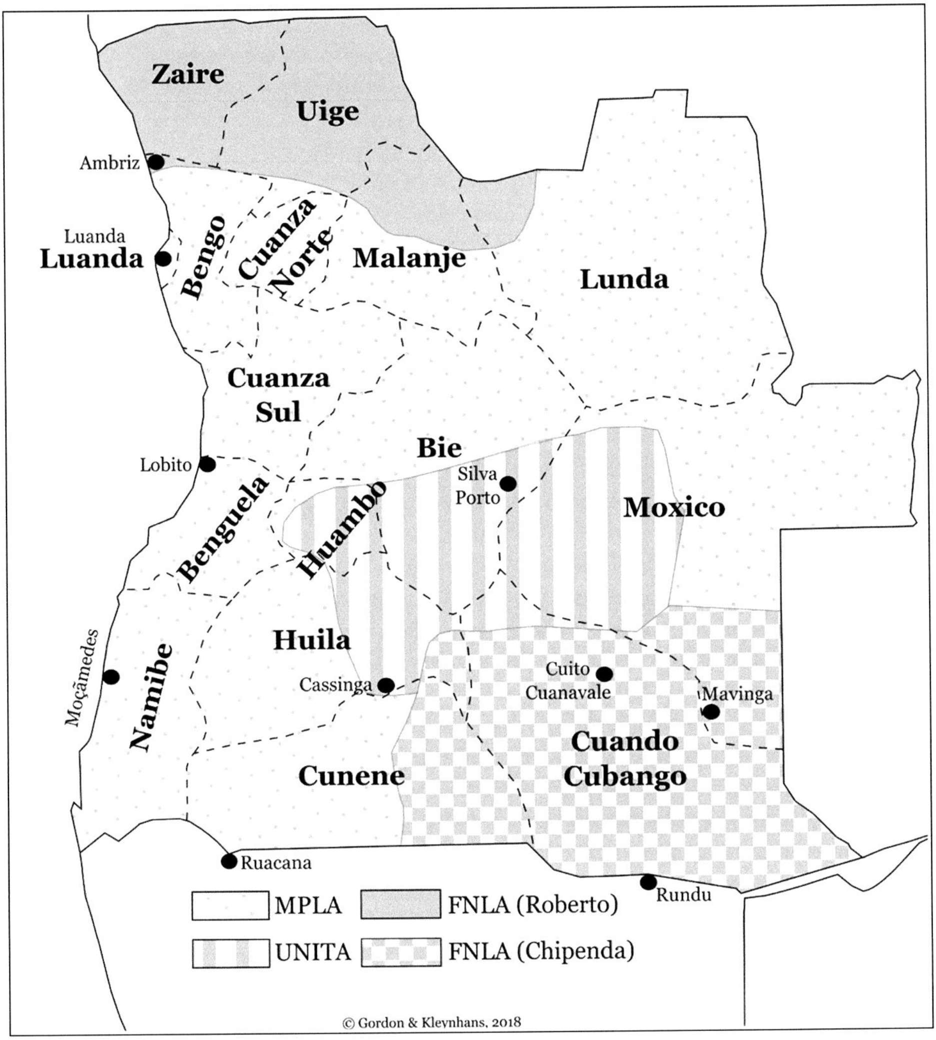

Areas of support for the Angolan liberation movements, 1975.

the SADF and not SWAPO. To maximise this support, the organisation envisaged that all Angolans in Namibia – estimated at between 38,000 and 80,000 – would have the right to vote in the Namibian elections.[21] While this made sense from a South African

21 DODDC, 32 Bn Gp 2A, Box 132, Inligting, Vol. 1, 32 Bn Sielkundige Fiksie, Minute about a session held on 30 November 1982 in Windhoek to discuss and appreciate basics for a establishment of a political, cultural, social organisation of Angolans in SWA/Namibia.

perspective – the more votes they could garner, the less likely SWAPO was to win an election – the impact of the enfranchising of Angolans cannot be underestimated. While Angola had held some form of elections following Portugal's departure, it is likely that, for the majority of Angolans, at least those serving with 32 Battalion, this was the first time in their lives that they were promised a role in determining their own future, even if that future was to Pretoria's benefit.

Perceptions

The early perception of ethnic units, such as 32 Battalion, against the backdrop of the Angolan socio-economic situation at the time, is fascinating. Writing as part of the 'Perspectives on southern Africa' series of books, commissioned by the University of California Press, in 1983 Kenneth Grundy illustrates both the secrecy that still surrounded 32 Battalion at that time, as well as the misconceptions that were, intentionally and otherwise, popularised regarding Pretoria's use of black troops, built around kernels of truth:

> Even more interesting is the 32 Battalion, known as the Buffalo Battalion, a 1,000-man unit formed as a direct outgrowth of the Angolan Civil War and South Africa's military intervention therein. Large numbers of refugees fled the fighting in Angola into Namibia ... Many were housed and fed by the South African authorities. In 1976 the SADF decided to recruit among these refugees, who were both black, white and mixed-race Portuguese speakers. Most of its ranks are former members of the FNLA's army. Black members of the Portuguese Army were signed on, too. They are under short-term contracts, normally for one year. If they have had military experience they are paid a bonus on signing of around $600, and at the end of their terms they are given an additional $1,900 bonus. Later a black Angolan who claimed to be a captain in the 32 Battalion reported that he was paid around $1,000 per month and $12,000 at the end of his contract.[22]

Unfortunately, Grundy does not reveal the source of his information. However, when compared to the impassioned pleas of the first Officer Commanding (OC) of 32 Battalion, Jan Breytenbach, to secure some sort of representative remuneration for his troops in 1976 (the source of which *is* available in the South African Department of Defence Documentation Centre), Grundy's contention almost seems comical. Breytenbach had to campaign aggressively to convince the SADF to pay platoon leaders of 32 Battalion R480 per year, with no guarantee of a bonus.[23] Table 3.1 provides a more comprehensive breakdown of Breytenbach's proposed salary scale, and indicates payment by the soldier's role in the unit. Of course, the Rand-Dollar exchange rate looked somewhat

22 K. W. Grundy, *Soldiers Without Politics; Blacks in the South African Armed Forces*. Los Angeles: University of California Press, 1983, pp.259–260.
23 DODDC, 32 Bn, Box 14, G/OPS/3/3, Vol. 1, Budgie – B Group, Salarisskaal: B Groep.

different in 1976 than it currently does, but the $24,000 that the so-called 'captain' claimed to be earning still equates to about R20,600 at the time.

There is no way that the SADF would have allowed Grundy to access documents relating to 32 Battalion in 1983 – those documents are still classified today and access to them continues to present a researcher with some difficulty – so his blatantly inflated claims can, perhaps, be overlooked. However, the inaccuracies in his account are indicative of what the global rumour-mill was grinding out in the early 1980s. In two comparatively balanced articles that appeared early in 1981, British newspaper *The Guardian* nonetheless enhanced the popular misconception about conditions and circumstances in 32 Battalion. Based largely on interviews with a former 32 Battalion member who went absent without leave during a patrol and subsequently made his way to London, Trevor John Edwards, and a black Angolan, 'captain' Jose Ricardo Belmundo (there were no black officers in the unit at the time), *The Guardian*'s account, like Grundy's, illustrated more favourable conditions in 32 Battalion than reality proved. 'Captain' Belmundo claimed to have been part of the ex-FNLA group of soldiers who became the core of 32 Battalion during Operation Savannah in 1976, and that he was promoted to second lieutenant after undergoing 'commando training'. In a convolution of nomenclature, he claimed to have been part of a reconnaissance unit, Number Five, commander by Colonel Carpenter (Breytenbach's radio call-sign).[24]

A unit called 5 Reconnaissance Regiment did, of course, exist, but had no relation to 32 Battalion or its reconnaissance wings. Trevor John Edwards' interview was much more sensational than that of Belmundo. Edwards' accounts of unrestricted, uncontrolled violence, rape, and pillage would certainly have sold newspapers, but was devoid of all but the most humble kernels of truth.[25] The point of grouping these three accounts together is to illustrate what kind of information regarding 32 Battalion was permeating the SADF's layers of secrecy. For an Angolan, who had been waging war for most of his life and potentially did not have any skills other than fighting his enemies, the promise of unimagined riches as described by Grundy must have had strong allure. Additionally, Belmundo's alleged relatively quick promotion would have appealed to the Angolan soldiers, particularly those who were accustomed to operating under the direction and command of a politically-appointed *commissar*. Even Edwards' description of the opportunity to loot and pillage, virtually unchecked, would undoubtedly have appealed to the less savoury individuals that are inevitably found in any military organisation, but would also have been a means of empowering a group of people with limited opportunities. On a socio-psychological level, it might also have been perceived as an opportunity to assert an individual's masculinity, given that the socio-economic conditions in Angola had, from the perspective of the patriarch protecting and providing for his family, largely emasculated Angolan soldiers. Joanna Bourke, though writing about a form of warfare that was uncommon during the Border War, hand-to-hand combat,

24 J. Steele, 'Defector describes SA raids into Angola' in *The Guardian*, 2 February 1981.
25 Anon., 'South Africa's Secret War of Terror' in *The Guardian*, 29 January 1981.

nonetheless identifies a connection between the way in which soldiers reflect on their memories of killing in war that has distinct links with their masculinity and sexuality. Though the form of killing would differ, the links remained:

> Men preparing for a trench raid would pass 'caressing' hands over their bayonets, all the while preparing for that moment of bliss when the blade would be 'driven deep' into another man's chest 'so that his heart's blood spurts in a great jet onto the muzzle of the gun.' It is no coincidence that men bragged most frequently about their bayoneting exploits to mothers, sisters and girlfriends, rather than to fathers, brothers and male comrades.[26]

John Lynn argues that a distinction exists between 'the reality of war and the way in which a culture conceives of war: between the concrete and the conceptual.'[27] By extension, the way in which cultures perceive, and agree or disagree with, conflicts must necessarily influence the motivation of soldiers to participate in those conflicts. In the case of the future members of 32 Battalion, this distinction is blurred by the fact that they were well aware of the nature of the conflict in which they were involved. While the political ideology of the FNLA and the SADF differed, the reality of war largely remained the same for the men doing the fighting.

FAPLA and SWAPO

Even before the Border War escalated to the point where South Africa became involved on a larger scale, and before the MPLA became the ruling party in Angola, FAPLA and SWAPO, possibly because of their pro-communist orientation, cooperated closely with one another. After Angolan independence, FAPLA undoubtedly became the senior partner in the mutualistic relationship, because they were able to become a conventional defence force with the backing of a recognised government. Soviet aid further increased their combat capacity.[28] Nonetheless, the loose alliance between FAPLA and SWAPO continued, at times complicating the situation that the SADF faced, as they were, theoretically, only concerned with countering Namibian insurgents and did not want to engage FAPLA. However, several examples make it clear that this was a near-impossible task. On 16 February 1977, the SADF was involved in a skirmish with SWAPO forces on the Namibia-Angola border. SWAPO initiated the contact, but when the SADF forces returned fire, FAPLA called down mortar fire on the SADF forces. Although no casualties resulted, it was clear to the SADF that SWAPO 'fired on the Security

26 J. Bourke, *An Intimate History of Killing: Face-to-Face killing in twentieth-century warfare.* London: Granta Books, 1999, pp.54–55.

27 J. A. Lynn, 'Discourse, Reality and the Culture of Combat' in *The International History Review 27 (3)*, 2005, p.475.

28 C. Andrew & V. Mitrokhin, *The World was Going our Way: The KGB and the battle for the Third World.* Perseus Books, 2005, p.445.

Forces over the top of the MPLA, to ignite a confrontation between MPLA/RSA.'[29] A SAP informant also reported that SWAPO, in some cases, wore the same uniform as FAPLA,[30] further blurring the lines between the two organisations.

Illustrating the relationship between FAPLA and SWAPO allows the conclusion that the actions of FAPLA would, to a certain extent, reflect on SWAPO and, to a much greater extent, that the actions of SWAPO would have been linked to FAPLA. In other words, if SWAPO interacted with the local population in southern Angola or northern Namibia, it is unlikely that there would have been a clear distinction between the two groups in the minds of the civilians. This means that SWAPO's actions would also have influenced how FAPLA was viewed, and how this would have influenced the Angolan (and Namibian) population in choosing where to direct their support. To this end, an examination of a few SWAPO-practices is useful.

Continued dedication to the organisation was important to SWAPO, and they did not hesitate to impose harsh sentences, even on senior members of their ranks. An example of this can be found in an interview, conducted by the SADF, with one Raphael Shoopala. Shoopala was the SWAPO Secretary of Foreign Affairs, as well as the SWAPO representative in Botswana. Nonetheless, when he handed in his resignation, due to his perceived corruption within SWAPO ranks, in 1975, he was imprisoned in the Remand Prison in Lusaka for approximately 18 months.[31] While imprisoned there, Shoopala met 15 other SWAPO members, some of whom had been in prison for five years. According to Shoopala, these men had been classified as illegal immigrants by the Zambian government, at the request of SWAPO, and therefore had no recourse to Zambian courts. Their 'crimes' ranged from desertion from SWAPO to, like Shoopala, requesting resignations. According to Shoopala, though, these men had been the lucky ones, as SWAPO's leader, Sam Nujoma, had ordered the execution of some other SWAPO members, mostly Caprivians, who had attempted to leave the organisation to join the Caprivi African National Union.[32]

Angolans in 32 Battalion

In contrast to the South African component, few Angolans joined 32 Battalion for political or ideological reasons. The initial group of ex-FNLA troops, the *sete seis*, became part of the South African forces almost by accident. Many of the Angolans that joined early in 1976, immediately after Operation Savannah, would have had a choice between life – and the attendant uncertain future – in a refugee camp or, perhaps the more

29 DODDC, 32 Bn, Box 7, G/OPS/3/3, Vol. 1, Insam, Inligtingsamevatting 7/77 Tydperk 12 Feb to 25 Feb 1977. Afrikaans: *oor MPLA op VM gevuur het om konfrontasie tussen MPLA/ RSA te ontketen.*

30 DODDC, 32 Bn, Box 7, G/OPS/3/3, Vol. 1, Insam, Afdeling 1: SWAPO.

31 DODDC, 32 Bn, Box 8, G/INT/5/1, Inligting Samevatting, Onderhoud met Raphael, Shoopala alias Lucky, p.2.

32 DODDC, 32 Bn, Box 8, G/INT/5/1, Inligting Samevatting, Onderhoud met Raphael, Shoopala alias Lucky, pp.6–8.

pragmatic approach, joining the SADF in units such as 32 Battalion. To capitalise on this pool of available manpower, 32 Battalion gained access to nominal rolls of civilians that had acted in political capacities for the FNLA, as well as soldiers of ELNA. The list of civilians identified 193 people from 34 families[33] – the list includes dependents – that could potentially be beneficial to 32 Battalion, while the military list identified 116 men – excluding families – who had previous military experience with ELNA.[34]

Subsequently, Angolans joined the unit either because of misconceptions about the possibilities and opportunities within the unit, or because even the reality of life with 32 Battalion was preferable to the lives they had led previously. This does not mean that Angolans were apathetic towards the politico-military situation in their country. On the contrary, where South Africans were debating the rights and wrongs of protecting the sovereignty of their homeland in a war hundreds of miles distant, Angolans had been doing it on their doorstep for decades. The Medical Officer at Bravo Group in September 1976, Lieutenant (Dr) Jacobs, came to the same conclusion, claiming that the morale of the black troops was good, as they 'like being soldiers and strive towards winning back their country.'[35] This is certainly not the mentality of soldiers who only fought for money.

However, circumstances had led many Angolans to believe that their contribution to the independence struggle had been negated by the subsequent assumption of power by the MPLA and the attendant socio-economic imbalances. To a large extent, South Africa was seen as something of a saviour by many Angolans, particularly from the rural south. Even those that were not interested in joining the SADF, or unable to do so, still sought help from the South Africans, whether through official channels or otherwise. To that effect, in early 1977, it became commonplace for Angolan refugees to approach South African NSM with the expectation that the latter would be able to help address their problems.[36] The SADF did, in some cases, make promises to Angolans in their ranks, as with Staff Sergeant Kanganjo, who was promised that his wife and children would be relocated from Zaire and reunited with him.[37] How, exactly, the SADF planned to do this, is a mystery, but the incident serves to indicate that, at least, some Angolans expected something from the SADF in return for their service. In some cases, 32 Battalion did attempt to assist its soldiers in reuniting with their families, the most well-known case occurring in 1981 when 32 Battalion OC, Deon Ferreira, authorised a Reconnaissance Wing special operation into Angola to retrieve the family

33 DODDC, 32 Bn, Box 14, G/OPS/3/3, Vol. 1, Porto Vlugtelinge, Relação Nominal dos Civis da FNLA.

34 DODDC, 32 Bn, Box 14, G/OPS/3/3, Vol. 1, Porto Vlugtelinge, Relação Nominal dos Militares do ELNA.

35 DODDC, 32 Bn, Box 9, LOG/OPS/3/16/8, Vol. 1, Medies en gesondheid (Verslae, aanvrae, ens.), Report from Lt. Jacobs to Maj. Greeff, 8 Septemebr 1976. Afrikaans: *hou daarvan om soldaat te wees en … strewe om hulle land terug te wen.*

36 DODDC, 1 MG, Box 82, Troep Bew: Feb, Message SEC/636/JAN 77 from 13 Sub Area to 101 TM.

37 DODDC, 32 Bn Gp 2, Box 28, 104/12/1/1, Vol. 1, Letter from S.Sgt. Kanganjo to Cmdt. Ferreira, 23 July 1979.

of Rfn Shopota. The operation was successful, and Shopota continued to serve with 32 Battalion until retirement. His family still lives in Pomfret, where 32 Battalion relocated after the war.[38] This was, however, the exception rather than the rule.

An additional factor that would have influenced Angolans' decisions on where to enlist their support can be found in the MPLA's interaction with the local population in southern Angola. This may well have further persuaded some of them that it was better to fight alongside the South Africans. Although a South African intelligence report on MPLA (and Cuban) crimes against the local population should be taken with a grain of salt, even if the report were based exclusively on rumours, these had to originate somewhere: '...children are abducted and parents that resist are summarily shot ... children's parents have to pay ransom, in the form of large quantities of cattle, to the Cubans.'[39]

The opportunity to earn a respectable living with the South Africans was too good an opportunity for many to refuse,[40] although some did grow disenchanted with the rigours of being professional soldiers in the SADF shortly after joining, perhaps accustomed to the more relaxed atmosphere in the Angolan liberation armies. In May 1976, after 3 weeks' service with Bravo Group, seven Angolan members of the unit applied for a week's 'home leave'. This was either a serious miscalculation on their part, or a ploy that worked out exactly as they had hoped, because they were deemed 'not beneficial to the SADF', and their employment was terminated immediately.[41] These men were not isolated cases, and some Angolan members inevitably continued to find life at 32 Battalion far different from their expectation. In September 1978, the unit recorded 44 Angolan members as absent without leave (AWOL), including a sergeant and two corporals.[42] An additional 77 members (including three corporals and one lance corporal) were discharged for other, undisclosed, reasons, but this would not have been the case if they had accepted the life and discipline of the unit.[43] However, the men and women who chose to remain with the SADF did so despite being given the opportunity to return to Angola – or even Portugal, if they qualified to do so – by the Portuguese consul during a visit to Bravo Group's base in October 1976.[44] This offer should, however, be viewed in the context of the time it was made: those who qualified for Portuguese residency or citizenship may have been able to accept the offer of going to Portugal, but it was unlikely that the Angolans at Bravo Group would have received quite as warm a welcome back in Angola.

38 Nortje, *The Terrible Ones*, pp.600–602.
39 DODDC, 32 Bn, Box 7, G/OPS/3/3, Vol. 1, Insam, G/INT/1/0: Insam 5/77. Afrikaans: ... *kinders word ontvoer en ouers wat weerstand bied word summier geskiet ... ouers van kinders moet losprys in die vorm van groot getalle beeste aan die Kubane betaal.*
40 Interview with Hilton Husson (pseudonym), former 32 Battalion soldier, Centurion, 10-07-2019.
41 DODDC, 1 MG, Box 82, G/OPS/3/3/BRAVO, Vol. 1, Message PERS/132/MEI 76 from 101 TM to H Leer. Afrikaans: *nie 'n aanwins vir die SAW.*
42 DODDC, 32 Bn, Box 50, 107/2/3, Ontslag SP lede, Ontslag SP lede.
43 DODDC, 32 Bn, Box 50, 107/2/3, Ontslag SP lede, Discharge list: SP members.
44 DODDC, 32 Bn, Box 7, G/OPS/3/3/LETTA, Vol. 1, Letta, Message OPS/368/OCT 76 from 101 TF to C Army.

It is very likely that at least one of the armed organisations in Angola would have viewed them as deserters, at best, or enemies, at worst. Edwin Eduardo (pseudonym), son of a former soldier of 32 Battalion and a young child in 1976, remembers the uncertainty of life in a refugee camp for him and his family. He is quite certain that his father joined the unit primarily as a means of providing for his family, albeit by utilising the soldiering skills that were familiar to him during his days as a member of the FNLA:

> When we moved from Angola, it was as a result of the [civil] war ... We moved from Angola to a concentration [*sic*] camp in Calai ... That is where we were received by ... Colonel Breytenbach ... My father, whilst in Angola, was affiliated to FNLA; ... he was part of the group of ... ex-combatants. Growing up in a concentration [*sic*] camp ... I remember that the then South African Defence Force used to supply us with food parcels, with clothing ... [which] for some of us was a luxury.[45]

Another indication of the fate that would probably have awaited soldiers of 32 Battalion in Angola can be seen in the attitude of Angolan civilians towards black soldiers of Bravo Group in 1976: an Angolan soldier of the unit strayed from the 'camp' that his section occupied and made his way to a local village. When he asked for water, he was attacked, stabbed and left unconscious. He only returned to his section the next day, whereupon a patrol was sent to the village to investigate the incident. While the white members of the patrol, with the aid of a black translator, questioned some of the villagers, another attacked a different black member of the patrol with a club. The assailant was only deterred from his attack by a warning salvo fired by members of Bravo Group.[46] While nobody was permanently injured by either of the attacks on members of Bravo Group – indeed, the mental image of a civilian attacking an armed soldier with a club borders on the comical – the attacks are indicative of the mentality of the local Angolan population towards their former countrymen, now serving South Africa, during the early stages of the war.

The perception from Angolans that joining the SADF, and 32 Battalion in particular, would have positive consequences did not diminish significantly over time, and in 1985, Angolans still opted to enlist with the unit, with 16 new recruits joining in February alone. The impression of Captain Heyns, base commander at 32 Battalion's training base, was that they were 'very positive and looking forward to their training.'[47] The SADF did not, however, consider the fact that the Angolans of the unit came from six different ethnic groups, with inherent socio-cultural differences. As far as the SADF

45 Interview with Edwin Eduardo (pseudonym), son of former 32 Battalion soldier; Kimbo and Pomfret resident, Wonderboom, 24-06-2019.

46 DODDC, 32 Bn, Box 9, LOG/OPS/3/16/4, Vol. 1, Dissipline en regsaangeleenthede (verhoormagte ens), Report by Sgt. N Clack, 16/2/76.

47 DODDC, 32 Bn Gp 2, Box 262, 522/4, Vol. 1, Konf., Kong, Semnaar, Simposiums + Vergaderings: Vergaderings, Maandverslag Opleidingsbasis vir die maand Februarie 1985. Afrikaans: *baie positief en sien uit na die opleiding*.

was concerned, all the Angolan soldiers essentially had the same background. This was, of course, not the case. Former 32 Battalion soldiers remember: 'That is something about 32 that is dealt with … very softly … there were … six different tribes [*sic*] that came out of Angola and now became a unit; lived in the same town.'[48]

South Africa

Conscription

No study of, or including, the SADF would be complete without giving some attention to conscription. The overwhelming majority of South African manpower was obtained by means of conscription and, although SADF propaganda strove to paint a different picture, not everyone was equally keen to do their stint 'on the border'.[49] Conversely, however, not everyone was opposed to conscription to such an extent as has become fashionable to claim. Graeme Callister astutely observes that 'Duty in the townships and combat on the border, as opposed to simply being stationed in Namibia, were also not typical national service experiences … involving only a minority of conscripts.'[50] He contends that much of the anti-conscription argument has become entangled with the anti-apartheid discourse and has, therefore, become an argument about the morality of apartheid itself. Because morality is subjective by nature, this entanglement has legitimised the subjective critique of conscription in many current works.[51] Fanus Fourie, however, indicates how successful attempts by the SADF were in 'mobilising and preparing' the community in the Vaal Triangle (on the border of the then Orange Free State and Transvaal provinces) during the mid-1970s.[52] This could not have been the case in the face of concerted resistance to SADF policies. Craig Cameron holds the belief that 'culture [is] a means of selectively creating collective identities from disparate elements' and that 'race has always served as a strong glue to hold together people who disagree on other grounds.'[53] The SADF was, for the most part, successful in using culture and race as a unifying and binding factor in white South Africa.

48 Group discussion with former 32 Battalion soldiers, Centurion, 10-07-2019. Afrikaans: *Dit is 'n ding van 32 wat baie … saggies hanteer word … daar was … ses verskillende stamme wat uit Angola gekom het en nou 'n unit geword het; in dieselfde dorp gebly het.*

49 M. Alexander, 'The Militarisation of South African White Society, 1948–1990' in *Scientia Militaria: South African Journal of Military Studies, 30 (2)*, 2000, p.285.

50 G. Callister, *Compliance, Compulsion and Contest: aspects of military conscription in South Africa, 1952–1992.* Stellenbosch University: MA thesis, 2007, pp.13–14.

51 Callister, *Compliance, Compulsion and Contest*, p.14.

52 S. M. Fourie, 'Van Mobilisering na Transformasie: Die era van Suid-Afrika se militêre hoogbloei met die Vaaldriehoekse samelewing (1974–1994) as konsentrasieveld' in *Scientia Militaria: South African Journal of Military Studies, 30 (2)*, 2000, pp.296–301. Afrikaans: *paraatmaking*.

53 C. M. Cameron, 'Race and Identity: The Culture of Combat in the Pacific War' in *The International History Review 27 (3)*, 2005, p.565.

Although 32 Battalion did, for the most part, attract both NSM and PF members that were keen to get involved in the fighting aspect of the war, particularly after their existence, character and reputation became public knowledge, some of the doubts and uncertainties about conscription would, inevitably, have been present among the white leader group of the unit. Additionally, as illustrated by Callister, this is the very group who was most likely to have negative experiences of conscription. This section does not aim to be a comprehensive study of the phenomenon of conscription, but rather highlight those aspects that might have influenced the thoughts and actions of the men who were to join 32 Battalion, as well as highlight the anomalous way in which the men of 32 Battalion experienced their national service, compared to the rest of the SADF conscripts.

Daniel Conway presents an excellent assessment of the relationship between the state and conscription, as well as the way in which conscription influences social identity. Before stating that 'Conscription as a performative concept is premised on republican norms of citizenship as a practice where political status and agency are earned and acknowledged rather than automatically conferred,'[54] he claims that 'Citizenship's central role in defining an individual's relationship with the state connects it with other politicised forms of identity, such as race and gender, which are constructed to mark boundaries and to include or exclude, empower or disempower.'[55]

Conway's interpretation of conscription is particularly reminiscent of apartheid South Africa, where the state certainly did their utmost to distinguish between those that were included or excluded and empowered or disempowered. This process started at an early age, with the government holding great store by the cadet system, in which boys were compelled, and girls encouraged, to participate in drill teams.[56] The logical continuation of this practice into adulthood – the concept that political status, and the social identity that accompanies it, are earned rather than conferred – can be seen throughout interviews with former members of the SADF. The Historical Papers Research Archive at the University of the Witwatersrand houses several such interviews in their Missing Voices Oral History Project.[57]

The theory, perpetrated by the NP government, that South Africa faced a 'multidimensional threat … in the sense that the Republic's enemies attack the constitutional, the economic, the social and the security bases in accordance with a coordinated plan or strategy'[58] lay not only at the heart of conscription, but at the heart of white South African citizenship, or even identity. Failure to render military service when it was needed not only carried the stigma of being a 'bad' citizen, but detracted from the

54 D. Conway, *Stop the call-up: Masculinities, militarisation and the end conscription campaign; war resistance in apartheid South Africa*. Johannesburg: University of the Witwatersrand, 2012, p.20.
55 Conway, *Stop the call-up*, p.20.
56 Alexander, 'The militarisation of South African white society', p.286.
57 Historical Papers, Missing Voices, A30179, Interviews and documents, 2004–2012.
58 Van Deventer as quoted by C. Alden, *Apartheid's Last Stand: The Rise and Fall of the South African Security State*. London: MacMillan, 1996, p.68.

very being of the young, white, South African male. Although the concept of a 'multi-dimensional threat', as well as Pretoria's 'Total National Strategy'[59] to combat it, was only verbalised in the 1970s, the reasoning that underpinned it had been present in South African thought for much longer. James Roherty contends that South African Prime Minister PW Botha was 'basically of a managerial bent'[60] and that his natural inclination was to think from a managerial perspective, trying to find ways in which to manage the *status quo*, rather than implement new ideas. This may have been the reason why the Total National Strategy was only implemented in the 1970s, but former Regimental Sergeant Major (RSM) of the Rand Light Infantry, John Keene, illustrates that, in the mind of the average, white South African, the road to a Total National Strategy might have started in World War Two:

> I was born in 1946 ... At school ... most of our fathers had served in the Second World War ... And the mind-set that we had developed at that stage was that our fathers had fought a war for the liberation of the human race and that the world offered a lot. The big problem that seemed to be on the minds of our parents was the threat of communism.[61]

Additionally, by the mid-1980s, South Africans were increasingly becoming aware that 'The Border' was as much of an ideological construct as it was a reference to the boundary dividing Angola and Namibia.[62] In popular Afrikaans discourse, the ideological 'Border' had expanded to encompass the perceived greater communist threat, both in southern and South Africa. The recollections of an English-speaking NSM, called up in 1982, is indicative of the dichotomy between Afrikaans and English-speaking South Africans and might reflect why the NP government felt that it had become necessary to formalise their approach to protect South Africa:

> ...I didn't really believe in this whole Communistic [*sic*] onslaught and all of that. I sort of believed that ... affectively [*sic*] we were in Angola because of a buffer, and affectively [*sic*] it was to keep space between us and whatever. I didn't really believe in this, that there was a Red under every bed and under every tree. That was propaganda ... The Afrikaners believed that they were going to swarm over us.[63]

59 Cf. Alden, *Apartheid's Last Stand*, p.51.
60 J. M. Roherty, *State Security in South Africa: Civil-military relations under PW Botha*. New York: M.E. Sharpe, 1992, p.38.
61 Historical Papers, Missing Voices, A3079-D4-001, John Keene interviewed by Mike Cadman 19-09-07.
62 M. Drewett, 'Battling over Borders: Narratives of Resistance to the South African Border War Voiced through Popular Music' in *Social Dynamics 29 (1)*, 2003, p.84.
63 Historical Papers, Missing Voices, A3079-D6-001, National Serviceman (name withheld) 10-09-07.

While Anton Oberholzer, who graduated from an Afrikaans high school in 1985 and was conscripted in 1986, confirms this view of the 'Afrikaners' to a certain extent by claiming that 'There was a stigma attached to the guys whose family were [*sic*] rich and they were sort of sent to Portugal or wherever to gyppo the army … as a white South African you had to go and fight for your country, and the communist force was pretty strong and moving towards South West Africa.'[64]

Dr Colin Forbes recalls that not all English-speaking South Africans were against conscription:

> I never questioned National Service, whether there was an option of going or not. I was fully committed to going … I thought it was my sort of patriotic duty. And my belief was that I was going to be helping the cause in protecting South Africa and the country that I identified with, from becoming something akin to what Zimbabwe is today.[65]

This train of thought is supported by ex-32 Battalion officer, Kevin Fitzgerald. Reflecting on the motivation of NSM to do national service, he remembers that

> …they served their country, most of those National Service men [*sic*] honestly believed they were serving their country, not serving [a] political party … but serving their country, the country where they lived, grew up, their homes that were precious to them, their families that were dear to them … they believed they were protecting that, not necessarily protecting [a] political system[66]

In fact, some NSM relished their time as conscripts.[67] Whatever their motivation, whether it was ideological, based on experiences in the SADF, or merely because they enjoyed the military milieu, the request of two NSM instructors in 1976 illuminates the pro-conscription perspective: After completing their 18 months' National Service, these two instructors, with 'good experience in unconventional war' indicated that they would be willing to extend their service for a further six months, provided that they could be deployed 'somewhere near the front'.[68] If these NSM were negative about their conscription, it stands to reason that they would have taken the first opportunity to return to South Africa and put the SADF behind them, while they actually did the diametrical opposite and sought out postings where they would be more likely to encounter the enemy.

64 Historical Papers, Missing Voices, A3079-D8-001, Anton Oberholzer Ratel 20mm Gunner 17-01-08.
65 Historical Papers, Missing Voices, A3079-D9-001, Dr Colin Forbes 4-11-07.
66 Historical Papers, Missing Voices, A3079-B1-11-001, Kevin Fitzgerald Tape 0/11, A3079/B.21.
67 Group discussion with former 32 Battalion soldiers, Centurion, 10-07-2019.
68 DODDC, 1 MG, Box 82, G/OPS/3/3/BRAVO, Vol. 1, Untitled radio transcript. Afrikaans: *goeie ondervinding in ongereelde* [*sic*] *oorlog*; *iewers voor.*

Supplementary to conscripts' understanding that they were protecting their homes, families and country, the concepts of masculinity and conscription as a kind of 'rite of passage' played an important part in promoting acceptance of the policy. In fact, the very idea that it is the duty of a man to protect the things that he loves and cherishes is an embodiment of hegemonic masculinity.[69] This stems from the contention that 'Masculinity is never fully possessed, but must perpetually be achieved, asserted and negotiated.'[70] To achieve the ultimate embodiment of masculinity, males are constantly required to re-assert and re-establish their claim to it. Some of the accepted norms of masculinity form a small part of the process and are easily overlooked, while others are central to the definition of a 'man'.[71] The most important of these in apartheid South Africa, Conway contends, was inextricably linked to conscription: 'At the pinnacle of South Africa's 'performance' of masculinity and citizenship was soldiering; to refuse to be a soldier was to forfeit political agency … and to embody subordinate masculinity.'[72] Much of South African men's struggle with issues around masculinity in the present stems from this concept of masculinity. Robert Morrell paints a vivid mental picture when he contrasts the 'grim-faced, rifle toting soldier clad in camouflage gear, patrolling the streets of a township' with a more contemporary 'colourful cross-dresser, strutting his stuff in a gay pride march.' It is, of course, much more acceptable to 'strut one's stuff' in a society where political agency is *not* linked to masculinity, but, as Morrell illustrates, this certainly was not the case during the Border War. Additionally, the mind-set was not limited to white South Africans. Black South Africans also developed what Thokozani Xaba referred to as 'struggle masculinity'; in a society where it was difficult to find firm foundations for any identity, black men identified themselves with a masculinity that was against anything that originated from the apartheid government, and were committed to 'political militancy'.[73] However, struggle veterans were unlikely to join 32 Battalion, particularly during the early years of its existence. For that reason, their quest for identity and masculinity will not be evaluated in depth.

Resistance to Conscription

Although conscription, by means of a ballot system (similar to that used at the beginning of the US's Vietnam War) was introduced in South Africa in the early 1950s,[74] resistance was largely limited to a critique of the balloting system itself, rather than the concept

69 Cf. Bourke, *An Intimate History of Killing*, pp.44–49.

70 Roper & Tosh, as quoted by D. Conway, 'Every coward's choice? Political objection to military service in apartheid South Africa as sexual citizenship' in *Citizenship Studies 8 (1)*, 2004, p.29.

71 R. Morrell, 'The times of change: Men and masculinity in South Africa' in R. Morrell (ed.), *Changing Men in Southern Africa*. Pietermaritzburg: University of Natal Press, 2001, p.3.

72 Conway, 'Every coward's choice?', p.29.

73 T. Xaba, 'Masculinity and its malcontents: The Confrontation between 'Struggle Masculinity' and 'Post-Struggle Masculinity' (1990–1997)' in R. Morrell (ed.), *Changing Men in southern Africa*. Pietermaritzburg: University of Natal Press, 2001, pp.108–109.

74 Alexander, 'The militarisation of South African white society', p.274.

of conscription.[75] The fact that the balloting was predominantly done by Afrikaans-speaking, National Party supporters irked the general public, as well as some leading politicians. The perceived reluctance of Afrikaners to join the Allied war effort during World War II led Sir De Villiers Graaff, leader of the Opposition, to comment that the people who were responsible for the balloting of conscripts '…refused to fight during World War II. Now they are apparently listing the young South Africans who are to fight during World War III.'[76] Although the idea that South Africans fighting in World War II were almost exclusively from the English-speaking communities of the country has largely been debunked by researchers such as Albert Grundlingh,[77] this is, nonetheless, indicative of the concerns of 1950s and 1960s South Africa, a time in which many of the future leader group of units such as 32 Battalion joined the Defence Force. In practice, however, early conscription did not prove as disastrous as some had predicted. Despite the influence of the National Party in the balloting-process, the Defence Force continued to be viewed as a predominantly English-speaking force into the 1950s,[78] to the extent that a committee, chaired by World War II Veteran Brigadier H. B. Klopper, was established in 1953 to 'create a more even geographical and language distribution in relation to the manpower made available by the introduction of the ballot system.'[79] The net result was that, on socio-linguistic grounds, while there may not have been complete acceptance, there was little or no actual resistance to the policy of conscription during the 1950s and 1960s.

In a trend that was to continue until the 1990s, the early resistance to conscription mainly came from religious objectors. In the UDF, conscientious objection was allowed under the King's (later Queen's) Regulations, but the South African Military Code of 1957 – replaced by the Defence Act (No.14 of 1957) – effectively eliminated the possibility of conscientious objection. The only exception was that members of pacifist churches, notably Jehovah's Witnesses, could request to be assigned to non-combat roles in the SADF.[80] In 1967, the Defence Amendment Act (No.85 of 1967) instituted universal conscription of white men to replace the balloting system that had existed up to that point. While it continued the 1957 Act's provision for objection, a few factors are worth noting.[81] The 1967 Act allowed for 'allotment' or 'exemption' as outcomes of

75 G. Callister, 'Patriotic duty or resented imposition? Public reactions to military conscription in white South Africa, 1952–1972'. In *Scientia Militaria: South African Journal of Military Studies, 35 (1)*, 2007, p.53.
76 Graaf, as quoted by Callister, 'Patriotic duty or resented imposition?', p.53.
77 A. Grundlingh, 'The King's Afrikaners? Enlistment and ethnic identity in the Union of South Africa's defence force during the Second World War, 1939–1945' in *Journal of African History, 40*, 1999, p.354.
78 Callister, 'Patriotic duty or resented imposition?', p.53.
79 I. van der Waag, *A military history of modern South Africa.* Cape Town: Jonathan Ball, 2015, p.237.
80 Callister, 'Patriotic duty or resented imposition?', p.57.
81 For an excellent exposition of the legal implications of various amendments to the Defence Act, cf. L. Berat. 'Conscientious objection in South Africa: Governmental paranoia and the

objection. The outcome of both resulted in essentially the same possibility that the 1957 Act had provisioned: assignment to a non-combatant role. The difference, however, was that allotment could be decided by the 'registering officer' if he *knew* that the recruit belonged to a 'recognised religious denomination by the tenets whereof its members may not participate in war.' Exemption, on the other hand, had to be considered by an exemption board (not a single officer) who did not need to *know* about a conscripts religious affiliation, but had to be *convinced* of it.[82] In effect, the 1967 Act only made provision for *religious* objection, since the outcome of both exemption and allotment rested on a conscript's adherence to a specific, pacifist, religion. It made no provision at all for *conscientious* objection that stood independent of a particular religion. Equally significantly, despite the reliance on religion for successful objection, no church had any input in the decision-making process.

As South Africa moved increasingly towards a security state from the mid-1970s,[83] conscientious objection came to be viewed as dissent against the government. Conway holds that a 'key tenet of the state's claim to legitimacy is the right to organise for war and define the terms and content of the national security discourse.'[84] Civil disobedience and unrest within South Africa's borders were challenging the efficacy of the government,[85] pushing the state towards the precipice of increasingly severe retaliation. Pretoria had exhibited the practical implications of the national security discourse at Sharpeville in 1960, which resulted in a widespread international crisis of legitimacy for the government's internal policies, underlined by the doctrine of apartheid.[86] To combat internal pressures, the Defence Further Amendment Act (No.83 of 1974), while maintaining the provisions for religious objection from 1967, made it a criminal offence to incite, or even suggest, conscientious objection.[87]

The Soweto uprising, typified in 1976 by what is now commemorated in South Africa as Youth Day on 16 June, sensitised the broader South African public to the role of the SADF in suppressing unrest. At the time, the war in Angola and Namibia had not yet reached anything approaching a climax and, for the most part, conscripts were still keen, if somewhat uncertain, to do their national service. When it became apparent that their duty might not be to protect South Africa's borders against the ever-maligned 'Red Danger', but rather against internal unrest, questions started to be raised. Laurie Nathan holds that it was primarily the English-speaking universities and churches that were the initial catalysts for resistance to conscription, and claims that an average of 1,750

law of conscription' in *Vanderbilt Journal of Transnational Law* 22, 1989, pp.127–186.

82 Defence Amendment Act, No. 85 of 1967, section 40.

83 Alden, *Apartheid's last stand*, pp.70–71.

84 Conway, *Stop the call-up*, p.26.

85 T. Simpson, *Umkhonto we Sizwe: The ANC's Armed Struggle.* Cape Town: Penguin, 2016, pp.3–20.

86 United Nations Security Council resolution, S/RES/134, Question relating to the situation in the Union of South Africa, 1 April 1960.

87 Defence Further Amendment Act, No. 83 of 1974, section 10.

conscripts failed to report for national service from 1975–1978 and that 12 conscientious objectors were imprisoned between 1978 and 1982.[88] Nathan's contention is supported by a SADF intelligence report from 1978, which claimed that the Youth Christian Workers, a religious organisation supported, both financially and ideologically, by the Roman Catholic Church in South Africa, not only had great influence among South Africa's black population, but was also 'reactivating' the conscientious objection movement to influence the (white) South African youth against conscription.[89]

Gavin Cawthra contends that the white South Africans who chose exile over national service in the 1970s and 1980s were sympathetic to the plight of black South Africans, but found it difficult to gain acceptance within Black Consciousness (BC) movements. Many of the anti-apartheid, anti-conscription movements and organisations that were established by exiled conscripts were 'driven by the exigencies of their exclusion from the liberation struggle by BC activists.'[90] Notably, Cawthra identifies a 'fault-line' running through the main proponent of BC, the Pan-Africanist Congress, as well as the ANC and the South African Communist Party: all these organisations were motivated by clear divisions, either along racial or class lines. The fact that white South African exiles chose to establish their own organisations abroad, when they were excluded from established ones historically from South Africa again indicates that white resistance to conscription was primarily motivated by Pretoria's domestic policies, rather than opposition to the external deployments of the SADF.

In addition to 'black resistance to white domination' from organisations like the United Democratic Front (UDF),[91] dissent from within, in the form of conscientious objection, from one of the pillars of the South African security state, became an increasingly vexing problem to Pretoria. The Conscientious Objector Support Group (COSG) and the National Union of South African Students (NUSAS) became more vociferous in their support of conscientious objection and their opposition to militarisation. Although it has become unfashionable to admit as much, the NP still enjoyed the overwhelming support of the white South African electorate and, by extension, the majority of white South Africa still supported the NP policy of conscription and were largely uncritical of the way in which the SADF was deployed. The government was sufficiently concerned about the activities of organisations such as COSG and NUSAS to introduce the Defence Amendment Act (No. 34 of 1983) in 1983. Probably in an attempt to garner the support of the South African clergy, this act explicitly provided the opportunity for *religious* objectors (as opposed to *conscientious* objectors),

88 L. Nathan, 'Marching to a different beat: the history of the End Conscription Campaign' in J. Cock, & L. Nathan, (eds), *War and Society; The militarisation of South Africa.* Cape Town: David Philip, 1989, p.309.

89 DODDC, 32 Bn, Box 12, 205/4, Insam – Intsum, Insum 9/78 + Briefing Report.

90 G. Cawthra, 'The South African War Resistance Movement 1974–1994' in *Scientia Militaria: South African Journal of Military Studies, 43 (2)*, 2015, p.115.

91 L. Nathan, 'Troops in the townships, 1984–1987' in J. Cock, & L. Nathan (eds), *War and Society; The militarisation of South Africa.* Cape Town: David Philip, 1989, p.67.

who refused to serve in any armed force, to perform their National Service in government departments other than the SADF, albeit at one and a half times the length of military service.[92] On the other hand, the sentence for *conscientious* objectors, or those who specifically refused to serve in the SADF, was increased from a maximum of two to six years.[93]

The contention that garnering support from the clergy was a contributing factor in Pretoria's decision to change the attitude towards religious objection is reflected in the way in which the Exemption Board, deciding on applications for exemption from national service on religious grounds, had to be constituted. According to the stipulations of the 1983 Act, the chairman of the board had to be a judge or retired judge of the Supreme Court of South Africa. The other five compulsory members of the board had to be three theologians (the wording of the Act does not make it clear whether 'theologians' had to be interpreted in the academic sense of the word, or whether ordinary clergy would suffice) of different denominations and two members of the SADF, one of which had to be a chaplain.[94] A board that has to make decisions about religious objection is bound to contain a high percentage of theologians, but the excessive weighting in favour of men of the cloth over lawmen would also have given churches a sense of having a hand in their own destiny. If the SADF was prepared to rely so heavily on expertise from outside of its own ranks, surely, the church must have reasoned, they must be making a genuine attempt to accommodate religious objectors.

The various amendments to the Defence Act had several consequences. Firstly, Pretoria prevented South African churches from joining forces against conscription (and other political policies). The Afrikaans-speaking churches had always been more sympathetic towards the NP than the English-speaking ones, but the mollification provided by the Act soothed many a conscience among Afrikaans theologians. The largest Afrikaans denomination, the *Nederduitse Gereformeerde Kerk (NGK)* (commonly referred to as the Dutch Reformed church [DRC] in English) remained a stalwart supporter of the National Party for another decade and never actively entered the debate about the validity or the morality of conscription. Other Afrikaans churches largely followed suit and the English churches remained the spiritual voice of caution. This is exemplified by the number of successful applications granted in 1984 in terms of the 1983 Amendment Act: 101 Jehovah's Witnesses, two from the Worldwide Church of God, three Anglicans, two Methodists, one Baptist, one Seventh Day Adventist, and five Christadelphians.[95] Secondly, by creating a clear dichotomy between *religious* objection

92 K. Satchwell, 'The power to defend: an analysis of various aspects of the Defence Act' in J. Cock & L. Nathan (eds), *War and Society; The militarisation of South Africa.* Cape Town: David Philip, 1989, p.42.
93 Nathan, 'Marching to a different beat', p.309.
94 Satchwell, 'The power to defend', p.42.
95 Editor, 'Wet erken godsdiensbeswaar teen diensplig' in *Die Hervormer.* September 1984, p 4. *Die Hervormer* is the official newspaper of another of the Afrikaans mainstream churches, the *Nederduits Hervormde Kerk van Afrika* (Dutch Reformed Church of Africa).

and *conscientious* objection, Pretoria maintained the aforementioned 'right to organise for war and define the terms and content of the national security discourse'[96] and protect her own political legitimacy. Religious objectors were now no longer as much of a threat to the perceived sovereign rights of the State, as their protest was now diverted to spiritual, rather than political, spheres. At the same time, the government had provided itself with a mandate to act decisively against those who did oppose them politically. This is clearly reflected in the comments of the judge that sentenced David Bruce, who refused to do national service, to a term of imprisonment of six years in 1988:

> no State exists where the final authority is not vested in an organised Defence Force. The competence to apply an armed force in order to combat any armed resistance and thereby securing and maintaining State security, law and order results typically from the historical foundation of any State. In South Africa too, the State has the duty to protect all individuals by securing law and order. In that regard the State is competent to compel and prescribe to its subjects in order to compile an effective defence force.[97]

Ironically, conscientious objection, at a psychological level, deals with morals, ethics and values, issues that should have been at the forefront of the religious discourse at the time. Because conscientious objection was mainly in reaction to the internal deployment of the SADF, rather than the more traditional external deployment, the observations regarding the psychological experiences of conscripts on township duty of clinical psychologist, Diane Sandler, are significant. Her description of the psyche of the soldiers shows that society has a rich history of embodying the 'hero as warrior'.[98] Heroes achieve their status through violence, specifically killing or destroying their enemies. The more visible and public the setting of this violence, the greater the hero's social gain. In doing so, the focus of the hero's killing is not on the destruction of life, but the preservation of the ideals that the hero represents. Killing confers 'honour, fellowship, and something close to a state of grace' on the hero.[99] The hero cannot achieve this by his own devices, though. He 'requires some kind of initiation process, a symbolic form of death and rebirth that may and usually does coincide with his attainment of adulthood. In that rite (now called basic training), his civil identity with its built-in restraints is eradicated, or at least undermined, and set aside in favour of the warrior identity, with its central focus upon killing.'[100]

96 Conway, *Stop the call-up,* p.26.
97 As quoted by Satchwell, 'The power to defend', p.46.
98 D. Sandler, 'The psychological experiences of white conscripts in the black townships' in J. Cock & L. Nathan (eds), *War and Society; The militarisation of South Africa.* Cape Town: David Philip, 1989, p.82.
99 Sandler, 'The psychological experiences of white conscripts', pp.82–83.
100 Sandler, 'The psychological experiences of white conscripts', p.83.

Sandler argues convincingly that the psychology of the warrior-hero was deeply ingrained in South African society. The many recollections of former NSM that they were protecting what was dear to them, thereby essentially doing an honourable duty, supports her argument. This is vividly exhibited in a letter from the father of a deceased, white, South African soldiers who had served in 32 Battalion. He wrote to thank the Logistics Officer, Major Ken Greeff, for visiting and returning their son's belongings to them. He then proceeded to narrate salient events in his son's life, from his desire the enter Christian Ministry after his National Service, to his decision to join the Permanent Force, rather than continue his theological training. Significantly, the father informed Major Greeff that his son did not consider it a hardship to serve with 32 Battalion, but rather 'considered it a privilege to serve his country in this way.'[101]

Though the psychological make-up of the majority of conscripts allowed them to embrace the concepts illustrated here, the conscientious objectors obviously recognised some of the flaws in its reasoning. Some objectors inevitably used conscientious objection as a convenient excuse not to do national service, for reasons other than a genuine concern about the validity of the application of the policy. Nonetheless, it could legitimately be argued that those who gave the matter sufficient thought, and objected to military service because of their morals and ethics, were actually more spiritually orientated than the religious objectors, who refused to do national service on the basis of theological dogma. It is unfortunate, and reflects shamefully on the clerical leaders of the time, that churches failed to recognise that the state was creating an artificial schism between the two types of objection and were satisfied with the mollification of the concessions of the 1983 Defence Amendment Act made to religious objectors. Significantly, despite these attempts by the SADF and NP to combat objection to conscription and undermine the efforts of the End Conscription Campaign (ECC), the situation had escalated to a point where, at an Infantry Training Conference in July 1988, it was emphasised that, under the emergency regulations in force until June 1989, SADF members had the power to arrest anyone 'that makes, writes or publishes an undermining declaration', explaining that such declarations included promoting boycott actions, attacking the government or criticising conscription and promoting the execution of the powers granted to the SADF under the state of emergency. The paragraph concluded with the insightful phrase 'The church leaders and organisations like the ECC are thus effectively neutralised.'[102]

101 DODDC, 32 Bn, Box 9, LOG/OPS/3/16/13/3, Vol. 1, Pers Welsyn (Dood, siekte van naasbestaandes, uitstel van opl), Letter from Andries Keulder to Ken Greeff, 20 March 1977. Afrikaans: *het dit as 'n voorreg beskou om sy land op hierdie wyse te kan dien.*

102 DODDC, 32 Bn Gp 2, Box 262, 522/1/1, Vol. 7, Bevelvoerderskonferensies, Notule van 'n Infanterie Opleidingskonferensie gehou te SA Leërkollege oor die tydperk 5–6 Julie 1988. Afrikaans: *wat 'n ondermynende verklaring maak, skryf of publiseer; Die kerliers* [*sic*: *kerkleiers*] *en organisasies soos die ECC word dus effektief aan bande gelê.*

South Africans in 32 Battalion

No South African serving in the SADF during apartheid could have been immune to, or even unaware of, the political agenda that underpinned the SADF's doctrine and its relation to the NP government. Although it has become fashionable to deny supporting the apartheid government, and the defence force that served her, enough South Africans *did* support the government for apartheid to be perpetuated for a far longer time than would have been possible if everyone who retrospectively claims to have opposed the policy had, in fact, done so. Whether by chance or by design, indoctrination was a part of everyday South African life. It is against this background that many of the men who served in 32 Battalion joined, or were conscripted into, the SADF. Objection to conscription was frowned upon and objectors were ridiculed and emasculated. The psychological perceptions promoted by the NP government permeated the psyche of South African society. This is reflected by the number of applications received by 32 Battalion for extension of service, or transfers to the unit, from both NSM and PF soldiers for the one year period May 1976 to May 1977.

Table 2.1: Applications for transfer to / extension of service with 32 Battalion, May 1976–May 1977[103]

Rank					Period requested			
NCO	WO	Jnr Off	Snr Off	Total	< 1 yr	> 1 yr	Perm	Total
6	1	15	3	25	9	2	14	25

While the PF-applications can be understood in light of the fact that active service inevitably looks good on a professional soldier's record, the number of requests from NSM, either to extend their service, or to transfer to the PF, provided that they could stay with 32 Battalion, is a certain indicator that the war was not as unpopular as it is now made out to be. In fact, one officer felt so strongly about continuing his service with 32 Battalion that he wrote a letter to Jan Breytenbach, informing him that he was studying towards a degree in Strategic Studies at the University of South Africa (UNISA) but, as UNISA is a correspondence university, felt that he would be able to continue his studies while serving with 32 Battalion. He preferred this to waiting three years, until he had completed his studies, before returning to his old unit.[104]

After 32 Battalion relocated to South Africa in 1989, it suddenly became desirable to be identified with a unit that boasted as distinguished a combat record as 32 Battalion. On the other hand, during the Border War 32 Battalion experienced constant difficulties in maintaining adequate levels in its leader group, indicating that most South African

103 Compiled from DODDC, 32 Bn, Box 9, LOG/OPS/3/16/13, Vol. 1, Personeel beleid (Vrywillige diens ens.).

104 DODDC, 32 Bn, Box 9, LOG/OPS/3/16/13, Vol. 1, Personeel beleid (Vrywillige diens ens.), Letter from Lt. Van der Merwe to Col. Breytenbach, 4 January 1977.

NSM were more interested in completing their national service than in achieving something during their time in the Defence Force. Nonetheless, those South Africans, of all ranks, who did gain some experience with 32 Battalion were often eager to continue their affiliation with the unit. Table 2.1 indicates requests for transfer to, and extensions of service at, 32 Battalion very early in its existence. It appears that, despite the National Party's apartheid policies, the cosmopolitan mix of 32 Battalion's soldiers did not pose an inherent problem to white South African NSM.

Conclusion

The SADF had recognised, shortly after Operation Savannah, that the press had an influence on soldiers. In the case of Operation Savannah, the problem was that soldiers had to maintain a stance that had clearly become a lie – that South Africa did not have troops in Angola[105] – but the principle applies in general: soldiers tend to believe what they read. The tragedy of the press's perpetuation of the misconceptions indicated above would only really become apparent three decades later. While the Angolan soldier who was persuaded to join 32 Battalion by these, and similar, rumours might have been disenchanted at first, the reality of life in 32 Battalion was not altogether bad. Officers, for the most part, had a genuine concern for the wellbeing of the men under their command and the apartheid policies, that were such a breeding ground for discontent within the borders of South Africa, were not rigorously enforced in 32 Battalion. Although Edwin Eduardo (pseudonym) is of the opinion that:

> the political climate in Angola is not so stable … with my cousins and people of my age group that I left in Angola, when I go back to Angola to see them, I'm better off … I look at them and I think: it's actually a pity that you didn't travel the journey that I did,[106]

a strong argument can be made that, today, the Angolans who remained in Angola are better off than the now-abandoned ex-Angolans of 32 Battalion. In a 2007 study for the ISS Monograph series, focusing on former UNITA soldiers, 77 percent of 'ex-combatants' consider themselves to be reintegrated in civilian life, following the cessation of hostilities in Angola.[107] Although 32 Battalion drew most of its initial manpower from the FNLA structures, the survey of UNITA troops is still indicative of the current Angolan social dynamic towards former combatants in Angola's five decades of war.

105 DODDC, 32 Bn, Box 41, 309/1/5, Vol. 1, Lesse geleer gedurende Op Savannah, Lesse geleer gedurende Op Savannah.
106 Interview with Edwin Eduardo (pseudonym), son of former 32 Battalion soldier; Kimbo and Pomfret resident, Wonderboom, 24-06-2019.
107 J. Gomes Porto, I. Parsons & C. Alden, 'From soldiers to citizens; the social, economic and political reintegration of UNITA ex-combatants' in *ISS Monograph Series No. 130,* 2007, p.104.

The former 32 Battalion soldiers, many of whom now live in Pomfret, have not been polled in a similar way, but the conditions of extreme poverty that are prevalent in Pomfret are indications that these men would not consider themselves part of South African civilian life.

The ideological gulf between the South African and Angolan members of 32 Battalion should have resulted in an untenable marriage. The South Africans who served in the unit inevitably came from the group that accepted conscription, at least as a necessary evil, or were not sufficiently critical of the policy to actively oppose or resist it. The ideologies and psychological assumptions that accompany an acceptance of conscription have been illustrated. All predictions should, therefore, have pointed to an ideological clash between the implicit supporters of the apartheid South African government and their black brothers-in-arms; the 32 Battalion-anvil should, by all indication, have remained a pipedream. From the Angolan point of view, the myths and half-truths about 32 Battalion would have influenced the decision of some members to join the unit. The disillusion of reality could easily have resulted in discontent among the Angolan contingent. Additionally, the segregation of the greater SADF would have been foreign to them. Despite their vast sociological, psychological, economic and political differences, the men of 32 Battalion succeeded not only in enduring one another's presence, but in forging a cohesive, coherent unit that functioned more efficiently than many of its more homogenous counterparts.

3

'The Hammer': The Fighting Battalion

At the start of Operation Savannah in 1975, South Africa was largely unprepared for war. Speaking metaphorically, the SADF did not have a hammer with which to pursue the conflict with its enemies. The majority of the infantry component of the South African forces consisted of hastily trained foreign troops under South African leadership; a makeshift hammer, at best, at the time. These troops were to become the nucleus of 31 and 32 Battalion of the SADF. The experiences during Savannah made it clear to the SADF that its doctrine and equipment would have to be re-evaluated and adapted. From its inception during Operation Savannah, 32 Battalion evolved from irregular infantry using whatever weaponry and equipment could be pilfered, acquired, and appropriated, through the days of pseudo-operations and guerrilla warfare, to a conventional infantry battalion armed with some of South Africa's latest doctrine and cutting-edge equipment by the end of the war. Throughout the existence of 32 Battalion, the SADF also went through a process of evolution, from the hastily assembled battle groups of Operation Savannah to one of the most modern armies in Africa. Comparisons can therefore be drawn between the different roles of 32 Battalion and the perceived requirements of the SADF.

Operation Savannah

South Africa was already involved in the civil war in Angola when Luanda declared independence in 1975. The MPLA was deemed the least desirable of the three nationalist organisations competing for power and the SADF was keen to support either the FNLA or UNITA. The latter organisations both approached South Africa for assistance in their fight against the MPLA and were assisted to a greater or lesser extent.[1] Unfortunately for South African strategists, the FNLA proved an unreliable ally and an

1 C. Andrew & V. Mitrokhin, *The World was Going our Way: The KGB and the battle for the Third World.* Perseus Books, 2005, pp.450–451.

ineffective fighting force, despite the material and advisory assistance from South Africa and the USA. This is clearly indicated by the rapid state of deterioration of morale and equipment within the FNLA. A newspaper report in March 1975, stating that 'FNLA soldiers have a neat uniform, modern arms, good pay and allowances, efficient transport and their discipline and behaviour are excellent'[2] contrasts markedly with the first impressions that the South Africans had of them at Mpupa in August of the same year: 'The base was in a filthy state. The approaches were through a several hundred-metre-wide minefield of human excrement … the stench was all-pervading … all of the men showed signs of starvation … none of them had decent footwear.'[3]

This left UNITA as the only viable opposition to the MPLA, unless support to the FNLA was increased dramatically and to a more practical level. In addition, South Africa was not well prepared for a large-scale conflict in Angola. Conscription was still in its infancy and the Citizen Force pool was not as large as it would be when the SADF planned and executed the later large cross-border operations. To compound the problem, Army Headquarters had, on 19 March 1975, concluded that there was 'no conventional threat to the RSA.'[4] This meant that the SADF planning was focused on low intensity, low manpower, COIN warfare, rather than conventional operations in a foreign country. South Africa required manpower if they were to increase their influence in Angola without a large mobilisation effort in the Republic, which was curtailed both by time constraints and potential political repercussions. In accordance with the direction provided by the Joint Interdepartmental Counterinsurgency Committee, which had been established in 1974 'To formulate joint strategies to oppose counterinsurgency and to coordinate counterinsurgency-actions, thereby ensuring that insurgency in 1 Military Area (1 MA) is eradicated in the most effective way possible,'[5] the SADF simply did not have sufficient manpower in 1975 to launch an effective, semi-conventional, operation.

Daniel Chipenda played a crucial, though unintentional, part in assisting the SADF to fill this manpower void. A former member of the MPLA, Chipenda had fallen out with Agostinho Neto, the MPLA leader, and joined the FNLA as assistant secretary general in 1975.[6] Although some of the MPLA support base – approximately 2,000

2 As quoted by F. J. du T. Spies, *Die Angolese Burgeroorlog*. Pretoria: Militêre Informasieburo, 1980, p.187.

3 J. Breytenbach, *The Tempered Sword: Forged in Battle Revisited; Operation Savannah and the birth of 32 Bn*. Bushwarrior.com, 2011, pp.22–24.

4 DODDC, 32 Bn, Box 14, G/OPS/3/3, Vol. 1, Focus, Aanhangsel B by Operasionele Instruksie No 1/75. Afrikaans: … *geen konvensionele militêre aanslag teen die RSA nie.*

5 DODDC, 32 Bn, Box 72, HVS/206/36/4, Beplanningsraad, Stigting van die Gesamentlike Interdepartementele Teen-Insurgensiekomitee (GITK), p.2. Afrikaans: *Om … gesamentlike strategieë vir die bekamping van teeninsurgensie te formuleer en om die teeninsurgensie optredes te koördineer, om sodoende te verseker dat insurgensie in 1 Militêre Gebied (1MG) … op die mees doeltreffende manier uitgewis word.* Despite the rather clumsy use of the phrase 'to oppose counterinsurgency', the Afrikaans makes it clear that the author's intended meaning was actually 'to oppose insurgency'.

6 P. Nortje, *The Terrible Ones: A complete history of 32 Battalion*. Cape Town: Zebra, 2012, p.49.

soldiers – followed Chipenda to the FNLA, they did not espouse their new organisation wholeheartedly and remained a faction within the FNLA. One of the first acts of Chipenda's faction, under Oginga Odinda,[7] was to establish a presence in southern Angola, something the FNLA had been unable to do effectively up to that point.[8] The FNLA had approached South Africa House in Trafalgar Square for aid in the war effort against the MPLA as early as 28 February 1975,[9] during the period when American aid was still sufficient to keep the movement in the field but by May Chipenda had apparently come to the conclusion that South African aid had become crucial. In an attempt to secure this for his faction, he visited Rundu on 24 May and Windhoek on 28 May.[10] Perhaps disheartened by Pretoria's decision to limit FNLA support to supplying Holden Roberto with military hardware, rather than his own faction, Chipenda left the next meeting with the South Africans to Oginga Odinda, who on 8 July informed the South Africans at Calai of the presence of about 300 Chipenda-FNLA troops at Mpupa, about 60km to the north. Odinda promised that, with South African help, these men would take the fight to SWAPO inside Angola.[11] At a follow-up meeting initiated by Chipenda's brother-in-law, Pilisso, on 11 July, the South Africans were presented with a more accurate picture of the situation at Mpupa: there were only about 150 men who, between them, only had 15 rifles.[12] In addition, Chipenda was no longer taking an active part in the leadership of this part of his FNLA faction. The SADF quickly realised that this situation could be turned to their advantage, identifying the Angolan soldiers as a potential SADF proxy force.

Major General Constand Viljoen, then Director General of Operations at Army Headquarters (HQ), tasked Jan Breytenbach to move to Angola and commence a training programme. Breytenbach, given 11 Reconnaissance Commando (Recce) operators to assist him with the task,[13] arrived at 1 MA in Namibia on 28 August 1975. The next day, Breytenbach met with Brigadier Dawie Schoeman, Commandant M. Knoetze (South African Military Intelligence) and representatives from the FNLA to establish a training programme. In an attempt to keep South African involvement in Angola a secret, the FNLA delegates were informed that the white SADF personnel that would be in charge of the training programme was a mercenary force employed by the South African government.[14] Although this deception was successful in keeping SADF activities secret for a few more months, the epithet 'mercenary' would stay with 32 Battalion for the remainder of its existence. Nonetheless, a detailed training plan was drawn up,

7 Sometimes written 'Odinda Odinda'.
8 DODDC, HS Ops, Gp 1, Box 9, HS/1//3/14, Vol. 1, Waardering oor die moontlike gebruik / aanwending van Chipenda / FNLA tot voordeel van RSA.
9 Spies, *Die Angolese Burgeroorlog,* p.296.
10 Spies, *Die Angolese Burgeroorlog,* p.299.
11 Nortje, *The Terrible Ones,* p.60.
12 Spies, *Die Angolese Burgeroorlog,* p.312.
13 Breytenbach, *The Tempered Sword,* pp.16–17.
14 Spies, *Die Angolese Burgeroorlog,* p.315.

ostensibly based on FNLA reports of their own strength and capabilities at Mpupa. Although Breytenbach's recollections of the training indicate a haphazard, makeshift approach,[15] the events that he recalls digress only slightly from the training plan that he submitted to Brigadier Jannie Geldenhuys, Director Operations at Army Headquarters, on 3 September 1975.[16]

When Jan Breytenbach arrived at the FNLA base at Mpupa on 5 September 1975 on a fact-finding mission, he discovered that even the more realistic image, sketched by Pilisso on 11 July, had significantly overstated the reality of the situation at Mpupa. Breytenbach is scathing in recollecting his initial impression of the troops,[17] but applied himself and his small core of South African officers and NCOs to the abbreviated training that they had planned. After addressing the most immediate concern – feeding the starved FNLA troops – Breytenbach organised them into two rifle companies of three platoons and a support company with a mortar, machinegun and anti-tank platoon. Training focused on physical fitness, section and platoon drills, weapons training and offensive drills.[18] The actual training differed from the planning only in the addition of the anti-tank platoon, which was not initially envisaged and added by Breytenbach only because he had been supplied with 3.5" rocket launchers by the SADF and an ex-Portuguese army soldier, by then part of Chipenda's FNLA, claimed to be an anti-tank expert.[19] True to the reputation that he had acquired and was fast developing, Breytenbach did not let the opportunity, however improbable, of adding additional firepower to his makeshift force slip through his fingers. The agreement between the SADF and the FNLA envisaged that the latter would gradually provide additional troops for training at Mpupa until the force under Breytenbach's command came up to battalion strength,[20] but in reality it was rather the news that spread of the improved conditions now prevalent at Mpupa under South African leadership that inspired enough 'recruits' to turn up to enable Breytenbach to establish a third rifle company.[21]

Although this third rifle company lagged behind the other two in training that was already cut down to a minimum they would still, contrary to the initial planning, be deployed during Operation Savannah. This lack of training, knowledge and discipline had regrettable consequences when Task Force Zulu's Bravo Group, as Breytenbach's command was now known, ran into a FAPLA ambush near Mupa during the initial stages of Operation Savannah. In the confusion of battle, Charlie Company established positions on either side of a road, after which the two parts of the company started firing on one another. Two soldiers of Charlie Company were wounded and one of them later

15 Cf. Breytenbach, *The Tempered Sword*; J. Breytenbach, *The Buffalo Soldiers: The Story of South Africa's 32-Battalion 1975–1993*. Alberton: Galago, 2002.
16 Spies, *Die Angolese Burgeroorlog*, p.317.
17 Cf. Breytenbach, *The Tempered Sword*; Breytenbach, *The Buffalo Soldiers*.
18 Nortje, *The Terrible Ones*, p.71.
19 Breytenbach, *The Tempered Sword*, p.41.
20 Spies, *Die Angolese Burgeroorlog*, p.316.
21 Cf. Breytenbach, *The Tempered Sword*, pp.27–37; Nortje, *The Terrible Ones*, pp.68–72.

died of his wounds.[22] Because of this incident, Breytenbach kept Charlie Company in reserve for the rest of the campaign. In turn, this meant that Charlie Company never acquired the combat experience of the first two companies, Alpha and Bravo, while under Breytenbach's command. At the Battle of Ebo, when Charlie Company was detached to Battle Group Foxbat, Charlie Company's inexperience cost them dearly when they were confronted by a well prepared, well executed FAPLA ambush.[23]

Perhaps due to the SADF's inexperience in using proxy forces, or due to the poor track record of the FNLA, the equipment provided to Breytenbach's men was – with the exception of the FN / R1 rifles – almost exclusively inferior and of World War Two vintage.[24] The 3" mortars, with an effective range of around 1,000 metres, were hopelessly outclassed by the more modern Soviet 82mm mortars of FAPLA that could fire up to 3,000 metres. At first glance, the water-cooled Vickers machineguns seemed prehistoric alongside FAPLA's RPDs and PKMs. The Sten submachineguns (SMGs) that were used as personal weapons by the support platoons might have gained a brutal reputation in townships in South Africa, particularly at Sharpeville in 1960, but were of arguable use against a well-equipped opponent using significantly newer weapons and equipment.[25] The Stens were unpopular with the support weapons platoons from the outset[26] and were eagerly exchanged for Soviet PPSh SMGs as soon as these were captured during Operation Savannah.[27] Possibly due to security concerns, the SADF recalled all the FN / R1 rifles that were issued to Bravo Group shortly after the start of Operation Savannah, but it was impossible to exchange them for AK47s, as proposed by 1 Military Area Headquarters, while Bravo Group was actively deployed.[28] In contrast to the SADF's reluctance to issue Bravo Group with newer, more efficient weapons during Savannah and regardless of the rushed training of the troops, the SADF did not see a problem with issuing Bravo Group with explosives, including 50,000lbs of PE4 and 10,000lbs of TNT, in February 1976, shortly after Operation Savannah.[29]

Despite the challenges facing him and the men under his command, Breytenbach succeeded in moulding an effective fighting force from his demoralised FNLA troops. Three aspects, that would become hallmarks of 32 Battalion in later years, stand out in the fighting efficiency of Bravo Group. Firstly, the innovative use of whatever equipment they had at hand increased the efficiency of obsolete weapons. The most obvious examples of this kind of innovation were the mounting eight Vickers machineguns on the back of

22 Nortje, *The Terrible Ones,* pp.78–79.
23 Breytenbach, *The Tempered Sword*, pp.215–223.
24 Breytenbach, *The Tempered Sword*, pp.66–68.
25 DODDC, 32 Bn, Box 7, G/OPS/3/3, Vol. 1, Insam, Insidentelys tot Insam 7/77, periode 110600B Feb 77 tot 180600B Feb 77.
26 Breytenbach, *The Tempered Sword*, p.35.
27 Nortje, *The Terrible Ones,* p.87.
28 DODDC, 1 Militêre Gebied, Box 82, G/OPS/3/3/BRAVO, Vol. 1, Bravo, Message 004/222/0830 From 1 MA to 101 TF.
29 DODDC, 1 Militêre Gebied, Box 82, G/OPS/3/3/BRAVO, Vol. 1, Explosives for Bravo Group.

a flat-bed truck and using this in broadside offensives against FAPLA strongpoints[30] or mounting machineguns on Land Rovers and using these vehicles as armed scout cars.[31] Secondly, superior tactical awareness and application negated many of the advantages that FAPLA's superior weapons and tactically defensive positions gave them. This is evident from the organisation of Breytenbach's column during the advance into Angola: the Land Rovers led the way, followed by the machinegun and mortar companies. The rifle companies formed the rear of the column.[32] In this way, Bravo Group was able to bring very heavy fire to bear on any enemies that they encountered, in a short space of time. It also positioned the mortars further towards the front of an engagement, thereby enabling them to have some effect on the outcome of the battle despite their limited range, though endangering the mortar crews in the process. Thirdly, Breytenbach did not hesitate to appoint black, non-SADF personnel in key positions. This was partly due to a shortage of SADF NCOs and junior officers, but astute judgement in these appointments gave the FNLA soldiers both a sense of continuity and importance. Initial planning had strongly suggested that white, South African leadership would be essential to achieve success. This was the contention both of the SADF, with Breytenbach stating that '...the success of the operation is dependent on good control at low level, in other words white, South African control...'[33] as well as the FNLA, who requested '...that we assist them not only with training, but also with the actual planning and control of operations.'[34] Nonetheless, when it became apparent that enough 'white, South African' personnel were not available and that elements of the FNLA command structure were, in fact, capable leaders, Breytenbach digressed significantly from his planning brief in order to make optimum use of the forces at his disposal. Operation Savannah showed the importance of leadership by example, which was absent in the FNLA, and the men chosen by Breytenbach formed the nucleus of the permanent leadership of 32 Battalion.

The three aspects illustrated above seem to be asynchronous with military culture. Cornell University's historian Isabel Hull defines military culture as 'the actions that result consciously from applied doctrine and training, and the habitual actions that seem obvious by virtue of unquestioned assumptions or necessary by virtue of the unintended consequences of regular military procedure.'[35]

It is doubtful that Breytenbach would have articulated his actions in this way, but it appears that he realised that traditional military culture would not work in the early days of his unit. Breytenbach's only action that bears any resemblance to the SADF's

30 Nortje, *The Terrible Ones,* p.71.
31 Nortje, *The Terrible Ones,* p.77.
32 Breytenbach, *The Buffalo Soldiers*, p.40.
33 Breytenbach as quoted by Spies, *Die Angolese Burgeroorlog,* p.317. Afrikaans: ...*die sukses van die operasie [hang] af van goeie beheer tot op lae vlak, d.w.s. wit Suid-Afrikaanse beheer...*
34 As quoted by Spies, *Die Angolese Burgeroorlog,* p.317. Afrikaans: ...*dat ons hulle moet bystaan, nie alleen met opleiding nie, maar ook met die fisiese beplanning en beheer van operasies.*
35 I. V. Hull, *Absolute Destruction: Military Culture and the Practices of War in Imperial Germany.* Ithaca: Cornell University Press, 2005, p.94.

'doctrine and training' in the mid-1970s is an emphasis on superior tactical ability. His use of weapons and his training methods were certainly not applied according to SADF doctrine. Similarly, the very nature of Operation Savannah disqualifies it from being 'standard military procedure' and the 'unquestioned assumptions' of apartheid South Africa differed significantly from Breytenbach's view of his troops. It is ironic, then, that 32 Battalion's own military culture almost developed from a rejection of military culture by Breytenbach, another aspect that highlights the unique nature of the unit.

Integration and early deployment

Although Operation Savannah was a tactical success, with South African battle groups advancing more than 3,000km into Angola in a little more than a month,[36] Pretoria's strategic decision to withdraw to southern Angola left Bravo Group with no immediate prospects of employment. A large part of the white leader group had already been evacuated because of malaria and Brigadier Schoeman of 1 Military Area Headquarters planned to withdraw the remainder and replace them with newly-arrived South Africans. However, Breytenbach realised that Schoeman's proposal would be problematic both ways: the FNLA troops were unlikely to take kindly to leaders who had not proved themselves and the South Africans would probably underestimate the value of the FNLA troops. Fortunately, the bonds that had been forged during Operation Savannah proved strong enough and Breytenbach and the remainder of his leader group took a firm stance: if they came back to Namibia, the Angolans under their command came with them.[37] With the MPLA assuming power in Luanda, the future looked bleak for their opponents, who had opposed them both as part the FNLA and the SADF. Common sense prevailed, and unofficial arrangements were made for the troops of Bravo Group to reconvene at Mpupa and Calai in January 1976, following a period of leave for the South Africans.[38] By that time, the influence of the FNLA had diminished considerably, effectively leaving UNITA as the only viable opposition force in Angola. This meant that former FNLA supporters had nowhere to go within Angola, as UNITA was as much an enemy as the MPLA, resulting in a large number of refugees trying to enter Namibia. The South Africans made the most of this situation, hand picking the best of the former FNLA troops from among the refugees to join Bravo Group.[39] In addition to the soldiers recruited in this way, skilled civilians from amongst the refugees were also informally attached to Bravo Group.[40] These two recruitment drives were so successful that Bravo Group found it difficult to stem the influx of former Portuguese soldiers and

36 L. Scholtz, *Die SAW in die Grensoorlog: 1966–1989*. Cape Town: Tafelberg, 2013, p.19.
37 Nortje, *The Terrible Ones*, pp.127–128.
38 Breytenbach, *The Tempered Sword*, pp.240–241.
39 Nortje, *The Terrible Ones*, pp.144–153.
40 DODDC, 32 Bn, Box 9, LOG/OPS/3/16/13/4, Portugese / Angolese, Indiensneming: Portugese.

civilians. In July 1976, they repeatedly had to inform 101 Task Force (TF) that they did not require any more Portuguese personnel.[41] The eagerness with which 101 TF passed Portuguese refugees on to Bravo Group could also be down to the fact that it then, effectively, removed the responsibility for those refugees from 101 TF and passed it on to Bravo Group, who were already experiencing difficulties in providing for their existing complement of soldiers and civilians.

Having managed to increase the size of the force under his command significantly, Breytenbach set about getting official SADF recognition for his new force. The focus of the SADF had by now returned to a counterinsurgency role aimed at combating PLAN infiltrations into Namibia, rather than direct action against FAPLA. South African intelligence had established that the Angolan government was supporting SWAPO and PLAN,[42] providing them with bases of operation inside Angola, and the USSR had promised to provide PLAN with arms and ammunition to continue their fight against the SADF.[43] Reports of increased PLAN activity in southern Angola and Owamboland had also started coming in from November 1975 and South Africa's Chief of Staff Intelligence was under the impression that 'operations in s[outhern] Angola only influenced SWAPO's operational planning to a limited extent.'[44]

Breytenbach therefore envisaged that the former FNLA could be employed as a guerrilla force in the south of Angola, recreating something of the *cordon sanitaire* which PLAN forces would have to cross in order to infiltrate Namibia. To achieve this, he needed to legitimise the presence of his former Angolan troops in South African controlled territory. Although 'few of them would qualify for employment' in the SADF, the office of the Chief of the Army was informed that, should no arrangements be made to accommodate these troops, Alpha Group's strength would be halved and Bravo Group would cease to exist.[45] The Chief of the Army was also informed that 'success of COIN ops in the Kavango is directly linked to the presence of Alpha and Bravo Groups...'[46] Having initiated the administrative processes necessary to ensure that the Angolans would stay with the SADF, Breytenbach then requested logistical support

41 DODDC, 1 Militêre Gebied, Box 82, G/OPS/3/3/BRAVO, Vol. 1, Message PERS/026/ JUL 76 from 1 MA to 101 TF.
42 DODDC, 32 Bn, Box 8, G/INT/5/1, Inligting Samevatting, Insam 20/76, 250600B – 010600B Okt 76, No. 28.
43 DODDC, 32 Bn, Box 8, G/INT/5/1, Inligting Samevatting, Onderhoud met Raphael Shoopala alias Lucky.
44 DODDC, SWA HK (Ops), Box 19, G/OPS/3/3, Vol. 2, Hoër In, Signal from HIS to HSAW, HS DG Ops, HLeër D Ops, HLM, EVAL/315/DES 75. Afrikaans: *operasies in S Angola slegs in 'n mindere mate SWAPO se operasionele beplanning beinvloed* [*sic*] *het.*
45 DODDC, 1 Miltêre Gebied, Box 82, G/OPS/3/3/BRAVO, Vol. 1, Message PERS/975 from 1 MA to C Army. Afrikaans: *baie min van hulle sal kwalifiseer vir indiensneming.*
46 DODDC, 1 Miltêre Gebied, Box 82, G/OPS/3/3/BRAVO, Vol. 1, Message PERS/975 from 1 MA to C Army. Afrikaans: *sukses van teinops in die Kavango hou direk verband met Alpha en Bravo se teenwoordigheid...*

from 101 Task Force Headquarters,[47] which had been established in November 1975 to provide a more effective command structure over the SADF's increasingly large theatre of operations.[48] They duly complied, and authorisation for the training of 1,000 men was given. During Operation Savannah, the SADF had repeatedly denied that South African forces were operating in Angola until FAPLA paraded captured South African POWs in front of the media. Perhaps in a bid to avoid a repeat of this embarrassment, Bravo Group was to be equipped with captured Soviet PPSh SMGs for their new counterinsurgency role, rather than the standard SADF FN / R1 rifle that they had used during Operation Savannah.[49] This added a layer of protection to the SADF, but also made sense for a force set to operate inside enemy territory. However, the Department of Military Intelligence realised early in 1977 that equipment captured from SWAPO invariably included the latest model AK47s.[50] For Bravo Group to combat assault rifles with their SMGs would have been enough of a challenge, but facing the newest weaponry available to their adversaries might have been asking too much of them, and their equipment was updated later in 1976.

Bravo Group was now recognised as a quasi-South African force, and the Chief of the Army, Constand Viljoen, authorised their withdrawal, as well as that of their families, to Namibia together with the rest of the South African forces. The last South Africans were officially set to leave Angola by 27 March 1976.[51] This decision initiated the move to Pica Pau (Woodpecker) and later Buffalo, the home of 32 Battalion for the next 13 years and the first group of Bravo Group soldiers and civilians arrived at Pica Pau on 2 March.[52] World War Two surplus equipment was given a new lease of life again, with 15' × 15' tents used as housing for the soldiers.[53] Civilians had to make do with what they could find. On 2 March 1976, the SADF agreed to start paying salaries to the Angolan soldiers, the first sign of formal integration, at an annual rate of R60 for riflemen, R120 for lance corporals and R180 for corporals.[54] On 15 July Breytenbach requested a review of the salary scale, indicated in Table 3.1.

For comparative purposes, it is notable that, earlier in the same year, the Owambo Cabinet indicated to 2 Military Area (2 MA) that they were willing to 'spend R100,000 per annum for the employment of 500 Home Guards,'[55] which equates to R200 per guard per year. Although it is unclear whether this amount was earmarked exclusively

47 Nortje, *The Terrible Ones,* p.155.
48 Spies, *Die Angolese Burgeroorlog,* p.554.
49 Nortje, *The Terrible Ones,* p.155.
50 DODDC, 32 Bn, Box 7, G/OPS/3/3, Vol. 1, Insam, Inligtingsamevatting 7/77 Tydperk 12 Feb tot 25 Feb 1977, p.5.
51 Spies, *Die Angolese Burgeroorlog,* p.932.
52 Nortje, *The Terrible Ones,* p.159.
53 DODDC, 1 Militêre Gebied, Box 82, G/OPS/3/3/BRAVO, Vol. 1, Bravo, Message 022/106/1230 From 1 MA to 101 TF.
54 Nortje, *The Terrible Ones,* p.161.
55 DODDC, 32 Bn, Box 7, G/OPS/3/3/LETTA, Vol. 1, Signal Ops/555/Aug 76 Deel drie van drie.

for salaries, Breytenbach's proposed salary scale seems to be in greater sync with the prevalent socio-economic climate than the initial SADF allocation. Additionally, the fact that Breytenbach refused to rest on his laurels following his successful campaign for getting official recognition for his unit appears to indicate a genuine concern for the wellbeing of his men and their families.

Table 3.1: Breytenbach's proposed salary scale for black soldiers[56]

Role	Proposed Annual Salary
Trainee Rifleman	R120
Rifleman	R300
Section Leader	R360
Platoon Sergeant	R420
Platoon Leader	R480

After the rushed training programme at Mpupa, the frenetic pace of Operation Savannah and the struggle to get SADF recognition for his former FNLA troops, Breytenbach now found time to reflect on the composition of his unit. He realised that he had black men from at least seven different ethnic groups as well as white men from vastly divergent backgrounds and cultures under his command.[57] Undaunted, Breytenbach's mind turned to the expansion of his command. Not satisfied with a single battalion, he envisaged that his command could encompass two battalions, 32 and 33, with one continuously deployed operationally and the other training or recuperating. In addition to the two battalions and usual support elements, Breytenbach also wanted a 'Mounted Group', consisting of a 106mm recoilless rifle troop, a 12.7mm machinegun platoon and an 81mm mortar platoon.[58]

Hindsight shows that this was too much for the SADF to contemplate and Breytenbach had to be satisfied with a single battalion. Nonetheless, encouraged by the potential shown by Bravo Group, he started to foster an *esprit de corps* among his soldiers. Recognising that the reasons for which his men had become soldiers in the first place – the desire for an independent country in which to live – was no longer a motivating factor, Breytenbach embraced the motto of the French Foreign Legion: *Legio Patria Nostra* (The Legion is Our Fatherland). The inherent mentality within the unit would not be that black Angolan troops are fighting a white, apartheid, South African government's war, but rather that they are fighting for the unit itself. In return, 32 Battalion would provide a safe haven for them and their families. When viewed in light of the fact that the MPLA government in Angola was starting to

56 DODDC, 32 Bn, Box 14, G/OPS/3/3, Vol. 1, Budgie – B Group, Salarisskaal: B Grocp.
57 Breytenbach, *The Tempered Sword*, p.279.
58 DODDC, 32 Bn, Box 8, LOG/OPS/1/16, Vol. 1, Admin Orders en Instrs, Spesiale Eenheidsorder Deel 1 No 4/77. Afrikaans: *Berede Gp*.

refuse entry into Angola to refugees that wished to return,[59] the value of a guaranteed home increases significantly. However, this could only be achieved if the white South Africans in the unit embraced Breytenbach's philosophy with the same vigour as the blacks. From the outset, the white leaders were regarded as part of the unit, rather than elite instructors. If white leaders found themselves unable to adapt to the unusual circumstances at 32 Battalion, they were soon returned to their former units. A case in point can be found in the return of a captain from 4 South African Infantry Battalion (SAI) to his parent unit. The report that 32 Battalion sent to the General Officer Commanding (GOC) 101 TF as well as the Chief of the Army claimed that 'The black soldiers are loyal to the white men and success can only be guaranteed in the presence of mutual respect and trust... To prevent irreparable damage to the black/white relationships, Capt. [x] is being returned to his parent unit, 4 SAI, on the 1 Feb 77 flight.'[60]

The fact that the officers of 32 Battalion, in particular Breytenbach, placed the well-being and success of the black members of the unit above that of a white SADF captain speaks volumes in itself. This contrasts markedly with the concern of SADF intelligence about the fact that black Namibians in the Caprivi were resigning from the SAP because of inequality between them and their white counterparts.[61] At the same time, white junior officers of 32 Battalion quickly came to realise that their black senior NCOs had a wealth of information and experience to impart to a 19-year-old platoon commander, and the ingrained South African division between black and white soon diminished, at least when members were either at Buffalo or Pica Pau. A former resident of the Kimbo – the area where civilians associated with 32 Battalion lived – recalls that he was not aware of any racism at Buffalo, although he did experience racism after the unit's move to South Africa in 1989:

> [In Namibia,] the separation was there, [in] how we lived and how we socialised … but when it came to working together, we always worked together and we always had … a good relationship … When I was still at 32, I was not really aware of [any] racism … Only later, when we came to Pomfret, I started realising that … there was [a form of] racism. But in my upbringing at 32, I never experienced that.[62]

59 DODDC, 32 Bn, Box 7, G/OPS/3/3 – LETTA, Vol. 1, Bravo Group, Higher in Sitrep from 101 TF to C Army.

60 DODDC, 32 Bn, Box 9, LOG/OPS/3/126/4, Vol. 1, Dissipline en regsaangeleenthede (verhoormagte, ens.), Message from 32 Battalion to GOC 101 TF 28 January 1977. Name omitted by author. Afrikaans: *Die swart soldate is lojaal aan die witman en sukses kan slegs verseker word as daar wedersydse respek en vertroue bestaan … Om te verhoed dat onherstelbare skade aan swart/wit verhoudinge gedoen word, word kapt.* [x] *op die vlug van 1 Feb 77 teruggestuur na sy tuiseenheid 4 SAI.*

61 DODDC, 32 Bn, Box 8, G/INT/3/2, Inrap: Nov 76, Inrap 518/76 from 101 TF to C Army.

62 Telephonic interview with Brian Baloyi (pseudonym), son of former 32 Battalion soldier; Kimbo and Pomfret resident, Centurion, 17-03-2019.

Predictably, not everything went according to plan and there were some Angolans who misjudged the situation at 32 Battalion. Possibly anticipating more favourable circumstances than those that actually existed, a number of Angolans requested a leave period of one week, after serving in the unit for just three weeks. Interpreting this as a reluctance to accept 32 Battalion's ways of life, a request was made to the office of the Chief of the Army to arrange for the repatriation of these troops to Angola.[63] Additionally, some white officers did not accord black NCOs the respect that they deserved, in the eyes of 32 Battalion's command structure, and had to be reminded to address black NCOs by their rank.[64]

The HQ of 32 Battalion was located at Rundu, giving rise to the need for a transit camp there. The construction of this camp clearly indicated that the greater SADF was not yet comfortable with the desegregated views of 32 Battalion and in 1979 the General Officer Commanding South West Africa Command specifically instructed the SWA Engineer Squadron to pay attention to the construction of segregated ablution facilities at Rundu.[65] This indicates that SADF members who felt unable to embrace the attitude of equality within 32 Battalion would find a more comfortable fit in other, more traditional, SADF units, and they were soon reassigned, either by their own design or that of senior 32 Battalion officers.[66] The use of Angolans as NCOs filled a manpower void and ensured a measure of continuity, both along the chain of command and when SADF officers left.

Bravo Group, destined to become known as 32 Battalion in October, shortly before Commandant Gert Nel assumed command, received their official tasking from 101 TF on 18 May 1976. Their primary task was 'to deny SWAPO an area of 50 kilometres north of the South West African border by means of clandestine operations'[67] and they were specifically instructed to avoid contact with FAPLA and the armed forces of other neighbouring countries.[68] This directive necessitated two developments: establishing a training facility – which was done at Dodge City in the eastern Caprivi[69] – and establishing an operational base at Omauni in the east of Owamboland, since Buffalo was too far from the theatre of operations. Dodge City was chosen as a training facility because the area around Pica Pau was not big enough for the more intensive training that

63 DODDC, 1 Militêre Gebied, Box 82, G/OPS/3/3/BRAVO, Vol. 1, Message PERS/132/MEI 76 from 101 TF to C Army.

64 DODDC, 32 Bn Gp 2, Box 260, 522/1, Vol. 1, Konferensies, Kongresse, Seminare, Simposiums en Vergaderings: Konferensies, Notule van Basiskonferensie gehou te 32 Bn Buffalo op 28 Maart 1980, p.7.

65 DODDC, 1 MG Sektor 20, Box 78, 302/6/C63, Vol. 1, Projek Carpenter, Letter from GC SWA Cmd to C Army, 13 June 1979.

66 Breytenbach, *The Tempered Sword*, pp.279–289.

67 DODDC, 32 Bn, Box 14, G/OPS/3/3, Bevelsdirektiewe, Bevelsdirektief No 15/76 Ops 34. Afrikaans: *...om 'n strook van ongeveer 50km Noord van die SWA grens aan SWAPO te ontsê deur klandistiene* [*sic*] *optredes...*

68 Nortje, *The Terrible Ones*, pp.168–169.

69 Nortje, *The Terrible Ones*, pp.166–168.

was now taking place at 32 Battalion.[70] In order to execute the directive, Breytenbach requested more contemporary weapons for Bravo Group, including RPG7s to replace the 3.5" rocket launchers and 40mm grenade launchers, which he considered ideally suited to the task that 101 TF had assigned Bravo Group. In addition, because he now had the ability to train his men in its use, he requested equipment, such as camouflage nets, to use in training at Dodge City as well as on deployment.[71] Following their official recognition, Bravo Group was better equipped, though still not to the standard of a regular SADF infantry battalion. At least World War Two equipment had given way to more contemporary weaponry. This included captured Soviet AK-47 and Portuguese FN G3 rifles, FN MAG light machineguns and South African 60mm and 81mm mortars, though the machineguns and mortars were in very short supply and Breytenbach's request for rocket-propelled grenades (RPGs) and 40mm grenade launchers seems to have been ignored.[72] Initially, 32 Battalion deployments were similar to those of regular SADF infantry units, but, in an effort to address the manpower shortage that hampered 'high-intensity operations in infected areas,'[73] 32 Battalion patrols took place inside Angola and over periods considerably longer than other SADF patrols, typically lasting six weeks. David da Silva (pseudonym), a former soldier of 32 Battalion, explains that during a typical deployment soldiers

> carried 30 kilograms continuously … were resupplied, if … lucky, every two weeks, carried between eight and sixteen litres of water … loads of ammunition, [mortar] bombs, medical supplies, radios, two weeks' rations … hand grenades. … [Soldiers] stayed in the bush for that [six week] period, … walked in the bush, kept a pace of four kilometres per hour, carrying that load, in African condition, in the hot sun, soft underfoot.[74]

The fact that platoons were also led by more junior officers than elsewhere in the SADF was an initial cause for concern within 101 TF,[75] but the combination of South African training and Angolan experience proved sufficient. The nature of the 32 Battalion deployments, in which forces were seldom larger than a platoon, led Gert Nel to assign platoon commanders (usually white South Africans) and platoon sergeants (normally black Angolans) the responsibility of training their platoons.[76]

70 Nortje, *The Terrible Ones*, pp.169–171.
71 DODDC, 32 Bn, Box 14, G/OPS/3/3, Vol. 1, Budgie – B Group, Points submitted for discussion at OC's Conference.
72 Nortje, *The Terrible Ones*, p.170.
73 DODDC, 32 Bn, Box 55, 522/1, Vol. 1, Konferensies: 101 TM, Notule van Bevelvoerderskonferensie gehou op 16 Feb 77 te HK 101 Taakmag. Afrikaans: *hoë intensiteitoperasies in besmette gebiede*.
74 Interview with David da Silva (pseudonym), former 32 Battalion soldier, Pretoria, 20-06-2019.
75 DODDC, 32 Bn, Box 14, G/OPS/3/3, Vol. 1, Budgie – B Group, Higher Inrep from 101 TF to C Army.
76 Nortje, *The Terrible Ones*, p.253.

Although junior officers and NCOs were also responsible for platoon training in the rest of the SADF, the training at 32 Battalion was different in the fact that platoon commanders functioned autonomously and did not, as in the regular SADF, operate according to a set training plan. This meant that it was left to the platoon leaders to decide on which areas of training to focus within their particular platoons as well as, if the need arose, develop training methods and drills to improve the combat effectiveness of their platoons. Although the SADF informally had a culture of decentralised command, with lower ranking officers given a large degree of freedom in which to operate, in 1977 the idea that black soldiers were capable of leading and training South African forces differed radically from the views of the Apartheid government. Nel's concept made sense, though, in light of the fact that white members of 32 Battalion were either NSM, assigned to the unit for a limited time, or PF officers who had commitments to the SADF outside of 32 Battalion. A year later, in July 1978, an internal report on training at 32 Battalion, while acknowledging that training was efficient, continued to reflect this problem, stating that the 'Problem, however, is that training officers are young PF officers who are committed to attend promotion courses…'[77] The frequent replacement of white personnel meant that the presence of, and authority given to, black NCOs provided a sense of continuity to training at 32 Battalion, which would have been absent if training had followed regular SADF patterns. Additionally, this training method nurtured the innovative spirit of 32 Battalion, established from necessity during Operation Savannah, and was an efficient way of increasing the level of training and combat effectiveness of the Angolan troops. By translating combat experience into training programmes, 32 Battalion found a way in which 60mm patrol mortars could be lightened and still fired accurately: '[32 Battalion] improvised their 60mm mortars… The base plates of the mortars were made smaller … to reduce the weight. They were quite accurate [when used in this way].'[78]

Ironically, the SADF took the diametrically opposite view to command and control structures. The Chief of the Army compiled a document entitled 'Lessons learnt during Op Savannah' which states:

> The command and control structure of the SADF has been designed to function efficiently not only during peace-time, but also during war-time. To change this organisation and operate on an ad-hoc basis during an operation not only results in confusion among lower formations, but, as has been proved during Savannah, also causes unco-ordinated [*sic*] action and ineffective control. We must stick to our existing organisations and doctrine.[79]

77 DODDC, 32 Bn, Box 41, 309/1/ALG, Vol. 1, Spesifieke Operasies: Gesamentlik, Persoonlike verslag aan Bev 32 Bn deur Bev Buffalo Basis, p.11. Afrikaans: *Probleem is egter dat die opl offe jong sm offe is wat verpligtinge van bevorderingskursusse het…*

78 Interview with David da Silva (pseudonym), former 32 Battalion soldier, Pretoria, 20-06-2019.

79 DODDC, 32 Bn, Box 41, 309/1/51 (Savannah), Vol. 1, Lesse geleer gedurende Op Savannah, Lesse geleer gedurende Op Savannah.

This seems to disregard the successes achieved by units functioning on the very ad-hoc basis that is reviled in the document. Nonetheless, the caveats that the Chief of the Army issued are poignant when viewed in the light of later command and control failures that had disastrous results, particularly in the case of 32 Battalion.[80]

Pseudo-Operations and Reconnaissance Wing

Driven by the lack of intelligence on SWAPO, Breytenbach came up with the idea of pseudo-operations late in 1976. Intelligence gathering was, at the time, a hot topic in the SADF, as the realisation started to dawn that South Africa was probably now involved in a protracted war in Namibia and Angola. Studies were done on both the philosophy and praxis of intelligence gathering and, in typical army fashion, guidelines were established for efficiency.[81] The concept was based on the Rhodesian Selous Scouts and the idea was that a group of black 32 Battalion soldiers could masquerade as SWAPO cadres, hopefully gaining the trust of the local population and gathering intelligence from them.[82] Breytenbach again exhibited his willingness to use the assets at his disposal by appointing an Angolan sergeant, who had undergone guerrilla training in the USSR and China while serving in the FNLA, together with two other black Angolans and two South Africans as instructors.[83] The prevalent thought was that 'to apprehend SWAPO, you have to do what SWAPO do [*sic*], and do it better.'[84]

Thirty soldiers were trained, but, in accordance with guidelines from 101 TF envisaging teams of eight blacks under the command of one white NSM officer,[85] only 10 were selected for the first pseudo-operation, an infiltration of the Opepela area. The group successfully made contact with the local population and they were accepted as SWAPO cadres after spending some time among them. After nearly a month of posing as SWAPO insurgents, the group withdrew. Because of a communication breakdown between 32 Battalion, 101 Task Force and SADF Army HQ, the operation had taken place without the knowledge of the SADF. When they became aware of it, further operations of such nature were prohibited.[86] Soon thereafter, an OC's Conference was hosted by 101 TF on 16 February 1977,[87] followed by another at 2 MA HQ on 12 March, specifically emphasising the importance of intelligence gathering as a whole

80 Cf. 'Conventional Operations' below.
81 DODDC, 32 Bn, Box 7, G/OPS/3/3, Vol. 1, Konferensies, Voorvereiste vir die veiligheid van die staat.
82 Nortje, *The Terrible Ones,* p.274.
83 Nortje, *The Terrible Ones,* pp.274–275.
84 Interview with David da Silva (pseudonym), former 32 Battalion soldier, Pretoria, 20-06-2019.
85 DODDC, 32 Bn, Box 55, 522/1, Vol. 1, Konferensies: 101 TM, Notule van Bevelvoerderskonferensie gehou op 16 Feb 77 te HK 101 Taakmag.
86 Nortje, *The Terrible Ones,* pp.275–276.
87 DODDC, 32 Bn, Box 7, G/OPS/3/3, Vol. 1, Konferensies, Opvolging van punte bespreek op Bev Konf te 101 TM HK op 16 Feb 77.

but, to an even greater extent, intelligence gathering done in the prescribed, army way.[88] Intelligence Instruction 4/76, discussed at these conferences, states explicitly 'The largest possible measure of cooperation and trust between different intelligence organisations is vital.'[89] It is not a large leap of imagination to envisage 101 TF, chagrined at Breytenbach's independent attempts at intelligence gathering, pre-empting further such attempts at these conferences. Although Breytenbach (or any other delegate from 32 Battalion) did not attend these conferences, pseudo-operations ceased to form an integral part of 32 Battalion activities. Pseudo-operations therefore only form a small part of the fighting history of 32 Battalion, but are indicative of their adaptability and willingness to embrace new challenges. The fact that the concept of pseudo-operations was effectively implemented without the knowledge of Army HQ also illustrates the efficiency of the leadership in conceiving and implementing novel approaches to warfare.

The 32 Battalion Reconnaissance Wing (Recce Wing) was also born from the need for accurate, up-to-date intelligence. SADF intelligence doctrine of the time placed a premium on the rapid dissemination of intelligence and information, to the extent that it was considered worthless after a sufficient time lapse.[90] Nel recognised that the SADF Recces would never be a large enough group to provide intelligence for the whole of the SADF and set out to provide his own.[91] The first Recce Wing training commenced in 1978 and closely resembled that of the Recce Commandos. As with the Recce Commandos, training started with a selection phase, designed to eliminate soldiers that lacked either the physical prowess or the mentality to become members of the Recce Wing. Those that were selected then embarked on an intensive programme that included intensive navigation, bushcraft, tracking and minor tactics training in addition to a strenuous physical fitness regime.[92] This resulted in soldiers that were, in the eyes of their peers, 'tough as nails'.[93] Soldiers that completed both the selection phase and the Recce Wing training were then based at Omauni, closer to 32 Battalion's area of operations than Buffalo and therefore quickly able to deploy when the need arose,[94] and were organised into teams of five: a white team leader (usually a second lieutenant), a white NCO (usually a corporal) as the team's second in command, and three black troops (some of which had the rank of corporal). The rigidity of the composition of the teams, when compared to normal 32 Battalion platoons, was due to the fact that Recce Wing training attracted NSM from

88 DODDC, 32 Bn, Box 7, G/OPS/3/3, Vol. 1, Konferensies, Notule van Bevelvoerderskonferensie gehou te 2 MG HK Oshakati om 10h30 op 12 Maart 1977.
89 DODDC, 32 Bn, Box 7, G/OPS/3/3, Vol. 1, Konferensies, Inligtingsinstruksie No 4/76: Insameling van informasie en inligting. Afrikaans: *Dit is van kardinale belang dat daar die grootste mate van samewerking en vertroue heers tussen die onderskeie inligtingstawwe.*
90 DODDC, 32 Bn, Box 7, G/OPS/3/3, Vol. 1, Konferensies, Inligtingsinstruksie No4/76: Die beginsels van inligting.
91 Nortje, *The Terrible Ones,* pp.332–333.
92 Nortje, *The Terrible Ones,* pp.335–340.
93 Interview with David da Silva (pseudonym), former 32 Battalion soldier, Pretoria, 20-06-2019.
94 Interview with Hilton Husson (pseudonym), former 32 Battalion soldier, Centurion, 10-07-2019.

outside 32 Battalion. These newcomers could not always comprehend the fluidity of the command structures within the unit, and a more traditional approach to the Recce teams went some way to alleviate the concerns of some potentially invaluable NSM.[95] The ability to gather intelligence from within their own ranks significantly reduced the time it took for 32 Battalion to act on such information. The success and efficiency of the Recce Wing soon led to it acquiring something of an elite status within 32 Battalion and it was eventually deployed for reconnaissance duties with other SADF formations in addition to providing intelligence for internal operations.[96] Later in the war, the emphasis of the Recce Wing shifted from providing combat intelligence to 32 Battalion and the SADF to gathering intelligence on infiltration routes used by the ANC and other resistance organisations that posed a threat to South Africa's internal security.[97]

Conventional Operations

By 1977, 32 Battalion had had time to organise and institute proper training programmes. These were still based on Breytenbach's vision, that 32 Battalion would be employed in an unconventional, counterinsurgency capacity, and were not targeted at conventional deployments. The training embraced the fact that 32 Battalion was not constituted in the same way as regular SADF units, and was tailored specifically to the unit. This led Constand Viljoen, Chief of the Army, to note that 'This HQ is definitely aware of … the 'differentness' of the unit … The manpower problem remains an issue and it is recognised, but attempts should nonetheless be made at achieving uniformity in training, in terms of doctrine.'[98]

Despite Viljoen's misgivings, he also noted that 32 Battalion's attitude towards training and operations was 'very positive' and that morale and fitness in the unit were high.[99] Notably, though, his assessment was based on rural counterinsurgency training, not training for conventional operations. Viljoen's desire for uniformity in terms of doctrine might be an indication that he envisaged a more conventional role for 32 Battalion, but this was not explicitly stated; an omission that would have significant consequences for 32 Battalion.

95 Nortje, *The Terrible Ones*, p.380.
96 Nortje, *The Terrible Ones*, p.670.
97 Interview with Ian Ines (pseudonym), former 32 Battalion soldier, Centurion, 10-07-2019.
98 DODDC, 32 Bn, Box 41, 309/1/EVAL, Vol. 1, Gesamentlike Ops: Eval van Anderskleuriges, Na-opl Evaluasie: 32 Bn: TEIN Plattelands. Afrikaans: *Hierdie HK is definitief op hoogte van … die 'andersheid' van die eenheid … Die mannekragprobleem bly 'n faktor en dit word besef, maar nogtans moet daar gepoog word om eenvormigheid in opl tov leerstellings en doktrine te verkry.*
99 DODDC, 32 Bn, Box 41, 309/1/EVAL, Vol. 1, Gesamentlike Ops: Eval van Anderskleuriges, Na-opl Evaluasie: 32 Bn: TEIN Plattelands, p.3. Afrikaans: *baie positief.*

In October 1977, 32 Battalion had well-established counterinsurgency training programmes, and was rapidly gaining experience in the guerrilla warfare aspects of patrolling and dominating an area, but had not deployed in a conventional role since the makeshift days of Operation Savannah. The availability of 'equipment and ordenance [*sic*]'[100] for use during training exercises and the availability of SADF officers and NCOs also continued to be a problem, to the extent that 101 TF accused 32 Battalion of 'grapping [*sic*: grabbing]' two second lieutenants en route to 1 MA at Rundu.[101] Such unconventional 'recruiting' tactics not only did nothing to endear 32 Battalion to the rest of the SADF, but compounded the command and control issues that already existed. Operation Kropduif, the assault of a SWAPO base at Eheke, executed together with the Recces, was 32 Battalion's first attempt at conventional warfare as formal SADF troops and vividly illustrated their leadership crisis.[102] Although SWAPO forces were successfully engaged, the large number of casualties suffered by a casualty-shy SADF led the operation to fail. The main reason identified for the failure of Operation Kropduif is a lack of command and control, at all levels and all times.[103] Potentially due to security concerns, little information about the operation was given to 32 Battalion during the planning phase. Considering that the Angolan soldiers had no formal SADF conventional warfare training, this lack of detail seriously hampered training for Operation Kropduif, which was a very different form of warfare than the guerrilla patrols that they were used to. In addition, close cooperation with other units, in this case the Recces, was alien to the 32 Battalion way of war up to that point, which was waged almost exclusively at platoon level. In fact, in order to minimise the risk of friendly fire casualties, it was custom for different 32 Battalion platoons on patrol to actively avoid each other's area of operations. Finally, adhering to a given timetable was key to the success of a conventional operation such as Kropduif, whereas the patrolling with which 32 Battalion was familiar, were much less time-critical. These factors combined in costly fashion to highlight the inexperience of 32 Battalion in conventional operations, despite 101 TF attempting to improve command and control by transferring soldiers from 32 Battalion to the Recces[104] and temporarily returning Recce operators, that had been part of Bravo Group, to 32 Battalion.[105]

Fortunately for the SADF, the men of the unit, though stunned by experiences of Kropduif, were not deterred from attempting future conventional operations, but were

100 DODDC, 32 Bn, Box 9, LOG/OPS/3/126/4, Vol. 1, Dissipline en regsaangeleenthede (verhoormagte, ens.), Orders given to Comdt. V.d. Spey.
101 DODDC, SWA HK (Ops), Box 7, 309/1, Vol. 1, 32 Bn, Signal from HQ 101 TF to 1 MA / 32 Bn, Q/OPS/151/JUL 77.
102 Cf. Nortje, *The Terrible Ones*, pp.302–321.
103 Nortje, *The Terrible Ones*, p.304.
104 DODDC, SWA HK (Ops), Box 7, 309/1, Vol. 1, 32 Bn, Signal from 32 Bn to 101TF, Q/OPS/428/SEPT 77.
105 DODDC, SWA HK (Ops), Box 7, 309/1, Vol. 1, 32 Bn, Signal from 101 TF to 2 MA, Q/OPS/457/AUG 77.

rather motivated to improve their capabilities in this regard. The minor part in Operation Reindeer,[106] the controversial assault on Cassinga, provided some more conventional experience, but it was only the arrival of Colonel Deon Ferreira as OC on 9 January 1979 that saw 32 Battalion become thoroughly proficient at conventional warfare. Tasked by Constand Viljoen to 'strike a balance between Breytenbach, who only wanted to shoot, and Nel, who only wanted to write,' Ferreira had an operational focus from the outset.[107] He quickly identified a number of problems in his new command, mainly centred on a lack of experience, training and planning. To rectify this, Ferreira initiated an intensive eight-week retraining programme as well as an evaluation of the – mostly black – permanent leader group, which had the additional effect of enhancing discipline within 32 Battalion.[108] Ferreira's emphasis on effective preparation was such that, towards the end of his command of 32 Battalion, he was able to outline his annual goals as 'inflicting maximum losses on SWAPO and disrupting them abroad to such an extent that they cannot continue their work domestically... to ensure minimum losses to own forces through good combat drills, deployment drills, preparation, training, accountability and aggression...'[109]

Emphasis was no longer placed on either the most basic of training to increase troops' chances of survival or exclusively on counterinsurgency, but had progressed to the point where Ferreira could accept that the men under his command could adhere to various drills, plan and execute an operation or exercise and, by extension, take on a more conventional role if the need arose. Training programmes included courses for black platoon sergeants and section commanders, new recruits and assault pioneers, as well as retraining courses for companies and mortar sections.[110] These courses were presented in addition to the normal training, at platoon or section level, that took place continuously throughout the year. Despite Ferreira's attempts to bolster 32 Battalion's conventional capabilities, training in this regard was still much weaker than regular SADF training, which consisted of a 26-point plan, including aspects such as navigation, ground and air cooperation, security and information, survival, advanced marksmanship and spiritual preparation, and took place over the course of 368 training periods.[111] Nevertheless, 32 Battalion had progressed to a point where they were able to liaise effectively with the rest of the SADF during combat operations. As this occurred ever more frequently, mutual respect deepened, particularly between 32 Battalion and the South African Air Force

106 Cf. Nortje, *The Terrible Ones*, pp.355–359.
107 Nortje, *The Terrible Ones*, p.377.
108 Nortje, *The Terrible Ones*, p.386.
109 DODDC, 32 Bn Gp 2, Box 260, 522/1, Vol. 1, Konferensies, Kongresse, Seminare, Simposiums en Vergaderings: Konferensies, 32 Bataljon doelwitte: 1982. Afrikaans: *Maksimum verliese aan SWAPO toe te dien en hom buitelands so te ontwrig dat hy nie sy werk binnelands kan voortsit nie... om deur middel van goeie gevegsdrils, ontplooingsdrils, voorbereiding, opleiding, verskilligheid en aggresiewiteit* [*sic*] *die minimum verliese aan eie magte te verseker...*
110 DODDC, 32 Bn Gp 2, Box 260, 522/1, Vol. 1, Konferensies, Kongresse, Seminare, Simposiums en Vergaderings: Konferensies, Aanhangsel B by 32BN/522/1 DD FEB 82.
111 DODDC, 32 Bn Gp 2, Box 262, 522/1/1, Vol. 7, Bevelvoerderskonferensies, Bestaande doelwitleerplan.

(SAAF). David da Silva (pseudonym), a 32 Battalion soldier at that time, remembers that '...the chopper guys – the Alouette pilots, gunship pilots – ...it's amazing how they contributed [to the success of 32 Battalion's operations]. The Pumas [troop transport helicopters] took us out of situations that you would not think a Puma could go in... Those guys were brave.'[112]

Regardless of whether Ferreira had an inkling of what was to come, or whether he just happened to provide the right kind of influence at 32 Battalion at the right time for the SADF, his time as OC saw an increase in their conventional deployment. This culminated in Operation Tiro-Tiro, an attack on a FAPLA base at Savate in support of UNITA from 17 to 24 May 1980. Drawing on experience gained from smaller deployments since Operation Kropduif, as well as Ferreira's influence on the morale and outlook of his troops, planning for Operation Tiro-Tiro was thorough to a fault.[113] Extensive reconnaissance and intelligence gathering was done beforehand that, although not flawless, was a vast improvement over the confusion of Kropduif.[114] 32 Battalion suffered heavy casualties during Operation Tiro-Tiro, but this time it could not be attributed to a lack of experience, planning, training or coordination. The UNITA forces that were supposed to support 32 Battalion did not live up to the expectations of the SADF,[115] but Ferreira was able to effectively adapt his battle plan, and effectively communicate this to his subordinates, to compensate for UNITA's lack of support.

In addition to enhancing the conventional capabilities of 32 Battalion, Ferreira also introduced 'air-mobile sweep operations' or 'butterfly operations', similar to the Rhodesian 'fire force' concept,[116] which required the coordination of three or more companies and, at times, artillery support, with helicopters from the SAAF. Butterfly operations took place concurrent with the normal COIN patrols. Ferreira significantly increased the command and control structures and capabilities of 32 Battalion, which in itself gave them a greater conventional capability. Coupled with the increased standards of training and experience gained during smaller parts in operations, conventional combat effectiveness had increased dramatically. At the end of Ferreira's tenure as OC 32 Battalion, training of black leaders was a firmly established priority at the unit. Specialised courses, specifically for black platoon sergeants and section leaders, was officially acknowledged as one of the key goals that would contribute to future success,[117] culminating in the commissioning of black members of 32 Battalion as some of the first officers in the SADF.[118]

112 Interview with David da Silva (pseudonym), former 32 Battalion soldier, Pretoria, 20-06-2019.
113 Cf. Nortje, *The Terrible Ones,* pp.493–502.
114 Nortje, *The Terrible Ones,* pp.497–502.
115 Nortje, *The Terrible Ones,* p.531.
116 Nortje, *The Terrible Ones,* p.557.
117 DODDC, 32 Bn Gp 2, Box 260, 522/1, Vol. 1, Konferensies, Kongresse, Seminare, Simposiums en Vergaderings / Konferensies, Aanhangsel B by 32BN/522/1 DD FEB 82.
118 Interview with Abel Agostin (pseudonym), former 32 Battalion soldier, Pretoria, 14-12-2018.

Late War

When Colonel Eddie Viljoen took over as OC from Ferreira in 1982, the emphasis that 32 Battalion placed on the relationship between officers and men, as well as their concern for the wellbeing of their men, was beginning to stand in stark contrast to the greater SADF. In 1983, the office of the Chief of the Army saw the need to circulate a letter among the SADF. This letter was titled 'Application of the concept 'The soldier is the most important asset of the SADF'' and tasked units' leader groups to ensure that troops felt and experienced that they were important to the SADF, in particular by paying more personal attention to them.[119] Once again, 32 Battalion seems to have been ahead of the SADF in recognising the importance of leading by example and inspiring troops. The very success of Bravo Group in the early years had been based on the fact that the Angolan soldiers had seen that their officers were willing to put themselves at risk for their men and had responded to this practical leadership. Seven years later, when the SADF also recognised that officers needed to provide inspirational leadership, this concept was ingrained at 32 Battalion and, far from needing to convince their troops that they meant something to the SADF, they were ready to evolve and adapt their combat capabilities.

Eddie Viljoen had seen the typical deployment of 32 Battalion change from patrols to deny SWAPO access to southern Angola to the support for UNITA against FAPLA. The MPLA was giving ever greater support to SWAPO and the distinction between FAPLA and PLAN combatants was becoming less clear. Pretoria also increasingly came to the realisation that it was impossible for the SADF and SWATF to effectively patrol the whole of the Angolan / Namibia border and that UNITA was needed as a buffer between Namibia and FAPLA / PLAN. Unfortunately for the South African strategists, UNITA was not able to offer effective resistance to FAPLA on their own and had to rely heavily on South African support. South Africa was able to provide UNITA with equipment, but international political pressure made it difficult to intervene directly on their behalf. Because the majority of the soldiers of 32 Battalion was black and spoke Portuguese, they became the natural choice when direct intervention was deemed essential. Pretoria was better able to deny involvement when confronted with evidence of black SADF troops aiding UNITA than with whites. As a result, 32 Battalion took on an increasingly conventional role, and by April 1986 Viljoen was able to assess the role of the unit as 'performing operations, conventional as well as COIN, in SWA and cross-border' in a letter to SWATF HQ.[120]

As a direct result of a meeting, held at Army HQ on 3 April and attended by Major General M.J. du Plessis from the office of the Chief of the Army, two brigadiers, nine

119 DODDC, 32 Bn Gp 2, Box 156, 522/1, Konferensies, Notule van Sektor-Sersant-Majoor konferensie gehou te Sektor 20 Hoofkwartier 261330B Jan 84. Afrikaans: *Toepassing van die begrip 'Die manskap is die belangrikste bate van die SA Leër'.*

120 DODDC, SWS 3, Box 52, 309/1, Vol. 1, TD Plan ter Onts van 32 Bn, 29 April 1986. Afrikaans: *die voer van ops konvensioneel sowel as TEIN in SWA en transgrens.*

colonels, two commandants (lieutenant colonels) and a major,[121] 1986 saw the attachment of Ratel 90 and Ratel ZT3 anti-tank Infantry Fighting Vehicles, Ystervark anti-air vehicles and multiple rocket launchers to the unit in anticipation of a FAPLA offensive against UNITA, which South Africa would support. The unit also received one of only two SA-9 surface-to-air missile systems in the SADF.[122] The unwillingness of the SADF, in 1977, to change the name of the unit from Bravo Group to 32 Battalion Group, on the grounds that the addition of the word 'group' implied the attachment of artillery, armour and other fighting elements,[123] now only served to illustrate to how great an extent 32 Battalion had outstripped the role originally envisaged for them. They were the first unit to operationally deploy the Ystervark and their ability to adapt and innovate was put to good use in developing the most effective drills to use on this type of weapon system. They were also able to suggest modifications to the system, such as the use of a different type of radio antenna, to the SADF in order to increase operational effectiveness[124] and point out shortcomings, such as the susceptibility of South African-manufactured ammunition links to stoppages.[125] Additionally, 32 Battalion was tasked with evaluating a new back-sight, called the 'S-point', for both R1 and AK47 rifles,[126] and as early as 1979, the SADF recognised that they were among the units that saw the greatest level of deployment and selected them to cooperate with Armscor in the development of a new backpack,[127] and webbing.[128]

For the rest of the war, 32 Battalion was, in some capacity, involved in the majority of SADF operations. They had established their competence in unconventional warfare and intelligence gathering / reconnaissance early in the war and had expanded their conventional capabilities under Ferreira and Viljoen. The SADF was therefore able to use them, in piecemeal fashion or otherwise, to fill the myriad of gaps that the increasing intensity of the war brought about. Although the 32 Battalion of 1989 was almost unrecognisable from the Bravo Group of 1975, the spirit of camaraderie that Breytenbach has initiated, and subsequent OCs had fostered, had stood the test of time. Censor reports for 1988,

121 DODDC, SWS 3, Box 52, 309/1, Vol. 1, Notule van 'n vergadering gehou by Leër HK (D Ops) 0310H30 Apr 1986 mbt 32 Bn.
122 DODDC, SWS 3, Box 52, 309/1, Vol. 1, Aanwending van die SA-9 GLM stelsel in 32 Bn.
123 DODDC, SWA HK (Ops), Box 7, 309/1, Vol. 1, 32 Bn, Signal from 101 TF to SSO Ops 32 Bn, OPS/364/JUN 77.
124 DODDC, SWS 3, Box 52, 309/1, Vol. 1, Signal from 32 Bn to C Army and SWATF, OPS/327/29 MEI 86.
125 DODDC, SWS 3, Box 52, 309/1, Vol. 1, Signal from 32 Bn to C Army and SWATF, OPS/260/201 MEI 86.
126 DODDC, 32 Bn Gp 2, Box 260, 522/1, Vol. 1, Konferensies, Kongresse, Seminare, Simposiums en Vergaderings / Konferensies, Notule van Bevelvoerderskonferensie gehou te 32 Bn HK.
127 DODDC, 32 Bn Gp 2, Box 262, 522/1, Vol. 1, Konferensies, Notule van bevelvoerderskonferensie gehou te 32 Bataljon Hoofkwartier op 12 Januarie 1979.
128 DODDC, Sektor 20 Gp 3, Box 72, 309/1, Vol. 1, Algemeen, Notule van SA Leër Inhuis Nabetragting tov Op Sceptic gehou te Blennie 150830B Jul 1980, p.3.

reflected in Table 3.2, indicate that the vast majority of 32 Battalion soldiers had positive experiences of the morale within the unit. It should be noted the most of these letters would have been written by white members, resulting in a somewhat distorted image, but the consensus is undeniable:

The unusually high percentage of negative comments about morale in the unit during June can probably be attributed to the fact that 32 Battalion's involvement in Operation Packer, the final of the contentious Modular / Hooper / Packer trilogy of operations around Cuito Cuanavale, ended on 30 April 1988.[129] Soldiers would, therefore, have had time to reflect on the operations and the indecisive outcome would undoubtedly have galled a unit that had become used to unequivocal results, if not successes. Even taking this into account, an average of one negative comment in more than 11 letters does not seem excessive.

Table 3.2: Frequency of reference to morale in letters from 32 Battalion soldiers

Month (1988)	Total letters censored	Mention of negative morale	Mention of positive morale	Percentage negative
March*	367	21	316	5.72
June†	338	66	215	19.53
July‡	268	17	88	6.34
August§	230	12	40	5.21
September|	291	22	128	7.56
October¶	289	23	64	7.96
November**	198	12	134	6.06
Total	**1,981**	**173**	**985**	**8.73**

* DODDC, SWA HK GM OATI, Box 105, SEK/202/02732, Vol. 1, DTI, Censor Report 01/03/88 to 31/03/88.

† DODDC, SWA HK GM OATI, Box 105, SEK/202/02732, Vol. 1, DTI, Censor Report 01/06/88 to 30/05/88.

‡ DODDC, SWA HK GM OATI, Box 105, SEK/202/02732, Vol. 1, DTI, Censor Report 01/07/88 to 31/07/88.

§ DODDC, SWA HK GM OATI, Box 105, SEK/202/02732, Vol. 1, DTI, Censor Report 01/08/88 to 31/07/88.

| DODDC, SWA HK GM OATI, Box 105, SEK/202/02732, Vol. 1, DTI, Censor Report 01/09/88 to 30/09/88.

¶ DODDC, SWA HK GM OATI, Box 105, SEK/202/02732, Vol. 1, DTI, Censor Report 01/10/88 to 31/10/88.

** DODDC, SWA HK GM OATI, Box 105, SEK/202/02732, Vol. 1, DTI, Censor Report 01/11/88 to 30/11/88.

129 Nortje, *The Terrible Ones*, p.1049.

Conclusion

From the earliest moments of 32 Battalion, when Jan Breytenbach started to train the FNLA troops at Mpupa, improvisation was necessary to achieve success. After Operation Savannah, Breytenbach recognised that he needed a focal point for the loyalty of the men under his command. He therefore consciously and actively fostered a culture of loyalty towards the unit, rather than the political or military structures controlling it. Less apparent, though, was the evolution of the culture of innovation that had germinated during Operation Savannah. Aided by the attitude of decentralised command prevalent within the SADF, 32 Battalion became adept at rapidly adapting to the changing nature of the Border War. In some cases, they started to address problems that the SADF had not yet recognised as such, and put invaluable resources at the disposal of the SADF, such as the Recce Wing. In addition, the unusual, from a SADF perspective, circumstances and experiences of 32 Battalion added valuable expertise to the SADF repertoire. By way of example, in July 1977, 101 TF was able to request that WO Pep van Zyl be detached to Windhoek for 14 days in order to assist with the training of (presumably white) instructors for six black companies. With this request, 101 TF tacitly acknowledged that 32 Battalion was the SADF's prime authority on the 'training methodology for black soldiers.'[130] 32 Battalion continually adapted existing, and developed new, ways of soldiering in order to increase the effectiveness as a fighting force, making optimum use of the resources at their disposal. The bludgeon of 1975 had turned into a multi-purpose hammer, still capable of delivering a crushing blow, but equally adept at the finesse required to provide the finishing touches to an ornamental piece. This is, perhaps, a defining example of how Williamson Murray describes military culture: 'Military culture represents the ethos and professional attributes ... that contribute to a common core understanding of the nature of war within military organisations... military culture obviously changes over time in response to changes in a society's culture, the advance of technology, and the impact of leadership.'[131]

The officers and men of 32 Battalion were certainly sensitive to the changing nature of the war in Angola and Namibia. Although Murray implies that military culture changes organically, an argument can be made that the changes were much more deliberate and focused in the case of 32 Battalion.

130 DODDC, SWA HK (Ops), Box 7, 309/1, Vol. 1, 32 Bn, Signal from 101 TF to 32 Bn, Q/OPS/356/JUL 77. Afrikaans: *metodiek van opleiding van swartes*.

131 W. Murray, 'Does military culture matter?' in *Orbis: A Journal of World Affairs 43 (1)*, 1999, p.27.

White instructors from 32 Battalion's Recce Wing training black soldiers in the use of the Heckler & Koch HK21 light machinegun.

A Valkiri 127mm Multiple Rocket Launcher, similar to that used by 32 Battalion late during the Border War.

Commandant Gert Nel,
32 Battalion's second
Commanding Officer,
1977–1978.

The unit at Buffalo.

Kempton Park, a suburb of Johannesburg, awarding 32 Battalion the Freedom of the City, 1991.

Major Hannes Nortmann (left) in front of one of the FAPLA T54/55s disabled by 32 Battalion's Ratel-ZT3s.

Black civilians being educated by an SADF teacher. Scenes like these took place throughout the Border War, as part of the SADF's ComOps-programmes.

A Ratel-ZT3, clearly showing the triple anti-tank missile launcher mounted on the turret.

Commandant Deon Ferreira (right), 32 Battalion's third Commanding Officer (1978–1982), after Operation Tiro-Tiro in 1980.

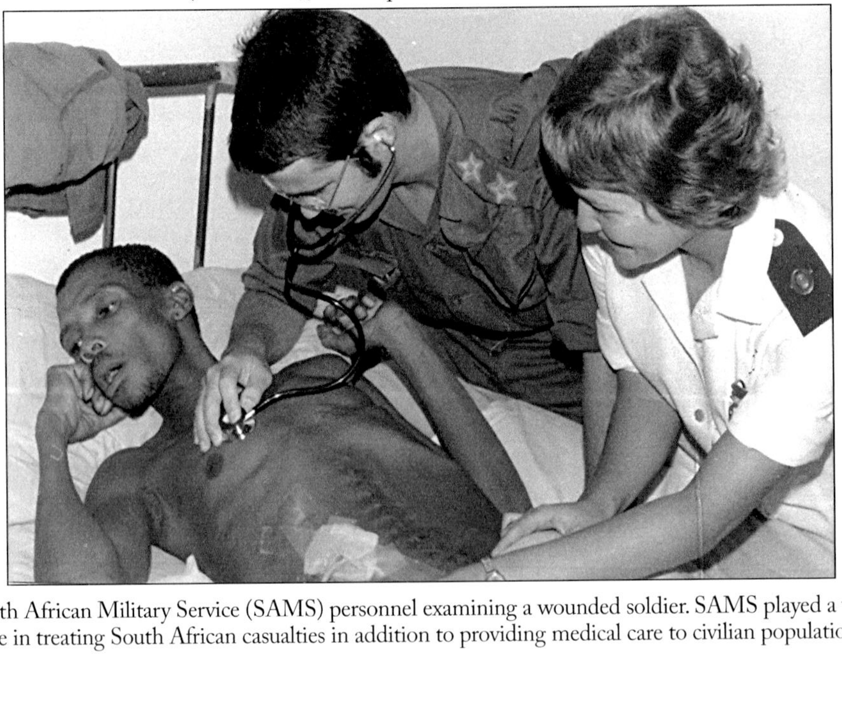

South African Military Service (SAMS) personnel examining a wounded soldier. SAMS played a vital role in treating South African casualties in addition to providing medical care to civilian populations.

4

'The Flux': Supplying the Battalion

Although the topic of supply and logistics in war has been studied extensively within the wider historiography, very little research has been done on supply during the Border War. Most of the authors of Border War memoires make only passing reference to supply and logistic issues. Piet Nortje's *The Terrible Ones* is an obvious exception, but his references to logistics are hidden within the larger narrative and are hard to find. Additionally, because it is not a focal point in his work, Nortje relies primarily on recollections and provides a perfunctory overview of the impact of supply and logistics on 32 Battalion. As flux provides better adhesion and integration between different metals during the forging process, logistics aided the meld not only of combat and society, of black and white, but also of South African and Angolan. This, if nothing else, makes it a vital consideration in any historical study of 32 Battalion.

Kenneth Macksey contends that

> The sheer intricacy of the logistical demands of modern warfare and the technological developments spawned by two world wars between them generated a complete revolution in both the control of the maintenance of forces deployed on operations and in attitudes towards the science of logistics. Now, even in the most inaccessible parts of the world ... it had become accepted that troops would be supplied with their essential needs despite the physical obstacles to movement.[1]

Martin van Creveld, writing in the 1970s when 32 Battalion was established, emphasised the challenges that Macksey identified by illustrating that

> ... it sometimes appears that the logistic aspect of war is nothing but an endless series of difficulties succeeding one another. Problems constantly appear, grow, merge, are handed forward and backward, are solved and dissolved only to reappear

1 K. Macksey, *For want of a nail: The impact on war of logistics and communications*. London: Brassey's, 1989, p.168.

> in a different guise. In face of this kaleidoscopic array of obstacles ... one sometimes wonders how armies managed to move at all, how campaigns were waged, and victories occasionally won.[2]

Van Creveld's contention is particularly applicable to 32 Battalion, where everything was done in a fairly haphazard manner, particularly early in their existence. Their successes in Operation Savannah, and thereafter, took place in spite of their logistic situation, not because of it. The added complication of the demands that the families of the fighting man placed on the SADF's logistical structures, highlighted by Macksey, makes a study of the way in which the unit was, and was not, supplied indispensable.

Supply, Logistics and Base Facilities

Although 32 Battalion's headquarters was in Rundu, their first 'base' was established in the Caprivi Strip. The base, initially called 'Pica Pau' (Portuguese for woodpecker) was soon renamed 'Buffalo' and remained the main base of the unit until their withdrawal from Namibia in 1989. 'Pica Pau' then became the name of the 'Kimbo', or civilian area. In addition to Buffalo, the need arose for a training base, and 'Dodge City' was established further east in the Caprivi in July 1976, but only remained in service with 32 Battalion until 1977, when it was taken over by the Engineer Formation. A new operational base was then established at Omauni (this was also the name of the base) in eastern Owamboland (to the west of Buffalo), to shorten the lines of supply and communication from base to operational area. Omauni was used as an operational base from July 1977 until July 1984, when it was handed over to the SWATF. Smaller operational bases were utilised on an as-needed basis, such as 'Charlie November', about 15km north-east of Elundu, which was taken over from 3 SAI to further simplify deployment into Owamboland and the so-called 'shallow' area, approximately 3km into the south of Angola.[3] The map on p. 108 reflects the approximate geographical positions of the important bases used by 32 Battalion, together with some well-known towns or cities for reference. The map indicates the distances that lines of communication had to cover between training bases, operational bases, headquarters and living areas, and highlights the challenges of supplying the unit.

2 M. van Creveld, *Supplying War; Logistics from Wallenstein to Patton*. Cambridge: Cambridge University Press, 1977, 231.

3 P. Nortje, *The Terrible Ones: A complete history of 32 Battalion*. Cape Town: Zebra, 2012, pp.166–175.

Table 4.1: Bravo Group requirements, 17 February 1976[4]

Item	Requested	Available	Available %
Trousers	4,000	500	11.1
Shirts	4,000	500	11.1
Boots	4,000 pairs	0	0
Socks	8,000 pairs	5,000 pairs	38.5
Hats	2,000	6,000	75.0
T-shirts	2,000	800	40.0
Ground sheets	2,000	1,000	33.3
Trainers (shoes)	2,000	1,000	33.3
Web belts	2,000	0	0
Webbing kits	2,000	0	0
Rucksacks	2,000	150	7.0
Tents	300	0	0
9-man cookers	24	0	0
Pots	30	0	0
Pans	30	0	0
Cutlery kits	2,000	150	7.0
Blankets	2,000	0	0
R1 Cleaning kits	3,000	110	3.7
LMG	20	2	9.1
R1	400	486	54.9
Browning .50	2	6	75.0
Browning .30	2	1	33.3
7.62 short ammo	120,000	668,000	84.8
7.62 ammo	200,000	2,706,920	93.1
.50 ammo	10,000	27,390	73.3
.30 ammo	100,000	400,000	80.0
AK47 ammo	20 cases	11 cases	35.5
12 gauge ammo	1,000	3,000	75.0
3.5" rockets	100	768	88.5
81mm mortar ammo	1,250	20,986	94.4
3.5" rocket launcher	9	14	60.9
81mm mortars	8	25	75.8

4 Compiled from DODDC, 1 Militêre Gebied, Box 82, G/OPS/3/3/BRAVO, Vol. 1, Benodigdhede vir Veggp Bravo.

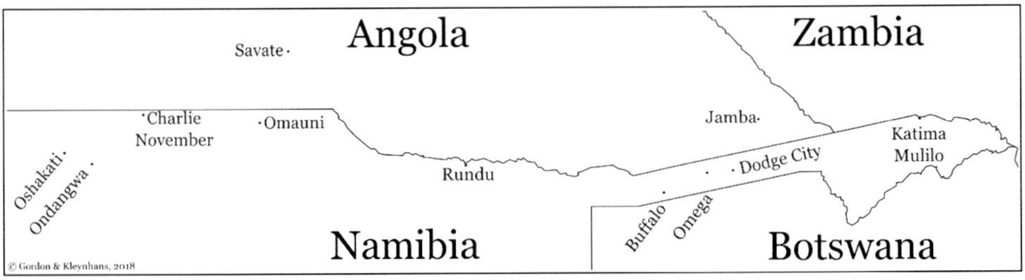

Bases used by 32 Battalion in northern Namibia.

Many difficulties were faced in securing a dependably supply-line. A comparison with the Vietnam War only serves to highlight the significant differences between that and the Border War: North Vietnam depended on the Ho Chi Minh Trail, through Laos and Cambodia, for a line of supply that was secure from American intervention. Upgrading work on this trail started in 1959, with 30,000 Vietnamese employed (or deployed) on the project.[5] By contrast, South Africa had the advantage of reasonably advanced infrastructure in Namibia, but neglected to utilise the period between 1966 and 1975, when the conflict escalated, to make significant improvements. The result was that, at least in the northern part of the country, securing supply lines to isolated bases, like Buffalo, continued to be a significant challenge.

On 12 February 1976, Commandant Van der Spuy of 2 Reconnaissance Commando, then serving with Bravo Group and tasked with training the former FNLA troops, reported that he was unable to continue with the training programme of the still relatively new Bravo Group soldiers, due to a lack of 'equipment & ordenance [*sic*]'.[6] He had therefore been forced to adapt the training to the equipment at hand, rather than pursue the goals set by the original training programme. Two years later, ammunition supply to Buffalo was still not up to the standard expected by the base commander, but it was noted that the Chief of the Army had reduced the supply of ammunition to be used for training in the whole of the SADF, so 32 Battalion was probably not alone in their chagrin at the lack of training supplies.[7]

A list of items requested by Bravo Group on 17 February 1976 indicates not the only extent of the shortages experienced by Bravo Group, but also the additional burden on the SADF supply chain, that would not have been anticipated even a year earlier, when even the concept of a unit like 32 Battalion did not exist. Table 4.1 compares the quantities of different store items requested to those actually available. This provides an insightful indication of the extent of the shortages experienced by Bravo Group during the early days of their existence. It is not clear which of the items were intended as

5 Macksey, *For want of a nail,* pp.174–175.
6 DODDC, 32 Bn, Box 9, LOG/OPS/3/16/4, Vol. 1, Dissipline en regsaangeleenthede (verhoormagte ens.), Orders given to Comdt. V.d. Spey.
7 DODDC, 32 Bn, Box 41, 309/1/ALG, Vol. 1, Spesifieke Operasies Gesamentlik, Persoonlike verslag aan Bev 32 Bn deur Bev Buffalo Basis.

replacements, and which were requested to achieve a full complement, so the assumption is made, throughout, that the sum of available and requested items constitutes the total requirement.

This table clearly shows that the SADF supplied Bravo Group fairly well with the equipment to wage war, but were far more frugal in their provision of items needed for day-to-day living. For example, Bravo Group had 93 percent of their 7.62mm (R1) ammunition requirement, but no blankets or tents and only 11 percent of the shirts and trousers that they needed to shelter and clothe the men that were expending the ammunition. Even heavier weapons, like rockets and mortars, had ammunition capacities of 89 and 94 percent respectively, but the men did not have a single pot or pan in which to prepare a meal. This possibly led to Bravo Group's – and later 32 Battalion's – reputation as notorious 'scroungers' and 'appropriators' of equipment, from the SADF as well as her allies, like UNITA.[8] Soviet equipment, captured from FAPLA and SWAPO, theoretically had to be handed over to the SADF, but was invariably put to good use with Bravo Group.[9]

Breytenbach complained to the GOC 101 TF on 24 April 1976 that his Bravo Group was not receiving adequate logistical support. In his unique style, which would later serve him well as an author, Breytenbach claimed that 'The logistical channel still is blocked solid – constipated' and that 'there is still an attitude of doing us a favour by supplying anything at all.'[10] He augmented his argument by referring to a case where he had wanted to have one of Bravo Group's vehicles camouflaged and the local workshop had given the Bravo Group soldier making the request a 'pot of paint and a brush' and told him to do it himself. Breytenbach contended that, in any other SADF unit, the camouflage would have been done 'within hours because it is an operational necessity.'[11] The attitude described by Breytenbach still seemed to be present over two years later, as reflected in a report on Buffalo by the base commander: 'Supply is not happening satisfactorily. During my term of service, nutria trousers were repeatedly requested and only 60 were received. On the other hand, there is a surplus of jackets and shirts. Supply of necessities, such as rifle cleaning kits, lilies [from piss-lilies: urinals] and toilets is also disappointing.'[12]

8 J. Breytenbach, *The Buffalo Soldiers: The Story of South Africa's 32-Battalion 1975–1993*. Alberton: Galago, 2002, pp.144–146.
9 J. Taylor, *A Whisper in the Reeds: 'The Terrible Ones': South Africa's 32 Battalion at war*. Solihull: Helion & Rugby: GG Books, 2013, p.50.
10 DODDC, 32 Bn, Box 14, G/OPS/3/3, Vol. 1, Budgie – B Group, Points submitted for discussion at OC's conference.
11 DODDC, 32 Bn, Box 14, G/OPS/3/3, Vol. 1, Budgie – B Group, Points submitted for discussion at OC's conference.
12 DODDC, 32 Bn, Box 41, 309/1/ALG, Vol. 1, Spesifieke Operasies Gesamentlik, Persoonlike verslag aan Bev 32 Bn deur Bev Buffalo Basis. Afrikaans: *Bevoorrading is nie na wense nie. Gedurende my dienstermyn is daar herhaaldelik aangevra vir nutria broeke en slegs 60 is ontvang. Daarenteen is daar 'n oorskot hemde en baadjies. Voorsiening van ander noodsaaklike items soos geweerskoonmaakstelle, lelies [pislelies] en toilette is ook teleurstellend.*

Buffalo also had a severe shortage of beds.[13] The availability of rations, on the other hand, had improved and rations were 'of the highest quality and always in sufficient quantities for everyone.'[14] It is, of course, possible that shortfalls in the quantities of rations may have been made up by shooting some of the local wildlife 'for the pot', an event which was not uncommon, particularly among the 'irregular' SADF units like 31 and 32 Battalions,[15] together with recreational hunting by senior SADF officers.[16] Nevertheless, residents of the Kimbo were, for the most part, satisfied with what the SADF provided: '…every single week [on] the first day of the week, they would provide us with food parcels for every home there … enough food for the whole month [*sic*] … there was more than enough.'[17]

In May 1976, the Bravo Group troops stationed in Luengue in Angola were experiencing significant supply shortages. Rations were reaching them infrequently and they did not have enough magazines for their rifles. Despite the Staff Officer, 1st Class (SO1) Logistics of 1 MA requesting assistance from 101 TF, both verbally and in writing, from February, the situation still persisted.[18] This is another indication of the difference in the way in which Bravo Group was perceived. Those that came into direct contact with them and were able to observe their capabilities became firm supporters of, and even campaigners for, the unit. In the wider defence force, though, they were still largely viewed as outsiders and not rated particularly highly.

In order to ensure that he did not lose part of his already thin crop of white leaders, particularly from the Permanent Force who were likely to stay on for longer periods than Citizen Force or national service leaders, Breytenbach was at pains to ensure that adequate housing was available for the men and families that were due to report at 32 Battalion headquarters at Rundu in December 1976 – January 1977. He specifically requested that portable, or terrapin, housing be requested from 101 TF for four officers, two NCOs and their families.[19] By contrast, almost a year later, some of the black troops were still lacking even tented accommodation. In September 1977, 250 more tents were en route to 32 Battalion, for use in the Kimbo, alleviating the problem with housing to a certain extent.[20]

13 DODDC, 32 Bn, Box 55, 522/1 (Bev), Vol. 1, Notule van bevelvoerderskonferensie gehou te 32 Bn om 231100B Jun 77.

14 DODDC, 32 Bn, Box 41, 309/1/ALG, Vol. 1, Spesifieke Operasies Gesamentlik, Persoonlike verslag aan Bev 32 Bn deur Bev Buffalo Basis. Afrikaans: *van hoogstaande gehalte en daar is altyd genoeg rate vir almal.*

15 Cf. J. Breytenbach, *Eden's Exiles: One soldier's fight for paradise.* Pretoria: Protea, 2015, pp.262–272.

16 Breytenbach, *Eden's exiles,* p.84.

17 Interview with Edwin Eduardo (pseudonym), son of former 32 Battalion soldier; Kimbo and Pomfret resident, Wonderboom, 24-06-2019.

18 DODDC, 1 Militêre Gebied, Box 82, G/OPS/3/3/BRAVO, Vol. 1, Message 'LOG/934/ MEI 76' from 1 MA to 101 TF.

19 DODDC, 32 Bn, Box 9, LOG/OPS/3/16/13/3, Vol. 1, Pers. Welsyn (dood, siekte van naasbestaandes, uitstel van opl), Behuising: Permanente lede S Mag: 32 Bn.

20 DODDC, 32 Bn Gp 2, Box 262, 522/1/BEV, Vol. 1, Konferensies, Notule van bevelvoerderskonferensie gehou te 32 Bn op 1 September 1977.

Nonetheless, despite 32 Battalion's liberal philosophy towards her black soldiers, the contrast between the housing arrangements for white officers and black civilians indicate that any claims of equality in 1977 would be an exaggeration.

By the end of 1976, 32 Battalion's command group had realised that they needed more permanent support staff and were unlikely to get this from the SADF in time for their requirements. In addition, Buffalo Base had expanded to such an extent that it was ready for the construction of cold storage facilities by November 1976.[21] The decision was therefore made to train three chefs for the Omauni operational base from the Portuguese soldiers that were already present at Buffalo. Eddie Viljoen, then a commandant at the unit, gave permission for three men to be temporarily promoted to expedite their training and deployment to Omauni.[22] Viljoen was able to reap the fruit of his own foresight during his tenure as OC 32 Battalion: in 1985, rations were effectively managed, shortages were infrequent and chefs provided an efficient service, not only in base but also in the training areas, where three were permanently employed.[23]

On 10 January 1977, the OC of 1 MA noted that the supply of clothing to 31 and 32 Battalions was insufficient. He added that the clothing in use by 31 Battalion (32 Battalion was not significantly better equipped) was only good for about three weeks in operational circumstances and issued guidelines for equipping 31 and 32 Battalions along the same lines as regular SADF units.[24]

Nonetheless, at an OC's conference on 24 February 1977, it was still noted that, 'In many cases, the equipment of personnel who are transported from Buffalo to Omauni is in a bad condition, weapons are unserviceable and equipment is incomplete.'[25]

This is indicative of either a lack of discipline, with regard to equipment, in the unit, or that shortages were still a very real problem, to the extent that troops being deployed operationally had to do so with unserviceable weapons.

By 1981, the supply problems at Buffalo and Omega (31 Battalion) had come to the attention of Sector 20. In particular, getting the necessary consumable produce, such as fresh rations, to these two bases, both of which also had an attached civilian component, was difficult. In an attempt at alleviating the pressure from ground transport channels, the OC of 6 Maintenance Unit investigated the possibility of transporting the

21 DODDC, 1 Militêre Gebied, Box 102, G/OPS/3/3/CARPENTER, Vol. 1, Operations (specific) Unconventional Operation Carpenter, Message 'D/GENIE/120/NOV 76' from H Leer to KMG.

22 DODDC, 32 Bn, Box 9, LOG/OPS/3/16/13/4, Vol. 1, Portugese / Ang'e, Promotions: NCO's: 33 Bn Omauni.

23 DODDC, 32 Bn Gp 2, Box 262, 522/4, Vol. 1, Konf., Kong, Semnaar, Simposiums + Vergaderings: Vergaderings, Maandverslag Opleidingsbasis vir die maand Februarie 1985, p.13.

24 DODDC, 1 Militêre Gebied, Box 82, G/OPS/3/3/BRAVO, Vol. 1, Herwaardering: Uitrustingskale 31 en 32 Bn.

25 DODDC, 32 Bn, Box 2, G/OPS/3/3, Vol. 1, Konferensies, Notule van bevelvoerder konferensie gehou op 24 Februarie 1977. Afrikaans: *Personeel wat vanaf Buffalo na Amaoni* [*sic*: Omauni] *gelig word se uitrusting is in baie gevalle swak, wapens is ondiensbaar, en lede se uitrusting is nie volledig nie.*

'± 18,000kg' of fresh produce required weekly by 31 and 32 Battalions by air.[26] The quantities involved and the fact that air transport was even considered illustrates the difficulties that the SADF encountered in supplying their frontline units. Despite investigating options such as these, supply of fresh produce continued to be a problem and the minutes of an OC's conference, held in December 1982, still notes that the supply of fresh produce to Buffalo is a problem.[27] The air transport option probably did not materialise, and the only alternative, road transport, clearly failed to achieve the desired results.

Progress on the construction programme at Buffalo is succinctly summarised in the minutes of an OC's conference, held on 19 September 1981:

> Currently, 440 houses have been completed and are inhabited. A further 20 houses are being built and 140 more have been approved. The sleeping quarters in the troop lines are progressing quickly and the first will be completed in two weeks. The water system should be functional within two weeks. No problems are being experienced with the power grid... The OC expresses his satisfaction with the progress of the overall building project.[28]

Despite the OC's satisfaction, it would still be a long time before the Kimbo had expanded enough to accommodate the needs of the soldiers and their families. Accidents contributed to this factor, and while the minutes of a terrain meeting in 1985 records that an additional 103 houses had been completed and signed over to the new occupants,[29] the same minutes also remarks that the cost of replacing the houses that had burnt down would not be covered by the SADF and would have to be financed by 32 Battalion itself, if they desired to replace them at all. The minutes also include the helpful suggestion that these costs could be budgeted for the following year, or could be through savings in other areas.[30] What the families who had lived in the burnt down houses were supposed

26 DODDC, 32 Bn Gp 2, Box 260, 522/1, Vol. 1, Konferensies, kongresse, seminare, simposiums en vergaderings / Konferensies, Notule van bevelvoerderskonferensie gehou te Rundu op 2511h00 Nov 1981.

27 DODDC, 32 Bn Gp 2, Box 262, 522/1/1, Vol. 2, Bevelvoerderskonferensies, Notule van bevelvoerderskonferensie gehou te Rundu op 4 Des 82.

28 DODDC, 32 Bn Gp 2, Box 260, 522/1, Vol. 1, Konferensies, kongresse, seminare, simposiums en vergaderings / Konferensies, Notule van bevelvoerderskonferensie gehou te Buffalo op 19 Sep 81. Afrikaans: *Daar is tans 440 huise voltooi en word bewoon. 'n Verdere 20 huise is in aanbou en nog 140 huise is goedgekeur. Die slaapsale in die troepelyne vorder vining en die eerste sal binne twee weke voltooi wees. Die waterstelsel behoort binne twee weke te funksioneer. Geen probleme word ondervind met die kragnetwerk nie ... Die bev spreek sy genoë uit met die vordering van die algemene bouprojek.*

29 DODDC, 32 Bn Gp 2, Box 261, 522/1, Vol. 1, Konferensies / Kongresse / Seminare / Simposiums / Vergaderings: Notules, Notule van terreinvergadering gehou te Buffalo Basis op 7 Februarie 1985, p.2.

30 DODDC, 32 Bn Gp 2, Box 261, 522/1, Vol. 1, Konferensies / Kongresse / Seminare / Simposiums / Vergaderings: Notules, Notule van terreinvergadering gehou te Buffalo Basis op 7 Februarie 1985, p.3.

to do in the meantime was not recorded. The Angolan population at Buffalo was not, however, idle. Many of them put the skills that they had acquired in Angola before the war to use at Buffalo. Brian Baloyi (pseudonym), a former resident of the Kimbo, recalls that '[at] 32 Battalion, there were different people with certain skills... If you were a medic before, if you studied medicine, they recruited you... The Kimbo had ... carpenters, there were teachers, everything. People ... had skills.'[31]

Although circumstances were far from perfect at Buffalo, by 1982 facilities at the base had progressed to such an extent that Buffalo was able to make some of their old building material available to Omauni, to be used for construction there. It came with the caveat that it had been in use at 32 Battalion for a long time and that is was no longer of the best quality. In view of this, a stern warning was issued to Omauni not to erect a 'squatter camp'.[32] In addition to the condition of the building supplies that Buffalo supplied to Omauni, the fact that a construction budget for Omauni had been approved would have contributed to the concern that the old Buffalo material could be used for non-essential, unsightly 'improvements' at Omauni. However, logistical issues played their part once again and the new material for Omauni was slow in arriving.[33] The old Buffalo material would have been a handy stop-gap measure. The insistence that the material be transported in mine-resistant vehicles[34] points to a measure of concern for the wellbeing of the logistic staff responsible for transport – in addition to illuminating the SADF's concerns about the security situation in the north of Namibia – but added to the delays in improving the efficiency of the operational base.

In an effort to address the supply problems experienced at Buffalo in 1982 the OC, Commandant Deon Ferreira, decided to send some of the black store clerks on an SADF training courses, both basic and advanced, to increase their efficiency in dealing with supply and logistics challenges.[35]

Although significant progress had been made in improving the buildings and accommodation available to both soldiers and civilians at Buffalo, by 1982 the rushed way in which these building programmes had been approached and the attendant lack of planning was starting to cause problems. At an OC's conference, it was noted that 'Buildings

31 Telephonic interview with Brian Baloyi (pseudonym), son of former 32 Battalion soldier; Kimbo and Pomfret resident, Centurion, 17-03-2019.

32 DODDC, 32 Bn Gp 2, Box 260, 522/1, Vol. 1, Konferensies, kongresse, seminare, simposiums en vergaderings / Konferensies, Notule van bevelvoerderskonferensie gehou te Buffalo op 19 Mei 1982. Afrikaans: *plakkerskamp*.

33 DODDC, 32 Bn Gp 2, Box 260, 522/1, Vol. 1, Konferensies, kongresse, seminare, simposiums en vergaderings / Konferensies, Notule van bevelvoerderskonferensie gehou te 32 Bn HK op 17 Mrt 82.

34 DODDC, 32 Bn Gp 2, Box 262, 522/1/1, Vol. 2, Bevelvoerderskonferensies, Notule van bevelvoerderskonferensie gehou te Buffalo op 21 Aug 82.

35 DODDC, 32 Bn Gp 2, Box 260, 522/1, Vol. 1, Konferensies, kongresse, seminare, simposiums en vergaderings / Konferensies, Notule van bevelvoerderskonferensie gehou te 32 Bn HK op 17 Mrt 82.

are signed over but are not up to standard and maintenance issues are predicted.'[36] The practical implications of this seemingly innocuous statement became apparent in 1985, when some of the older houses in the Kimbo started to fall apart. Although efforts were made to salvage the remains, only one new house could be built from the remnants of three collapsed ones.[37]

Nonetheless, by 1985 facilities at Buffalo had improved considerably, compared to the 1970s and early 1980s. Although most of the troops now had permanent housing, an air of indifference from the SADF was still apparent. When both the 'Denty' electricity generators in the troop lines became unserviceable, Major A. Williams of 24 Field Engineer Squadron (FES) informed Eddie Viljoen that the correct procedure for recovering, and replacing, the generators was to inform 24 FES HQ. The HQ would then inform the Sector 20 Technical Staff Officer, who would decide whether the generators would be repaired or replaced. Given that the 24 FES personnel at Buffalo, including Major Williams himself, considered one of the generators 'unserviceable' and the other 'burnt out', this delay in replacing them seems unnecessary.[38] It is an open question whether the engineers would have made more traditional, white, SADF units go through the same process in the same circumstances, or even if this would have been the case if the generators that supplied the 32 Battalion officers had become unserviceable. At least from the perspective of the Engineer Corps, and probably much wider, the black troops of 32 Battalion were viewed as a lesser priority than their white counterparts in the broader SADF. This is illustrated by the Director of Engineers' request that 32 Battalion provide an estimate of the cost involved in converting a 'kimbo' into an 'apartment for whites'.[39]

In 1986, 10 years after the formation of 32 Battalion, the SADF still seemed unsure how to effectively supply them. At a logistics conference on 14 May 1986, it was noted that there was still uncertainty about the supply channel for 32 Battalion, that the technical warehouse of Sector 20 was unable to supply 32 Battalion effectively, and that 'Problems with [equipment] issued directly from the RSA are still being experienced.'[40] However, the supply and preparation of foodstuffs, at least while the troops were at

36 DODDC, 32 Bn Gp 2, Box 260, 522/1, Vol. 1, Konferensies, kongresse, seminare, simposiums en vergaderings / Konferensies, Notule van Bevelvoerderskonferenise gehou te 32 Bn HK op 5 Feb 92. Afrikaans: *Geboue word afgegee maar is nie op standaard nie en onderhoudsprobleme word voorsien.*

37 DODDC, 32 Bn Gp 2, Box 261, 522/1, Vol. 1, Konferensies / Kongresse / Seminare / Simposiums / Vergaderings: Notules, Notule: Buffalo terreinvergadering 21 Mrt 85.

38 DODDC, 32 Bn Gp 2, Box 261, 522/1, Vol. 1, Konferensies / Kongresse / Seminare / Simposiums / Vergaderings: Notules, Notule van terreinvergadering gehou te Buffalo Basis op 7 Februarie 1985, p.1. Afrikaans: *ondiensbaar*; *uitgebrand.*

39 DODDC, 32 Bn Gp 2, Box 261, 522/1, Vol. 1, Konferensies / Kongresse / Seminare / Simposiums / Vergaderings: Notules, Notule van terreinvergadering gehou te Buffalo Basis op 7 Februarie 1985, p.2. Afrikaans: *blanke woonstel.*

40 DODDC, 32 Bn Gp 2, Box 155, 522/1, Konferensies, Notule van logistieke konferensie gehou te NL Kmdmt op 14 Mei 1986. Afrikaans: *Probleme word nog ondervind met direkte uitreikings aan 32 Bn vanaf die RSA.*

Buffalo, had obviously increased, as the high morale of 32 Battalion troops was, among others, put down to 'excellent food'.[41] In contrast, as late as 1987, the tendency to provide 32 Battalion with the equipment necessary to make war, but neglect humanitarian supplies, was still prevalent. At the discussion following an inspection at Buffalo on 10 June 1987, the quartermaster was tasked to request a resupply of items that the inspection had shown to be lacking. The majority of this list was made up of 'Esbit-stoves', used to prepare hot meals and drinks in the field.[42]

However much the provision of food to 32 Battalion might have improved, censor's reports for 1988 that food was still the issue that was complained about the second most, after issues affecting troops' morale. This did, however, decrease over the course of 1988, from 119 complaints in March to none in November. Table 4.2 indicates the four most common complaints from 32 Battalion soldiers in their letters: morale in the unit, the quality and quantity of food, the weather in Namibia and Angola and the dependability of the SADF's mail service. Complaints about the weather increased significantly during the rainy season. In March and November, the end of one rainy season and the beginning of the next, censors recorded 82 and 37 complaints, respectively, compared to a total of 18 for the five months from June to October.

Table 4.2: Complaints in letters from 32 Battalion soldiers, 1988[43]

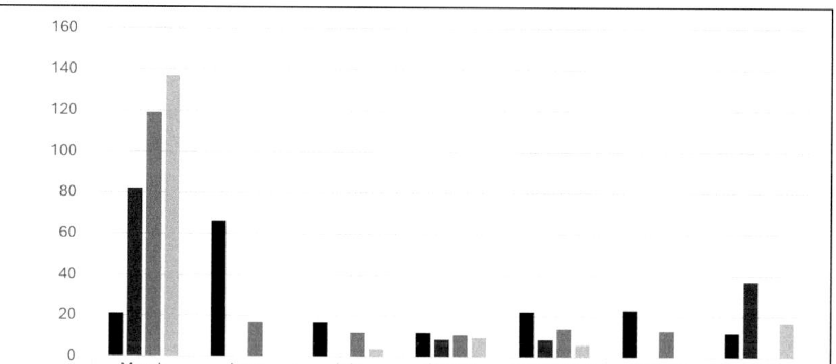

	March	June	July	August	September	October	November
■ Morale	21	66	17	12	22	23	12
■ Weather	82	0	0	9	9	0	37
■ Food	119	17	12	11	14	13	0
■ Mail	137	0	4	10	7	0	17

41 DODDC, 32 Bn Gp 2, Box 262, 522/4, Vol. 1, Konf., Kong, Semnaar, Simposiums + Vergaderings: Vergaderings, Maandverslag: Buffalo basis vir Januarie 1985, p.2. Afrikaans: *uitstekende kos*.

42 DODDC, 32 Bn Gp 2, Box 155, 522/1, Konferensies, Notule van bystaaninspeksie gehou te Buffalo op 10 Junie 1987.

43 Compiled from censors' reports in DODDC, SWA HK GM OATI, Box 105, SEK/202/02732, Vol. 1, DTI.

Supply, Support and Logistics in Battle

The logistical challenges that Jan Breytenbach experienced in getting supplies to the FNLA troops at Mpupa in 1975 were indications of the challenges that 32 Battalion would face over the coming years. Breytenbach recalls that, after he had met with the troops and their leaders for the first time, he reported to Brigadier Dawie Schoeman of 1 Military Area that he thought that the FNLA troops could be used by South Africa, but that they were in dire need of supplies. This led Schoeman to promise to supply Breytenbach with 'arms, combat fatigues and ammunition.'[44] He also authorised Breytenbach to draw rations for the troops that he was supposed to train, but this was much easier said than done, because the FNLA troops were not on strength in the SADF. In addition to these, fairly obvious, necessities, the supplies had to get from Namibia to Mpupa somehow. Breytenbach needed not only trucks, which he 'found' on the Angolan side of the border, but fuel and spare parts for them.[45] He also had to find a way in which to cross the Okavango river, which lay between him and Mpupa. In the end, he had to bribe an Angolan FNLA political leader to assist the river crossing with tractor.[46]

An example of the shortages experienced by Bravo Group is illustrated by the fact that the GOC authorised the issue of 30 AK47 rifles and 4,000 rounds of AK47 ammunition to Bravo Group on '14 Jun 74',[47] although from the context of the message, it is reasonable to assume that this should be '76'. By this time, Bravo Group was well established, had grown significantly from the three platoons of FNLA that had been the original manpower contingent, and was undertaking intensive training. To accomplish this with the addition of 30 rifles would have been challenging. A report by the Buffalo Base commander confirms this, indicating that the PF weapon smith who had inspected the weapons available to Bravo considered many of the weapons to be in poor condition.[48] Bravo Group's supply problems continued, leading to Breytenbach becoming 'quite' upset about the SADF's tardiness in delivering AK47 ammunition later that year.[49]

In contrast, Bravo Group had requested 300 AK47 rifles in April 1976. They were also experiencing shortages of Browning .50 ammunition, Browning .30 ammunition, 7.62 'Russian short' (AK47) ammunition and phosphorous grenades, requesting 20,000, 40,000 and 60,000 rounds and 200 grenades respectively. They were also eager

44 J. Breytenbach, *The Tempered Sword: Forged in Battle Revisited; Operation Savannah and the birth of 32 Bn*. Bushwarrior.com, 2011, p.28.
45 Breytenbach, *The Buffalo Soldiers*, p.25.
46 Breytenbach, *The Tempered Sword*, pp.28–29.
47 DODDC, 1 Militêre Gebied, Box 82, G/OPS/3/3/BRAVO, Vol. 1, Message 'Secret LOG/705/JUNE 76' from 101 TF to 1 MA.
48 DODDC, 32 Bn, Box 41, 309/1/ALG, Vol. 1, Spesifieke Operasies Gesamentlik, Persoonlike verslag aan Bev 32 Bn deur Bev Buffalo Basis.
49 DODDC, 1 Militêre Gebied, Box 82, G/OPS/3/3/BRAVO, Vol. 1, Transcript of radio message. Afrikaans: *redelik*.

to expand their heavier weapon capabilities, requesting 66 RPG7 rocket launchers.[50] Given that, on 17 August 1976, 101 TF issued an instruction to 16 Maintenance Unit to replace all R1 rifles in possession of Bravo Group with captured AK47 rifles as soon as possible,[51] the fact that they were experiencing shortages of ammunition for those rifles is significant.

In April 1976, 1 MA had sufficient confidence in the abilities of Bravo Group to authorise the issue of explosives to them, for use in operations.[52] Particularly against the backdrop of apartheid South Africa, issuing black troops with equipment that could potentially be used for sabotage indicates a significant level of trust. That Bravo Group garnered this much support from the SADF, outside of their immediate environment, is a significant achievement. Additionally, explosives seem to have been issued to Bravo Group without the soldiers who were supposed to use it being in possession of the necessary licences from the School of Engineers. When the issue of explosives to Alpha Group was discussed in February 1977, strong emphasis was placed on the fact that soldiers handling explosives had to be in possession of a valid licence from the School of Engineers.[53] Again, the fact that Bravo Group was allowed more leeway in obtaining explosives from the SADF stores is arguably indicative of a level of trust between black and white that was uncommon in 1970s South Africa.

Nonetheless, the issue of non-essential items, even combat equipment, continued to be a problem. In November 1976, Breytenbach replied to a letter from the mother of a South African NSM, addressing her concern that her son's boots were not suitable. While he was adamant that 'our boots are strong, well proven in the operational area', he conceded that 'most of my young second lieutenants wear all sorts of fancy footgear' and that 'I also wear a fancy pair of boots.'[54] These alternatives to the SADF boots, which Breytenbach not only allowed his white officers to wear, but wore himself, would not have been available to the black troops. Despite Breytenbach's defence of the SADF-issue boots, the prevalence of non-SADF footwear begs the question: how good were the SADF boots really?

The supply problems relating to non-essential equipment is further illustrated by an incident in March 1978, when the SADF attempted to increase the firepower of 32 Battalion by issuing them with additional machineguns. In light of the inventive and effective use that they had made of the Vickers machineguns available to them during

50 DODDC, 1 Militêre Gebied, Box 82, G/OPS/3/3/BRAVO, Vol. 1, Message 'LOG/797/APR 76' from 1 MA to 101 TF.
51 DODDC, 1 Militêre Gebied, Box 82, G/OPS/3/3/BRAVO, Vol. 1, Message 'Secret LOG/217/AUG 76' from 101 TF HW to 16 Maint Unit.
52 DODDC, 1 Militêre Gebied, Box 82, G/OPS/3/3/BRAVO, Vol. 1, Message 'LOG/803/APR 76' from 1 MA to 101 TF.
53 DODDC, 32 Bn, Box 55, 522/1/1MG, Vol. 1, Notule van bevelvoerderskonferensie gehou te Rundu op 18 Februarie 1977.
54 DODDC, 32 Bn, Box 9, LOG/OPS/3/16/13/3, Vol. 1, Pers welsyn (Dood, siekte van naasbestaandes, uitstel van opl), Letter from Col. JD Breytenbach to Mrs. DH Burman, November 1976.

Operation Savannah, the new weapons would undoubtedly have been put to effective use and increased the combat capability of 32 Battalion significantly. However, the weapons that were delivered to 32 Battalion HQ were 'incomplete', delaying distribution.[55] Additionally, 32 Battalion had limited ammunition available for training purposes. This shortage became so acute that the unit's acting second in command, Eddie Viljoen, had to issue an instruction in August 1978 that no automatic fire would be allowed on any shooting range,[56] though presumably automatic fire was still allowed on training exercises.

Despite the fact that the early lack of supply of combat arms and ammunition to 32 Battalion had speedily been rectified and they had been issued with sufficient weapons to accomplish their prescribed tasks quite early in their existence, the ease with which the transition was made to R4 rifles in 1983 stands in stark contrast to the early supply delays. By this time, 32 Battalion's worth had been recognised by the SADF and there was no longer any need to beg and cajole the logistics channels to receive weapons and ammunition. Furthermore, the R4s arrived in sufficient numbers to enable 32 Battalion to affect an efficient changeover, with the training on the new weapon that accompanies it. In fact, the SADF was so keen to provide 32 Battalion with the new assault rifle that there still seems to have been some concerns about the weapon at the time that 1,200 of them were supplied to the unit. In order to address this, Eddie Viljoen had to point out that the R4 was, in fact, a good weapon and that equipping 32 Battalion with it would ease logistic support and control, as the R4 was, by that time, the standard assault rifle in use with the SADF. Where the R1 was based on the Belgian FN FAL, a powerful but heavy 7.62mm rifle with a 20-round magazine, the R4, a 5.56mm rifle firing a less powerful round but weighing significantly less than the R1 and with a 10-round increase in magazine capacity, drew its inspiration from the Israeli Galil. Provision was therefore made for certain elements, such as the Reconnaissance Wings, to continue to operate with older weapons that were more suited to their particular requirements.[57]

The deployment of 32 Battalion for Operation Kakebeen in December 1986 stands in stark contrast to the deployment of Bravo Group during Operation Savannah 10 years earlier. Where the absolute minimum of military – particularly SADF – vehicles were available to Bravo Group in 1976, an early situation report for Operation Kakebeen recorded that the first deployment of troops was done with 17 vehicles, including a command Buffel and two tankers. The second deployment consisted of 12 vehicles, including another command Buffel, two more tankers and a recovery vehicle. Another 21 vehicles made up the third, and final, deployment.[58]

55 DODDC, 32 Bn Gp 2, Box 262, 522/1/BEV, Vol. 1, Konferensies, Notule van bevelvoerderskonferensie gehou te 32 Bn HK op 8 Maart 1978. Afrikaans: *onvolledig*.
56 DODDC, 32 Bn Gp 2, Box 262, 522/1/BEV, Vol. 1, Konferensies, Notule van bevelvoerderskonferensie gehou te 32 Bataljon Hoofkwartier op 23 Augustus 1978.
57 DODDC, 32 Bn Gp 2, Box 260, 522/1, Vol. 1, Konferensies, kongresse, seminare, simposiums en vergaderings / Konferensies, Minutes of Officer Commanding Conference held on 15 Sep 83 at Buffalo Training Base.
58 DODDC, 32 Bn Gp 2A, Box 132, File 01, Ops Kakebeen Sitrap, Message 'OPS/309/DES 86' from 32 Bn HQ to Sec 10.

However, this evolution, from the ill-supplied, unorganised Bravo Group of the early 1970s to 32 Battalion's new role as increasingly conventional infantry with increasingly conventional equipment, brought its own set of logistical challenges. By 1987, the supply channel for primary weapons and ammunition was running fairly smoothly. Nonetheless, the administration of the supply chain was still not streamlined enough for the OC 32 Battalion, Colonel K.V. (Jock) Harris, and he urged a review of the administration system from SWATF HQ's side.[59] Supply for supplementary weapons was still problematic, with 40mm grenade ammunition, 14.5mm heavy machineguns, sights for 120mm mortars and flame-throwing equipment being in short supply. The combination of these two issues was considered serious enough that the SO1, tasked with logistics liaison with South Africa, advised 32 Battalion to bypass the normal logistic channels and take up the matter of supply of these items directly with SWATF HQ.[60] The early difficulties of supplying of clothing and accommodation made way for issues with the supply of spare parts for the Valkiri, Ratel-ZT3 (Mongol) and Ystervark vehicles (cf. Table 4.3) with which 32 Battalion was now equipped, and spare parts for captured anti-aircraft weapons (used in a ground role for base defence) could not be found anywhere in the SADF.[61] In addition, 101 Workshop Troop – the unit responsible for issuing spare parts and workshop equipment to 32 Battalion – reported that they were 2 months behind schedule in supplying 32 Battalion. This was not quite as severe as the six-month backlog that they had for supplies to Sectors 10 and 20, and equal to the backlog for 61 Mechanised Battalion.[62] While 32 Battalion and 61 Mechanised Battalion were both frequently involved in SADF operations and actively deployed, it is insightful that they received roughly the same prioritisation for supplies from 101 Workshop Troop. In contrast to the early days of Bravo Group, it appears that, towards the end of the war, the SADF had come to recognise the potential of 32 Battalion as equal to that of traditional SADF units like 61 Mechanised Battalion, and strove to adequately supply them for their duties. Nevertheless, the fact that staffing at 101 Workshop Troop had decreased by almost 70 percent, from a total strength of 691 in December 1985 to 204 in January 1987,[63] inevitably affected the combat readiness and efficiency of two of the SADF's premier combat units to a greater extent than units that saw combat less often.

59 DODDC, 32 Bn Gp 2, Box 262, 522/1/1, Vol. 4, Konferensies, kongresse, seminare, simposiums & vergaderings: SD Leer Sektor 20, Stafbesoek Sektor 20, 32 Bn en Sektor 70 29 April 1987–1 Mei 1987, p.1.

60 DODDC, 32 Bn Gp 2, Box 262, 522/1/1, Vol. 4, Konferensies, kongresse, seminare, simposiums & vergaderings: SD Leer Sektor 20, Stafbesoek Sektor 20, 32 Bn en Sektor 70 29 April 1987–1 Mei 1987, p.4.

61 DODDC, 32 Bn Gp 2, Box 155, 522/1, Konferensies, Notule van 'n konferensie gehou te LBG op 091100B April 1987 om TD op Bouwerke en Log aangeleenthede te bespreek.

62 DODDC, 32 Bn Gp 2, Box 261, 522/1, Vol. 4, Log Konferensie, Personeel en logistieke knelpunte: 101 Werkplaaseenheid.

63 DODDC, 32 Bn Gp 2, Box 261, 522/1, Vol. 4, Log Konferensie, Sterkte NDP's en Staandemag lede.

Even though 32 Battalion was held in considerably higher esteem towards the end of the war than at the start of their existence, supply problems continued. In 1988, the unit was issued with five A68 radios to supplement the 15 serviceable radios already at the unit. While an increase of 33 percent in radio equipment would have been useful, the SADF neglected to issue antennae for the new radios, effectively making them useless until the problem was rectified.[64] This oversight would not be particularly significant if it were not for the workload that 32 Battalion carried in terms of time spent in operations, which far exceeded that of conventional SADF units.

Table 4.3: Unusual SADF vehicles, field-tested and used by 32 Battalion

	Ystervark*	**Mongol†**	**Valkiri‡**
Chassis	SAMIL-20	Ratel-60	SAMIL-20
Armament	1 × 20mm GAI-CO1 AA gun	Triple launcher for Ingwe missile system	24 × 127mm rockets per salvo
Purpose	Light, mobile, self-propelled anti-aircraft gun	Anti-tank guided missile system	Multiple Rocket Launcher

* S. Camp & H. Heitman, *Surviving the ride: a pictorial history of South African-manufactured mine-protected vehicles*. Pinetown: 30° South, 2014, p.222.

† Camp & Heitman, *Surviving the ride*, p.174.

‡ http://www.military-today.com/artillery/valkiri.htm [Accessed 07.10.2018].

Somewhat bizarrely, 32 Battalion's shortage of 'warm clothing for troops in the field' was a sufficient enough concern to be a point of discussion at the Sergeant Major of the Army's conference in 1988.[65] Whether this shortage was due to a supply problem, or whether problems with clothing arose due to the longer periods that sections from 32 Battalion spent in the field is unclear. Regardless, given the improvements that had been made in the supply chains between 32 Battalion and SWATF and the SADF, warm clothing should have been an issue that could easily be rectified. Additionally, some of 32 Battalion's equipment had been loaned to and/or used by other SADF units during Operation Modular and some of these units were tardy in returning the equipment to 32 Battalion after Modular.[66] This resulted in renewed shortages at the unit that was probably more actively involved in combat than the units holding on to their equipment.

64 DODDC, 32 Bn Gp 2, Box 261, 522/1, Vol. 14, Konferensies, Message 'SEIN/262/8 SEP 88' from 32 Bn to SWATF 33.

65 DODDC, 32 Bn Gp 2, Box 261, 522/1, Vol. 9, Notule van weeklikse monitor, Notule van die SWA Gebiedsmag Sers Maj se spanbou met Formasie Sers Maj'e en Snr RSM'e. Afrikaans: *warm klere vir trp in die veld.*

66 DODDC, 32 Bn Gp 2, Box 261, 522/1, Vol. 9, Notule van weeklikse monitor, Notule van die SWA Gebiedsmag Sers Maj se spanbou met snr Sers Maj'e gehou te Drywersdrift oor tydperk 13 tot 17 Junie 1988.

Logistical support to families

In April 1976, Bravo Group requested '75 (seventy five) 15 × 15 tents' from 101 TF to address the housing shortage at Buffalo.[67] This request for '75 tents 15 × 15' was repeated later in the same month, indicating that 101 TF was either not aware of the severity of the housing crisis at Buffalo, or were not yet particularly concerned about supplying the newest resource at the disposal of the SADF.[68] When the establishment of the base and Kimbo at Buffalo was approved by the SADF, priority was still not given to the basic needs of the soldiers and their families. Instead, the construction programme at Buffalo prioritised the building of storehouses.[69] Naturally, the SADF had to protect the supplies that it issued to its units, which makes the desire to construct suitable storage facilities for those supplies understandable. Nonetheless, the protection of the SADF's human capital, in the form of the black soldiers and civilians of 32 Battalion, should probably have been regarded at the same level.

In May 1977, the Warren huts that 32 Battalion had ordered, had arrived at 101 Engineering Support Squadron and were en route to Buffalo.[70] Supplies for the construction of housing in the Kimbo had also started reaching Buffalo.[71] However, it was decided that construction of the Kimbo could not proceed until all the building material that had been ordered was delivered.[72] Generally, this would be a sensible precaution, minimising the risk of reaching a certain stage of construction and not being able to continue. Given the urgent need for civilian accommodation at Buffalo, however, it might have been advisable to begin construction with whatever material was at hand, thereby speeding up the construction process and being able to provide accommodation to soldiers and their families sooner.

The lack of building supplies delivered to Buffalo was not the only factor that complicated the completion of Project Carpenter, the name given to the construction of living quarters and other amenities at Buffalo. When 11 FES took over the project from 21 FES in 1977, they reported that the equipment with which they had to accomplish their task was in poor condition and incomplete.[73] The SADF did, in time, accept

67 DODDC, 1 Militêre Gebied, Box 82, G/OPS/3/3/BRAVO, Vol. 1, Message 'LOG/805/APR 76' from 1 MA to 101 TF. Parenthesis original.
68 DODDC, 1 Militêre Gebied, Box 82, G/OPS/3/3/BRAVO, Vol. 1, Message 'LOG/927/APR 76' from 1 MA to 101 TF.
69 DODDC, 32 Bn Gp 2, Box 262, 522/1/BEV, Vol. 1, Konferensies, Notule van bevelvoerderskonferensie gehou te 32 Bn op 1 September 1977.
70 DODDC, 1 Militêre Gebied, Box 102, G/OPS/3/3/CARPENTER, Vol. 1, Operations (specific) Unconventional Operation Carpenter, Message 'G/115/MAY 77' from 101 Engr Supp Sqn to 1 MA 13 Sub Area.
71 DODDC, 32 Bn Gp 2, Box 262, 522/1/BEV, Vol. 1, Konferensies, Notule van bevelvoerderskonferensie gehou te 32 Bn HK op 5 Okt 77, p.3.
72 DODDC, 32 Bn Gp 2, Box 262, 522/1/BEV, Vol. 1, Konferensies, Notule van bevelvoerderskonferensie gehou te 32 Bn HK op 5 Okt 77, p.4.
73 DODDC, 32 Bn, Box 41, 309/1/PROJ CARP, Projek Carpenter, Sitrep Ingenieurs.

that 32 Battalion was an integral part of its order of battle. In order to facilitate the effective accommodation of soldiers and their families, R460,000 was allocated to Project Carpenter.[74]

In May 1977, phase 2 of Project Carpenter was under way. The order from the office of the Chief of the Army to the Quartermaster General to arrange the purchase of an additional 260 Warren huts, specifically for use in the Kimbo, illustrates that 32 Battalion and the SADF had started to consider the wellbeing of the families of 32 Battalion's Portuguese-speaking soldiers, as well as that of the military men.[75]

While considering the layout of the Kimbo in 1978, 32 Battalion and the SADF had to consider the provision of hot water to the residents. They decided on a 'donkey' system, where a fire, that had to be started and maintained manually, provided direct heat to water in a 44-gallon drum, to achieve this.[76] It is unclear how many people were supposed to draw water from such a system, but considering that the average household boiler is between 100 and 150 litres (approximately 22 to 33 gallons), shortages of hot water were sure to occur. A year earlier, 31 Battalion had rejected a suggestion to implement a solar system for their water heating requirements,[77] and it seems that this rejection had permeated to 32 Battalion, who never gave serious consideration to the system and chose to pursue the comparatively primitive 'donkey' system instead. This system had to supply the increasing demands of 32 Battalion and the Kimbo until 1987, when it was decided to provide each company with an electric boiler in order to solve the hot water problem.[78] Nonetheless, the housing that the SADF provided to the black Angolans in the Kimbo was still an improvement on the conditions in which many black South Africans had to live in the Republic, where they were forced to live in either townships or tribal homelands, were continuously monitored by the South African Police, had their movement restricted and had to make do with the most basic municipal infrastructure.[79]

As with many such major construction projects, bottlenecks occurred with Project Carpenter. The Warren huts that were intended for use by the civilians of 31 and 32 Battalions were delivered to Katima Mulilo and 13 Sub-Area at a greater rate than they were transported to Buffalo and Omega. At one point, a third of the huts intended for Buffalo were delivered at 13 Sub-Area and ready to be transported to

74 DODDC, 1 Militêre Gebied, Box 102, G/OPS/3/3/CARPENTER, Vol. 1, Operations (specific) Unconventional Operation Carpenter, Q/WKS/1 Projek Carpenter: Aanskaffing van boumateriale nie op staatskontrak: Totale waarde van bestelling per item bokant R1000.

75 DODDC, 32 Bn, Box 3, Q/WKS/1, Vol. 1, Warren Hutte, Message 'FAC/772/MAY 77' from C Army to QMG.

76 DODDC, 32 Bn, Box 41, 309/1/PROJ CARP, Projek Carpenter, 'Donkie' hot water system.

77 DODDC, 32 Bn, Box 41, 309/1/PROJ CARP, Projek Carpenter, Minutes of meeting to discuss Project Carpenter on 11 April 1977 in the office of Colonel Grobbelaar.

78 DODDC, 32 Bn Gp 2, Box 155, 522/1, Konferensies, Notule van die NDP komitee vergadering van HK kompanie gehou by 32 Bn (Buffalo) 08 23h00 B September 1987.

79 B. Ndaba & J. Smith, 'Steve Biko and the Rise of Black Consciousness' in B. Ndaba et al, *The Black Consciousness Reader*, Johannesburg: Jacana, 2017, pp.45–46.

Buffalo,[80] but the failure to do so resulted in some of the components of the huts becoming damaged and needing replacement.[81] While this might be put down to operational losses in other construction projects, the dire need of the civilians – and soldiers – at Omega and Buffalo made such a logistical logjam much more poignant and begs the question whether better planning could have resulted in a more expeditious improvement in the circumstances of the people at those two bases.

A report on the progress of Project Carpenter on 19 May 1978 indicates that, although apartheid and segregation was much less of an issue in 32 Battalion than in the rest of the SADF and South Africa, the SADF still preferred to take care of its own first. A list of works that had been completed by that date included the 'white mess', 'storehouses' and 'Zietsman building', among others. Works that had not been completed included accommodation for troops, though accommodation for 'whites' was also incomplete.[82] Nonetheless, the prioritisation of a mess and storehouse over the provision of accommodation strengthens the perception that the SADF was not greatly concerned about the wellbeing of their foreign troops. The fact that construction at the Omauni operational base was scheduled to be completed by April 1979,[83] well ahead of the construction at Buffalo, can be justified more easily. Omauni was a much smaller base than Buffalo, without the attendant civilian accommodation. Additionally, troops deployed on patrols and operations from Omauni, explaining the need to expedite construction. Nonetheless, the almost subconscious sense of superiority among the white SADF members – even the 32 Battalion personnel – towards their black troops is still evident in the combined prioritisation of construction projects at both Omauni and Buffalo.

Although planning for permanent accommodation was optimistically done early in 1980, accommodation, particularly in the Kimbo, continued to be a problem for several more years. The 1980 plan envisaged that, '500–600 houses will be built with water, electricity and sewerage systems … SP living quarters will be built in company lines.'[84]

80 DODDC, 32 Bn, Box 41, 309/1/PROJ CARP, Projek Carpenter, Minutes of meeting to discuss Project Carpenter on 11 April 1977 in the office of Colonel Grobbelaar.

81 DODDC, 32 Bn, Box 41, 309/1/PROJ CARP, Projek Carpenter, Message 'GENIE/975/25 APR 78' from 1 MA to SWA Cmd.

82 DODDC, 32 Bn, Box 41, 309/1/PROJ CARP, Projek Carpenter, Die volgende is punte wat met Brig. Moller bespreek is te Pta op 19 Mei 78. Afrikaans: *blanke menasie*; *pakhuise*; *Zietsmangebou*; *blankes*.

83 DODDC, 32 Bn Gp 2, Box 262, 522/1/BEV, Vol. 1, Konferensies, Notule van bevelvoerderskonferensie gehou te 32 Bataljon Hoofkwartier op 26 Oktober 1978.

84 DODDC, 32 Bn Gp 2, Box 260, 522/1, Vol. 1, Konferensies, kongresse, seminare, simposiums en vergaderings / Konferensies, Notule van basiskonferensie gehou te 32 Bn Buffalo op 28 Maart 1980. The suffix 'SP' was added to the force numbers of all black members of 32 Battalion, and became something of a shorthand, non-political way of referring to them. Former Angolan members of 32 Battalion had the suffix 'SP' to their force numbers. Afrikaans: *500–600 huise word opgesit met water, ligte en riool stelsels… SP woonkwartiere gaan in komp lyne opgesit word.*

Despite these optimistic estimates, a year later caravans that were assigned to 32 Battalion as a temporary measure to improve the housing problem at Buffalo failed to reach the base, material that was earmarked for the construction of permanent housing was never collected or delivered and got lost in the SADF logistic system, and it became apparent that ascertaining the feasibility of supplying water and ablution facilities to the intended housing project was neglected during the planning phase and only assessed retroactively.[85]

Although 32 Battalion experienced significant challenges in providing everyday necessities to its soldiers and civilians, they were able to provide a few luxuries as well. In 1981, a swimming pool was purchased for the Kimbo residents. The funding for this was generated by 32 Battalion, from sales at the base-shop (then still run by the unit itself) and from renting out one of the boats that they had captured in earlier operations for social events. Planning for the swimming pool was done at the same time as it was noted that 32 Battalion was having difficulty in maintaining adequate supplies of Liquefied Petroleum Gas (LPG), in part due to empty LPG bottles not being returned from outside bases.[86] Although it is not clear what the gas was used for, it is logical to deduce that cooking – and possibly refrigeration – was a prime consumer of LPG. While it is laudable that 32 Battalion paid attention to non-essential items, it appears that some of the energy expended in securing these items could have been better employed in securing necessities. This is particularly poignant in light of the fact that, two months before permission was given for the purchase of the swimming pool, 32 Battalion's Staff Officer, 2nd Class Logistics noted that 'The shortages of rations for the Kimbo appear to be a critical problem…' and the Buffalo Base commander was tasked to personally supervise the delivery of rations.[87]

Another factor that added to the frustration of life at Buffalo was caused by an administrative error on the part of 32 Battalion. In 1982, members were given the option of contributing to the construction of kitchens. A contractor was appointed to complete the construction but, crucially, no contract was signed between the contractor and the SADF or 32 Battalion. In 1983, the contractor lost interest in the project and refused to complete it. This resulted in 'much dissatisfaction' among members of 32 Battalion. The decision was taken that the kitchens would be completed as an internal building project, and several members had to be refunded to stem the tide of dissatisfaction.[88] With hind-

85 DODDC, 32 Bn Gp 2, Box 260, 522/1, Vol. 1, Konferensies, kongresse, seminare, simposiums en vergaderings / Konferensies, Notule van bevelvoerderskonferensie gehou te 32 Bn hoofkwartier op 6 en 7 Feb 81.

86 DODDC, 32 Bn Gp 2, Box 260, 522/1, Vol. 1, Konferensies, kongresse, seminare, simposiums en vergaderings / Konferensies, Notule van bevelvoerderskonferensie gehou te 32 Bn HK op 8 Apr 81.

87 DODDC, 32 Bn Gp 2, Box 260, 522/1, Vol. 1, Konferensies, kongresse, seminare, simposiums en vergaderings / Konferensies, Notule van bevelvoerderskonferensie gehou te 32 Bn hoofkwartier op 6 en 7 Feb 81. Afrikaans: *Die tekorte aan rantsoene vir die Kimbo blyk 'n kritieke probleem te wees…*

88 DODDC, 32 Bn Gp 2, Box 262, 522/1/1, Vol. 2, Bevelvoerderskonferensies, Minutes of Officer Commanding conference held on 15 Sep 83 at Buffalo training base.

sight, this incident is a rather poignant curtain-raiser to similar events at Pomfret 10 years later, though the outcome would be quite different.

In 1982, 32 Battalion transferred the administration of the shop at Buffalo to the South African Defence Force Institute (SADFI), apart from the sales of tobacco and alcohol, which would be done by SADFI but still be administrated by 32 Battalion.[89] The transfer almost immediately caused dissatisfaction in 32 Battalion. In an echo of the situation at the unit's sister-battalion, 31 Battalion,[90] soldiers, and civilians in the Kimbo, had to purchase their supplies from the SADFI shop at Buffalo. This monopoly inevitably led to problems, and in 1983 complaints were received that SADFI could not provide an after sales service on some of the goods that they sold. An example of this was the sale of paraffin fridges, but not paraffin with which to run them. Considering that the purchase of a fridge would have been a relatively large investment for many of the Kimbo residents, this problem would have been a larger issue than was apparent at first glance. The OC, Eddie Viljoen, reacted decisively and ordered the SADFI shop to carry all the after sales stock for items that they sold.[91] Fortunately for 32 Battalion, Viljoen's demand came at a time when SADFI was revaluating its business model, and was even prepared to run some of its more isolated shops at a calculated loss.[92] While the shop at Buffalo did not necessarily operate at a loss, SADFI would have been less inclined to agree to Viljoen's demands if they had been under pressure to deliver good financial statements. The fact that they could provide the level of service that 32 Battalion required, almost regardless of the impact on their bottom line, led to a marked increase in the efficiency of, and satisfaction with, the SADFI shop. By 1985, shortages occurred less frequently and were addressed sooner. In addition, an agreement was reached with the large SADFI shop[93] at 31 Battalion's Omega base, whereby the two shops could assist one another with supply shortages. This arrangement made the supply chain much shorter and decreased the time it took to rectify 'urgent shortages'.[94]

Although significant progress had been made in improving the civilians' circumstances in the Kimbo, and the 32 Battalion leader group made genuine attempts at addressing concerns that became apparent, supply problems continued to affect 32 Battalion. A school had been established for the children of serving members, but on 7 June 1983, SWATF HQ informed 32 Battalion and 201 Battalion that a large quantity of books and desks for their respective schools had been made available by the Department of

89 Nortje, *The Terrible Ones*, p.695.
90 F. Verster, *Omega, oor en uit: Die storie van 'n opstandige troep*. Cape Town: Tafelberg, 2016, p.19.
91 DODDC, 32 Bn Gp 2, Box 260, 522/1, Vol. 1, Konferensies, kongresse, seminare, simposiums en vergaderings / Konferensies, Minutes of Officer Commanding Conference held on 15 Sep 83 at Buffalo Training Base.
92 I. van der Waag, 'A History of the South African Defence Force Institute (SADFI) 1916–1991' in *Scientia Militaria: South African Journal of Military Studies, 21 (4)*, 1991, p.39.
93 Verster, *Omega, oor en uit*, p.68.
94 DODDC, 32 Bn Gp 2, Box 262, 522/4, Vol. 1, Konf., Kong, Semnaar, Simposiums + Vergaderings: Vergaderings, Maandverslag Opleidingsbasis vir die maand Februarie 1985, pp.13–14. Afrikaans: *dringende tekorte*.

Education, but had not yet been received by the units. The supplies available to the two units was of such a quantity that SWATF HQ envisaged that two Samil 50 trucks would be required to transport it.[95] While the progress in expanding the facilities and amenities available to the civilians at Buffalo is laudable, the fact that children had to make do without proper textbooks and/or desks because of logistical deficiencies seems avoidable.

A meeting held in the Kimbo to address the issues that the inhabitants experienced, illustrated the difficulties that were still prevalent in 1985. One of the concerns voiced by the Kimbo women was that 'Block 23' refused to supply water to the people living in tents.[96] A number of causes for concern are apparent from this statement: Firstly, it seems that the SADF and or 32 Battalion had not yet fully come to grips with the housing situation in the Kimbo and there were still civilians that were forced to live in tented accommodation. Secondly, this tented accommodation seems to have been quite rudimentary without access to running water and, therefore, sanitation. Thirdly, although it is only natural that it would occur, the fact that there was a social distinction between the civilians who had been given houses and those who were still living in tents was bound to complicate the administration of the base. Water supply continued to be a problem in 1986, when the filtration system in the Kimbo broke down. At the same time, a fresh water submersible pump was under repair at 39 Engineering Support Squadron, which led to water shortages at the HQ Company's housing area.[97]

Despite the logistical problems that 32 Battalion was experiencing, planning for the colour parade in 1985 included a significant logistical effort, including the civilians in the Kimbo. Because the women were expected to be 'well dressed for the occasion', an aeroplane was arranged to fly 70 of them to Windhoek for shopping.[98] It is not clear who the privileged 70 were, or how they were chosen, but arranging a flight for the exclusive purpose of providing the women of the Kimbo with the opportunity to visit the shops seems excessive, particularly in light of the shortages that they were experiencing in other areas.

Though some of the earlier, hastily constructed, houses in the Kimbo had started collapsing by 1985, 32 Battalion had gained invaluable experience in maintaining logistics channels with the SADF and in the intricacies of administrating a joint civil-military construction programme. This meant that, to a large extent, the deficiencies of the past could be rectified and the Kimbo, as well as the military facilities at Buffalo, could be expanded. A monthly report on Buffalo for January 1985 recorded that regular service

95 DODDC, 32 Bn Gp 2, Box 77, 309/1 B-Skool, Vol. 3, Buffalo Skool (Pica Pau), Message 'KOMOPS/MBD/420/17 JUN 83' from SWATF HQ to 201 Bn and 32 Bn.

96 DODDC, 32 Bn Gp 2, Box 156, 522/4, Vol. 1, Konferensies, Kongresse, Seminare, Simposiums en Vergaderings: Vergaderings, Notule van 'n roetine vergadering gehou by Kimbo saal te Buffalo 061200B om die algemene probleme te bespreek.

97 DODDC, 32 Bn Gp 2, Box 156, 522/1, Vol. 3, Konferensies, Kongresse, Seminare, Simposiums, Vergaderings: Konferensies, Terreinkonferensie gehou te Buffalo on 16 Jan 86.

98 DODDC, 32 Bn Gp 2, Box 156, 522/1, Konferensies, Minutes of meeting held on 8 August 1985 with Kimbo women at Buffalo Training Base.

and maintenance was being done on essential equipment such as water pumps, sewerage pumps and generators. Additionally, 100 new houses had been built in the Kimbo, three at the HQ complex, two burnt-down houses were rebuilt and three blocks of the old, by then decrepit, housing had been repaired.[99]

To the credit of both the SADF and 32 Battalion's command structures, a planning conference, held in July 1988, no longer listed the provision of housing in the Kimbo as a top priority. By that time, the provision of housing for 'white families' had overtaken the provision of accommodation for black families in the Kimbo, with the construction of five houses listed as a critical need and ten as important.[100] While this certainly does not indicate that the needs of the Kimbo residents had been completely met, it is indicative of the progress that had been made in accommodating the soldiers and civilians that lived in the Kimbo. Unfortunately, this progress also highlights the irony of the relocation of 32 Battalion, to South Africa, in 1989, when the whole process would have to restart and all the strides that had been made at Buffalo would be negated.

Medical supply

Anthony Feinstein was a medical doctor who completed his national service in Owamboland in the early 1980s. He had wanted to specialise in plastic surgery, but was instead assigned to psychiatry, with the useful explanation that, as the positions in plastic surgery had all been filled, psychiatry was next in line. Alphabetically,'PS comes after PL,' he was told.[101] While this was undoubtedly a shock to Feinstein, his recollections provide an invaluable insight into medical conditions in Owamboland, where 32 Battalion was based and from where much of their Namibian manpower derived, as well as South African townships, where Feinstein served during his 'camps', subsequent to his two-year conscription.

Feinstein recalls that, in regular SADF units, psychotic patients were sent home, the remainder of their National Service terminated. This was not the case, however, for 'those traumatised by war'. They had to complete their National Service, with the – inadequate – help of doctors like Feinstein. As an example of the latter group, Feinstein narrates the case of a signaller who was in a convoy that detonated two landmines, killing two South African troops. After an evaluation of the signaller, the SADF decided to terminate his National Service and send him home.[102] The details of the case mentioned above is not important in the context of this discussion, but rather the extreme contradiction

99 DODDC, 32 Bn Gp 2, Box 262, 522/4, Vol. 1, Konf., Kong, Semnaar, Simposiums + Vergaderings: Vergaderings, Maandverslag: Buffalo basis vir Januarie 1985, p.15.

100 DODDC, 32 Bn Gp 2, Box 261, 522/1, Vol. 14, Konferensies, Notule van 'n beplanningskonferensie om riglyne te gee vir die bedryf van 32 Bn vir die res van 1988 gehou te Buffalo 220730B Julie 1988. Afrikaans: *Blanke gesinne.*

101 A. Feinstein, *Battle Scarred: Hidden costs of the Border War*, Cape Town: Tafelberg, 2011, p.17.

102 Feinstein, *Battle Scarred*, pp.36–42

between regular SADF units and units such as 32 Battalion. While 32 Battalion had reasonably good medical care and facilities, a psychiatrist was virtually unheard of, and termination of service, far from being something desirable, would have meant the end of the only support structure that the men of the unit had.

This contrast is illustrated by a report submitted by a medical officer (MO), C. Klein, around September 1976 (the document is undated, but a reply is dated 8 September 1976), 22 men were examined at Omauni. The medical officer concluded that 'Twenty two [*sic*] men, average age of 21.4 years + average duration in the bush of 28.6 months were examined. All but one had symptoms or signs which although mild could be due to vitamin (Niacin, Thiamine + vitamin C) deficiency. Further 14 of those examined also had symptoms or signs consistent with an anxiety state.'[103]

The vitamin deficiency could easily, and cheaply, be rectified, but the 'anxiety state' would have been much harder to address. The fact that 14 out of 22 men – nearly two-thirds – suffered from these symptoms indicates a desperate need for psychological and/or psychiatric treatment at the unit, already in the very early years of their existence, even if allowances are made for the potential inexperience or exaggeration of the MO. This, however, was a need that was sorely neglected.

31 Battalion was equipped with fairly advanced medical facilities, including an X-ray machine and, when the hospital at Buffalo was being planned, medical staff suggested that 32 Battalion could also make use of this.[104] Meanwhile, NSM Lieutenant Mike Damp, who had only qualified as a doctor in 1975, together with a NSM medic, W. F. Olivier, had to make do with a 'hospital' that consisted of 'two tents pitched side by side just over the road from the tiffies' vehicle park.'[105]

In April 1977, the visiting dentist at Buffalo noted that the dental care that was provided to the black members of the unit was insufficient. He was sufficiently chagrined at the situation to threaten to take up the matter with the Surgeon General, unless 32 Battalion undertook to improve the situation. 32 Battalion countered by stating that the problem was not of their own making and could be put down to the fact that the mobile dentist that was supposed to operate in the area did not have access to transportation.[106]

In response, however, the medical orderly at Buffalo contended that there had never been observable vitamin deficiencies at Buffalo, although he did concede that the addition of vitamins to the soldiers' diet could only be beneficial.[107]

103 DODDC, 32 Bn, Box 9, LOG/OPS/3/16/8, Vol. 1, Medies en gesondheid (verslae, anvrae, ens.), Medical report: Medical examination of 1x section.
104 DODDC, 32 Bn, Box 41, 309/1/PROJ CARP, Projek Carpenter, Report from Lt. H Adendorff to OC 32 Bn regarding new hospital.
105 Nortje, *The Terrible Ones*, p.255.
106 DODDC, 32 Bn, Box 9, LOG/OPS/3/16/8, Vol. 1, Medies en gesondheid (verslae, anvrae, ens.), Tandheelkundige behandeling: Lede 32 Bn Gp.
107 DODDC, 32 Bn, Box 9, LOG/OPS/3/16/8, Vol. 1, Medies en gesondheid (verslae, anvrae, ens.), Message from Dr. Jacobs to Maj. Greeff, 8 September 1976.

In a report on the medical situation at Omauni in March 1977, the medical officer commented that

> As things stand at the moment, the sick bay is large enough to cope with the everyday demands. This may not, however, be the case should there be an escalation in the military situation in the area. The facilities are adequate for the management of a wide spectrum of injuries + illnesses, from the casual sick parade ailments to the resuscitation of the wounded.[108]

The medical officer's impression of the facilities at Omauni is reflected in the medical supplies that were available at Buffalo in September 1977. Again, the supplies were adequate – or even excessive – for day-to-day medical situations, but would not be sufficient to treat any major cases or influx of patients, whether due to illness or combat.[109] This evidence contrasts markedly with Nortje's – and Lieutenant Damp's – recollections that '… the medical staff had to work with very primitive facilities. The doctor and nurse doing duty had to make do with the minimum medical supplies available…'.[110] This difference in opinion highlights the inherent differences between archival sources and recollections: there can be little or no doubt that the medical supplies at Buffalo *was* adequate. Nortje and Damp's recollections, however, may well have been coloured by the passage of time.

For the period 21 April to 17 July 1978, the base commander at Buffalo considered the medical support at the base 'a problem' due to a lack of equipment and medical supplies, but predicted that completion of the 'hospital' under construction would alleviate the problem.[111]

In 1979, the South African Medical Service issued order SAWO 1/5/79 indicating that two Daraclor anti-malarial tablets per week had to be taken by all troops and visitors to the operational area.[112] Notably, the list of medical supplies at Buffalo two years earlier had not indicated the availability of any Daraclor,[113] nor was any requested at the time.[114]

108 DODDC, 32 Bn, Box 9, LOG/OPS/3/16/8, Vol. 1, Medies en gesondheid (verslae, aanvrae, ens), Monthly report on medical situation at Camp Omauni for the month ending March 1977.
109 DODDC, 32 Bn, Box 9, LOG/OPS/3/16/8, Vol. 1, Medies en gesondheid (verslae, aanvrae, ens), Medical Supplies Buffalo on 25-9-77. The author thanks former surgeon at 1 Military Hospital, Dr J.H. von Willich, for his comments on the list of supplies.
110 Nortje, *The Terrible Ones*, p.255.
111 DODDC, 32 Bn, Box 41, 309/1/ALG, Vol. 1, Spesifieke Operasies Gesamentlik, Persoonlike verslag aan Bev 32 Bn deur Bev Buffalo Basis.
112 DODDC, 32 Bn Gp 2, Box 21, 104/10/12/13, Instandhouding van personeel: Geneeskundige dienste: Mediese ondersoek beleid, Message 'MED/097/03 DES 81' from Sector 20 to Omega, Buffalo, Mpun Vlei, Musese, Kanjimi and Bagani.
113 DODDC, 32 Bn, Box 9, LOG/OPS/3/16/8, Vol. 1, Medies en gesondheid (verslae, aanvrae, ens), Medical Supplies Buffalo on 25-9-77.
114 DODDC, 32 Bn, Box 9, LOG/OPS/3/16/8, Vol. 1, Medies en gesondheid (verslae, aanvrae, ens), Medical requirements – Amaouni.

By 1980, the availability of supplies at Buffalo had increased to the extent that the OC could request relatively specialised medical equipment from 1 Military Hospital and reasonably expect to receive it. This included two wheelchairs and medical sheepskins (to prevent pressure sores) for a black member of 32 Battalion that had been injured and had become quadriplegic.[115] In an attempt to accommodate his wish to remain with 32 Battalion, he was employed as a cashier and provided with the necessary medical equipment to live comfortably, relative to many civilian Angolan and Namibian amputees. This case was not unique, and a precedent for accommodating 'medically unfit' members of 32 Battalion in non-combat roles had been set as early as 1977, at which time these members were employed at the Engineer Troop.[116] Despite the advances in medical supply by 1980, Buffalo was still experiencing difficulty in receiving adequate 'war supplies'. The problem seems to have become commonplace, and the tone in which it was mentioned at an OC's conference in December 1981 indicates an almost resigned acceptance of the fact that supply was, and always would be, a problem. This was particularly apparent in supplies from the Technical Service Corps.[117]

Despite the advances in medical facilities and supplies at 32 Battalion, emotional and psychological aid remained minimal. The accepted way for soldiers, both black and white, to deal with what would now be described as Post-Traumatic Stress Disorder was to drink heavily in an attempt to forget about the rigours of life on patrol, if only temporarily. The inefficacy of this, rather crude, method became tragically apparent in 1982, when Second Lieutenant Uys committed suicide and Lieutenant Du Plessis came close to killing Second Lieutenant Witheren when he shot him in the chest during a random, drunken shooting incident. Deon Ferreira attempted to remedy the situation by assigning long-serving white members of 32 Battalion to other postings, before returning to Buffalo.[118] No such measures were, however, put in place for black members of the unit.

As the base commander had predicted in 1978, the completion of the hospital at Buffalo and better management of the sickbay, improved the efficiency of medical services and supplies at the base. A clinic had also been built to provide basic medical services to the civilians in the Kimbo, and even though the target date for the completion of this project – the clinic still needed a water pump to provide running water – was March 1985,[119] a month earlier the base commander was able to report that 'Cmdt Smith

115 DODDC, 32 Bn Gp 2, Box 28, 104/12/1/1 (SP), Vol. 4, Instandhouding van personeel: Welsynsdienste: Gevallewerk: Individuele persone, 1MH/104/12/1/1/77880813SP/45/79.
116 DODDC, 32 Bn Gp 2, Box 262, 522/1/BEV, Konferensies, Notule van bevelvoerderskonferensie gehou te 32 Bn op 1 September 1977.
117 DODDC, 32 Bn Gp 2, Box 260, 522/1, Vol. 1, Konferensies, kongresse, seminare, simposiums en vergaderings / Konferensies, Notule van bevelvoerderskonferensie gehou te 32 Bn HK op 4 Des 81. Afrikaans: *krygsbehoeftes*.
118 Nortje, *The Terrible Ones*, pp.699–700.
119 DODDC, 32 Bn Gp 2, Box 262, 522/4, Vol. 1, Konf., Kong, Semnaar, Simposiums + Vergaderings: Vergaderings, Maandverslag Opleidingsbasis vir die maand Februarie 1985, p.14.

was here from Sector and conducted a stock-take at the Sickbay and Clinic. [He was] Very satisfied and congratulates us with the way in which the hospital is managed. [He was] Also satisfied with the administrative involvement of the doctors.'[120]

The completion of the clinic in the Kimbo had a particularly positive impact on morale. Residents felt that their needs were being met, and had confidence that they would receive adequate medical care if the need arose. Brian Baloyi (pseudonym) was born in the clinic and recalls

> If you get [*sic*] sick in Buffalo, we had a ... clinic in the community ... and if it was really bad, they would take you to the unit, ... to the military base, which had a hospital that was bigger than the clinic that we had within the community... If it was really severe [and] they couldn't treat you at the military base ... there was an emergency evacuation plan; ... then they would fly you to Pretoria, South Africa ... and they would treat you there.[121]

Edwin Eduardo (pseudonym), also a child in the Kimbo at the time, adds the military hospital at Grootfontein in Namibia as an additional step to the process described by Baloyi: 'We had a fully-fledged sickbay with doctors. In cases of emergency, some of us would go to Grootfontein; other would even travel to Pretoria, to 1 Military Hospital... From that point of view, I must say that we were taken care of.'[122]

Conclusion

While the SADF increasingly recognised the value of 32 Battalion in active deployments, they largely failed to recognise the unique needs of the unit and treated it, from an operational perspective, as any other SADF unit. Furthermore, although the majority of the white command group of 32 Battalion harboured a genuine concern for the well-being of the black men under their command – and were well ahead of the rest of white South Africa in moving towards the non-racial society of the Rainbow Nation – a racial divide was, nonetheless, apparent in the different attitudes towards the supply of resources to the black and white soldiers of the battalion.

120 DODDC, 32 Bn Gp 2, Box 262, 522/4, Vol. 1, Konf., Kong, Semnaar, Simposiums + Vergaderings: Vergaderings, Maandverslag Opleidingsbasis vir die maand Februarie 1985, p.16. Afrikaans: *Kmdt Smith was hier van Sektor en het 'n voorraadopname gedoen van Siekeboeg en die Kliniek. Baie tevrede en wens ons geluk met die wyse wat die hospital bestuur word. Ook tevrede met die administratiewe betrokkenheid van die dokters.*

121 Telephonic interview with Brian Baloyi (pseudonym), son of former 32 Battalion soldier; Kimbo and Pomfret resident, Centurion, 17-03-2019.

122 Interview with Edwin Eduardo (pseudonym), son of former 32 Battalion soldier; Kimbo and Pomfret resident, Wonderboom, 24-06-2019.

The SADF made undeniable progress with the supply and logistic channels to 32 Battalion. However, the increase in 32 Battalion's combat efficiency meant that they were deployed to a much greater extent than most other SADF units. The SADF was cognisant of this and prioritised the provision of 32 Battalion, along with other frequently deployed units like 61 Mechanised Battalion, but even with this prioritisation, supply issues continued to plague 32 Battalion throughout their time in Namibia. The SADF found ways to effectively provide 32 Battalion with the equipment that they needed to fulfil their immediate task – taking the war to South Africa's opponents – but was significantly less successful in the supply of non-essential equipment. This was particularly apparent in the SADF's attitude towards the civilians attached to 32 Battalion. Despite continuous progress in the provision of basic necessities, such as housing, rations and medical facilities, to the Kimbo, it was very late in the war before the Kimbo-infrastructure was comparable to the facilities available to white South Africans. Despite the efforts of 32 Battalion officers, a degree of racism was exhibited towards the unit throughout the war. Many white South Africans, particularly those who served, or came into contact, with 32 Battalion came to appreciate the contributions that they made towards South Africa's war effort, but their needs were never addressed with quite the same urgency as those of traditional, white units. In a sense, the SADF used a type of flux which aided considerably in some aspects of melding different strands together, but were largely unsuccessful in some others.

5

'The Crucible': Life in the Battalion

The origins of 32 Battalion led to the situation where not only soldiers, but also their families, depended on the SADF for their wellbeing. While it could be argued that this is the case in many military units, particularly garrison towns and bases, the dependency at 32 Battalion was much more direct. It was not a case of the soldiers earning a livelihood through the SADF and their families benefitting indirectly. At Buffalo, soldiers and civilians did not merely benefit from being associated with the SADF, they were utterly dependent on it for survival. The extent of this challenge is highlighted by the composition of the first group of Angolans to become members of 32 Battalion: in December 1975, shortly after Bravo Group's role in Operation Savannah had come to an end, a total of 651 people – 75 trained men, 39 untrained men, 26 youths, 40 older men, 229 women and 242 children – gathered at Mpupa, awaiting Jan Breytenbach's return from South Africa. This number rapidly increased over the following months, and eventually 1,800 men, women and children were selected to stay with Bravo Group and, eventually, move to Buffalo and the Kimbo.[1] By 1989, 3,162 civilians alone called Buffalo home.[2] In addition, the Angolan soldiers of 32 Battalion were not a homogenous group; they came from six different ethnic groups.[3] The map on p. 134 indicates the relative positions of Buffalo Base, the Kimbo and the unit's cemetery. The cemetery was the sight of the original base, where soldiers and families lived together. Soldiers were subsequently separated from their families and moved to the area that would ultimately become the Kimbo, when they moved, for the final time in Namibia, to Buffalo.

The majority of white, South African, members did not have their families living with them during their service. In addition, white members were entitled to official SADF support, even for social problems, should these arise. Black members only enjoyed this privilege long after the unit was established, and continually had to contend with being

1 P. Nortje, *The Terrible Ones: A complete history of 32 Battalion.* Cape Town: Zebra, 2012, pp.145–149.
2 DODDC, 32 Bn Gp 2, Box 61, 107/1/1, Vol. 2, Versekering / Assuransie: Groepsversekering, Message PERS/221/27JAN89 from 32 Bn Trg Base to 32 Bn HQ.
3 Interview with Hilton Husson (pseudonym), former 32 Battalion soldier, Centurion, 10-07-2019.

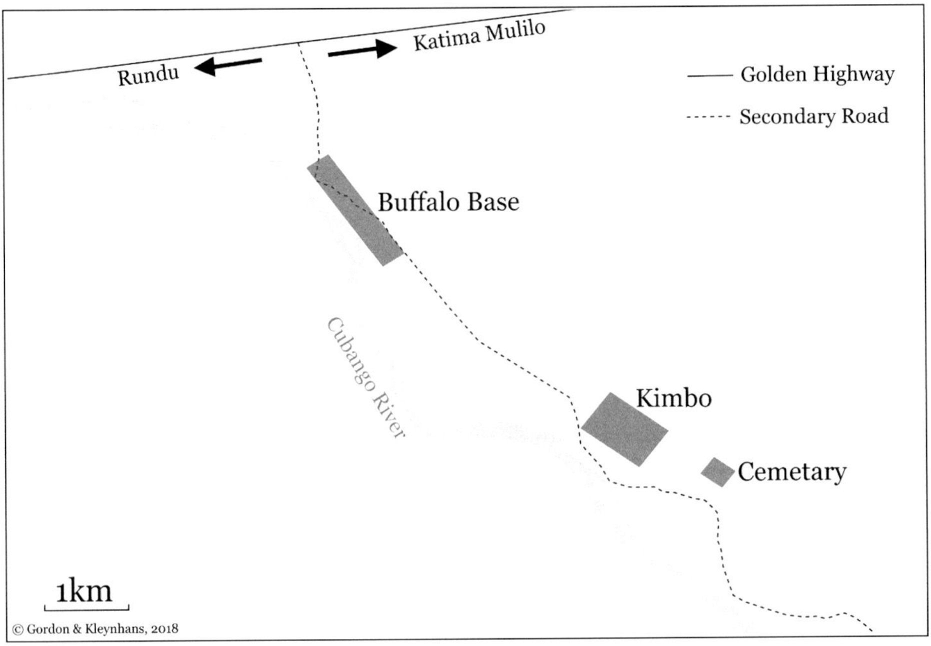

Buffalo Base, the Kimbo and the cemetery.

black in apartheid South Africa. This meant that they were much more dependent on the unit, itself, not only for its support structures, but in fact for their very identity, their *raison d'être*. Although 32 Battalion was, throughout its existence, primarily a frontline combat unit, the character of the unit was shaped in the crucible of society. The intense heat generated by introspection and reflection could only be found away from the rigours of war.

Immigration

From the start of 32 Battalion's existence, the fact that foreigners were being employed by the SADF was a problem. In addition to the potential international repercussions of South Africa employing 'mercenaries' to defend their apartheid policies, as the perception of Operation Savannah was increasingly becoming, Pretoria had to contend with an influx of refugees. The sensible course of action was to establish which of these refugees could be put to effective use in the service of South Africa, whether in a military sense or otherwise. The OC 32 Battalion at the time, Jan Breytenbach, embraced the opportunity to expand his fledgling force and recruited suitable candidates from among the Angolan refugees at Calai and Cuangar. However, by mid-1976, the SADF realised that this was happening and issued an instruction to 1 MA that proper immigration procedures had to be followed and that Angolans who did not meet immigration requirements could not be employed by the SADF.[4]

This prompted Breytenbach to write a letter to the office of the Chief of the Army, comprehensively illustrating why he thought that the SADF and, by extension, the Department of Home Affairs, should not rigidly enforce their immigration policies. He pointed out that both General Magnus Malan, Chief of the Defence Force, and Lieutenant General Constand Viljoen, Chief of the Army, were aware that additional black Angolans had been recruited by 32 Battalion after Operation Savannah. In addition, Breytenbach contended that Malan had authorised him to construct housing for the black Angolans, and their families, that were employed by 32 Battalion. He did concede, however, that he was aware of the fact that the black Angolans would not be allowed into South Africa, but was firm in his contention that they were accommodated in Namibia with permission from the SADF's most senior officers.[5] Realising that the SADF had slowly started to recognise the value of having units such as Alpha and Bravo Group at its disposal, Breytenbach astutely pointed out that the original members of these units were, from a legal perspective, in exactly the same boat as the refugees that were recruited later. Assuming that the SADF would be reluctant to lose Alpha and Bravo Groups, Breytenbach played his trump card: if the refugees had to be returned to Angola, the original Angolan component of the units would also have to be returned, effectively meaning that both Alpha and Bravo Groups would cease to exist.[6] The most important consideration, in Breytenbach's opinion, was that 'we promised to provide their families with a safe place to stay' and that returning the refugees to Angola would renege on this promise and place them in a social climate where civil discord between families supporting the different Angolan politico-military factions was rife.[7] In addition, offers of employment that had been made to these Angolans while they were still refugees, were accordance with orders from 1 MA at the time. This meant that the refugees had to choose between being transported to Portugal or entering service with the SADF. The information that had been passed on to them at the time enabled them to make an educated decision, and they could not be returned to Angola at the whim of politicians after they had received a firm offer of employment.[8] Breytenbach's final argument is indicative of the frame of mind that was prevalent in 32 Battalion, which differed greatly from the general thinking of apartheid South Africa: he argued that

4 DODDC, 32 Bn, Box 9, LOG/OPS/3/16/13, Vol. 1, Personeel Beleid (Vrywillige Diens ens.), Indiensenming: Portugese, p.1.

5 DODDC, 32 Bn, Box 9, LOG/OPS/3/16/13/4, Vol. 1, Portugese / Ang'e, Indiensneming: Portugese, pp.1–2.

6 DODDC, 32 Bn, Box 9, LOG/OPS/3/16/13/4, Vol. 1, Portugese / Ang'e, Indiensneming: Portugese, p.2.

7 DODDC, 32 Bn, Box 9, LOG/OPS/3/16/13/4, Vol. 1, Portugese / Ang'e, Indiensneming: Portugese, pp.2–3. Afrikaans: *ons belowe het om vir hul families 'n veilige tuiste te bied.*

8 DODDC, 32 Bn, Box 9, LOG/OPS/3/16/13/4, Vol. 1, Portugese / Ang'e, Indiensneming: Portugese, p.2.

the black Angolans were of much greater use to the SADF than white Angolans, and that allowing the latter to enter South Africa while disqualifying the former based on their race was folly. Breytenbach extolled the virtue of the black Angolans under his command, claiming that they were willing to perform under any circumstances, while the white Angolans were 'exceptionally unwilling to serve the country that has now provided him with refuge,'[9] thereby illustrating the oxymoronic nature of Pretoria's immigration policies.

The steps taken by 32 Battalion to ensure that they were able to recruit effectively and efficiently from among Angolan refugees and former soldiers stand in stark contrast to the difficulties that regular SADF units experienced in getting Angolans employed. In April 1976, Sector 10 wanted to employ two Angolans. However, despite them completing the required SADF medical examinations,[10] 'Internal Affairs [did] not want to support them and consider[ed] them classified foreign.'[11] Additionally, the two Angolans wanted to enrol their children in a school in Windhoek, to 'convert [a] purely Angolan approach to SA standards',[12] but, probably due to their immigration status, were unsuccessful. This, essentially, left the families of the two men stranded in Windhoek.[13] Events such as these provide a fascinating lens through which the actions that 32 Battalion took to ensure the wellbeing of the soldiers and civilians under their care should be viewed.

While it could certainly not be argued that 32 Battalion was the only unit with black troops that cared for its men, an incident in 1986, regarding a sergeant from 32 Battalion that had transferred to 1 Recce, is indicative of the complexity of the situation that the SADF faced. The soldier in question, a sergeant with 1 Recce had moved his family to Buffalo while he was still a member of 32 Battalion. On his transfer to 1 Recce, his family moved to a new home in South Africa. However, when the sergeant and his wife decided to get divorced, it had serious immigration implications for the family. Because of South African immigration procedures and racial policies, the family was no longer eligible for residency in South Africa. This information was passed on from 1 Recce to 32 Battalion, along with the request that the wife and children be allowed to return to the Kimbo, as this was where their only known relatives – and therefore only base of support outside South African borders – were living.[14] The location of 32 Battalion's base in the

9 DODDC, 32 Bn, Box 9, LOG/OPS/3/16/13/4, Vol. 1, Portugese / Ang'e, Indiensenming: Portugese, p.3. Afrikaans: *besonder onwillig om diens te lewer in belang van die land waarin hy nou 'n permanente tuiste gekry het.*

10 DODDC, 1 Militêre Gebied, Box 82, G/OPS/3/3/BRAVO, Vol. 1, Message A/PERS/38/1/920/APR 76 from 101 TF to 1 MA.

11 DODDC, 1 Militêre Gebied, Box 82, G/OPS/3/3/BRAVO, Vol. 1, Message PERS/704/APR 76 from 1 MA to 101 TF.

12 DODDC, 1 Militêre Gebied, Box 82, G/OPS/3/3/BRAVO, Vol. 1, Message PERS/704/APR 76 from 1 MA to 101 TF.

13 DODDC, 1 Militêre Gebied, Box 82, G/OPS/3/3/BRAVO, Vol. 1, Message A/PERS/5/2 from 101 TF to SWA Cmd.

14 DODDC, 32 Bn Gp 2, Box 28, 104/12/1/1, Message PERS/795/08 APR 86 from 1 Recce to HQ Special Forces, 32 Bn.

Caprivi undoubtedly gave it flexibility in terms of immigration that units based in South Africa could never hope to enjoy but the significance of 32 Battalion providing foster care to the families of other units is another illustration of the way in which social and military life intermingled in the unit.

Religion

Although military institutions across the Western World have historically used chaplains as 'moral spokesmen with the unique power to help incite the 'spirit of victory' and to bestow forgiveness afterwards'[15] – and South Africa was certainly no different in this regard – 32 Battalion required additional spiritual guidance. Firstly, the unit's very nature dictated that the majority of people to whom a chaplain would minister would not need incitement to victory, as they were civilians. Secondly, many of the men doing 32 Battalion's fighting did not necessarily do so out of a desire to win, nor did they necessarily feel the need for forgiveness afterwards. While every military unit is unique, and a theological or spiritual approach that worked for one might not work at another, chaplains and religious leaders at 32 Battalion faced particularly challenging circumstances.

On 17 February 1977, the chaplain of 1 Military Area, G. H. Theron, recognised that the composition of 32 Battalion created a unique challenge regarding religious and spiritual services to the unit. He noted that the white component of 32 Battalion spoke Afrikaans, English and Portuguese and that the languages of the black component included Portuguese and 'all the indigenous Angolan languages'. This, already significant, obstacle was compounded by the fact that members were from both Catholic and Protestant backgrounds. Although the white members were regularly visited by Theron and other visiting chaplains, the black troops received no personal spiritual guidance and were reliant on cassette recordings of sermons in Portuguese. In addition, the only Catholic clergyman available at the time was one Father Boniface from the mission nearby at Andara. However, Father Boniface could only speak Afrikaans, while the translator that was available could only speak English and Portuguese. This resulted in a situation that would have been comical, but for the inevitable difficulties that attended it: Father Boniface delivered his sermon in Afrikaans, whereafter someone translated it into English for the benefit of the translator. He then translated the English into Portuguese, for the benefit of the troops. While the Catholic part of 32 Battalion's black contingent derived at least some benefit from this inelegant solution, Theron claimed that 'The Protestants currently do not have any part-time chaplains.' This is a particularly strange remark, as the majority, if not all, of the chaplains that visited the white members on a regular basis would have been Protestant. The

15 J. Bourke, *An Intimate History of Killing: Face-to-Face killing in twentieth-century warfare*, London: Granta Books, 1999, p.270.

logical solution would have been to follow the same, admittedly clumsy, system as with the Catholic Father Boniface. Nonetheless, Theron did identify a former-refugee, then employed by the Evangelical Reformed Church of the Kavango, as a suitable candidate to minister to the needs of the black Protestants and urged the chaplain of 101 Task Force to employ him at 32 Battalion.[16]

Around a year later, in July 1978, the base commander of Buffalo Base reported to the OC 32 Battalion that the officers, men and civilians of the unit still did not have sufficient spiritual support. It seems that Father Boniface's efforts were insufficient and that the plan to appoint the Evangelical minister from the Kavango did not pan out. The base commander commented on the remarkably high level of religious education in 32 Battalion, but also highlighted that this came from two very different traditions, Catholicism and Protestantism. His suggested solution to the problem was that the Portuguese soldiers receive separate Portuguese-speaking clergymen, and church buildings, for the Protestant and Catholic groups, and he expressed the opinion that the contingent of white SADF members of 32 Battalion was sufficient to justify a permanent chaplain.[17] Despite these comments and attempts, as late as 1986, authorisation had not yet been received for a full-time chaplain. Protestant Chaplain Sydney Middlemost, a co-minister in Rundu,[18] was a regular figure at 32 Battalion, and a request had been made to have him permanently stationed there, but it had not yet been approved and the makeshift-ministry at the unit continued.[19]

The lack of a permanent solution to the ministry issues experienced at Buffalo is made more relevant by a comment of the OC, Eddie Viljoen, in 1983. At an OC's conference on 31 January 1983, he bemoaned the poor attendance of the previous year's Christmas service and 'warned that he would summarily dismiss any non-believer from 32 Bn.'[20] While encouraging troops to attend religious events, in order to provide a measure of stability in their turbulent lives through the moral advocacy of chaplains is not necessarily ill-considered, the threat of summary expulsion for non-attendance seems harsh. In addition, the difficulties experienced in providing regular, dependable access to clergymen compounds the hypocritical nature of this statement. In addition, it is a marked contrast to the management style of three years earlier, under Deon Ferreira. At that time, when Ferreira was faced with the problem of former Angolan troops, who all had force numbers

16 DODDC, 32 Bn, Box 9, LOG/OPS/3/16/13/4, Vol. 1, Portugese / Ang'e, Kapelaansdiens aan 32 Bataljon te 1 MG. Afrikaans: *al die inheemse tale van Angola*; *Die protestante het tans geen deeltydse kapelane … nie.*
17 DODDC, 32 Bn, Box 41, 309/1/ALG, Vol. 1, Spesifieke Operasies Gesamentlik, Persoonlike verslag aan Bev 32 Bn deur Bev Buffalo Basis, par. 15.
18 Nortje, *The Terrible Ones*, pp.912–913.
19 DODDC, 32 Bn Gp 2, Box 156, 522/1, Konferensies, Notulering van besprekingspunte tov personeelaangeleenthede deur Bevelvoerder soos bespreek op 4 Feb '86.
20 DODDC, 32 Bn Gp 2, Box 260, 522/1, Vol. 1, Konferensies, Kongresse, Seminare, Simposiums en Vergaderings: Konferensies, Notule van Bevelvoerderskonferensie gehou te Rundu op 31 Januarie 1983, p.5. Afrikaans: *gewaarsku dat hy enige ongelowige summier uit 32 Bn sal wegjaag.*

ending in SP, either resigning from 32 Battalion,[21] or going AWOL to Botswana for short periods, Ferreira ordered an investigation into the feasibility of selling 'strong liquor' in the Kimbo, and even wanted to know what 'the level of interest would be for a brothel for the SP members in the Kimbo.'[22] Ferreira obviously reasoned that, if he could not stop his black troops from going elsewhere for their indulgences, he might as well provide it to them in a controlled environment. It is only natural that different OCs would have different ideas about how a unit should be administered, and different ways of implementing their ideas. However, for the soldiers that had to bear the practical implications of these differences, it would have been difficult to understand how they could have gone from the lenient style of Ferreira to the puritanical demands of Viljoen.

Perhaps understandably, given the life-or-death nature of the existence of civilians during the early years of 32 Battalion, providing for the religious needs of the unit was not a high priority, and it took until 1988 before permanent church buildings, sufficient for the needs of the men, women and children of 32 Battalion, were erected. At this point, separate buildings were constructed for Protestants and Catholics, although the relationship between the groups had improved significantly.[23] Of course, the unit would only use these buildings for about a year, before relocating to Pomfret. The construction of churches did not, however, solve the linguistic challenges that the Portuguese-speaking inhabitants of Buffalo faced. Although 32 Battalion's ministry had much more structure, sermons for the Angolans still had to take place through an interpreter. Kevin Kambinda (pseudonym), a soldier at 32 Battalion in the late 1980s, recalls that '…sermons had to be given through a translator … at what we called chaplain's periods – I'm specifically referring to the Angolan population now – the whites … mostly spoke English, or Afrikaans.'[24]

Courts Martial and Discipline

Not all of the refugees recruited by Bravo Group embraced their new home with the same enthusiasm. From the onset, problems with discipline inevitably arose. As early as

21 DODDC, 32 Bn Gp 2, Box 260, 522/1, Vol. 1, Konferensies, Kongresse, Seminare, Simposiums en Vergaderings: Konferensies, Notule van Bevelvoerderskonferensie gehou te 32 Bn Hoofkwartier op 26 Jul 1980, p.3.

22 DODDC, 32 Bn Gp 2, Box 260, 522/1, Vol. 1, Konferensies, Kongresse, Seminare, Simposiums en Vergaderings: Konferensies, Notule van Bevelvoerderskonferensie gehou te 32 Bn Hoofkwartier op 12 Okt 1980, p.2. Afrikaans: *sterk drank*; *die belangstelling is vir 'n bordeel in die Kimbo vir SP lede.*

23 DODDC, 32 Bn Gp 2, Box 262, 522/1/1, Vol. 7, Bevelvoerderskonferensies, Notule van SWAGM Kapelaansdiens-konferensie gehou te Daan Viljoen Natuurreservaat van 20–22 Januarie 1988, p.10.

24 Telephonic interview with Kevin Kambinda (pseudonym), former 32 Battalion soldier, Centurion, 21-07-2019. Afrikaans: …*boodskappe moes [ge]gee word deur middel van 'n tolk … by wat ons genoem het kapelaansperiodes – ek praat nou spesifiek van die Angolese bevolking – die blankes het … meestal Engels gepraat, of Afrikaans.*

1976, some of the former refugees became known miscreants, even though this endangered their continued employment at 32 Battalion and the attendant degree of security for their families. The initial reaction of 32 Battalion officers was to try to resolve disciplinary issues informally and internally. To this end, corporal punishment was used. Offenders were spread-eagled on a 44-gallon drum, which became known simply as 'the drum' and lashed with a whip. After the punishment had been completed, the offender was given medical care, if required, and the matter was considered resolved.[25] This practice was discontinued in the late 1980s by the Officer Commanding, Michau Delport.[26]

From the start, however, 32 Battalion was not averse to taking more drastic and formal action if the situation warranted it. A pair of Angolans were discharged, and returned to a refugee camp with their families, in December 1976 because they continuously not only challenged the disciplinary regulations of 32 Battalion, but also contravened the law. Although they were never court-martialled, the list of their transgression included theft, threatening to kill all white Portuguese and, disconcertingly, throwing hand grenades in the Kimbo. They had been made to run with sandbags 'until they could not get up' several times before they were discharged, but despite this, matters got to the point where their platoon sergeants refused to accept them any longer, because of the discord and enmity they created within the platoon.[27] Keeping in mind that some of the platoon leaders were compatriots of the two discharged members highlights the effect that their actions had on the morale of the unit.

Courts martial were, however, held for more serious offences – though how throwing hand grenades in the Kimbo does not fall into this category remains a mystery. Recognising that some individuals were pushing their new boundaries at Bravo Group to try to establish what they could get away with, strict adherence to discipline, rules, regulations and law was imperative. To this end, a court-martial was convened to investigate a suspected case of rape in February 1976. It was chaired by a SADF commandant (lieutenant colonel) and the other three board members were a SADF lieutenant and two Angolan commandants (political titles, rather than military ranks). Two Angolan translators were present at the court-martial, the prosecution was done by a SADF warrant officer and the defence by a SADF lieutenant. It is not clear what units the South Africans belonged to. After the court-martial assumed that the defendant pleaded not guilty to the charge – they had to explain to him what rape meant and he did not, subsequently, enter a plea – the prosecution called three witnesses. A prominent member of the village where the alleged rape had taken place and his common law wife (also the sister of the victim) both offered damning evidence against the accused. The victim herself, 13 years old at the time, also recounted her version of events. Although the

25 Interview with Hilton Husson (pseudonym), former 32 Battalion soldier, Centurion, 10-07-2019; Interview with Jan Joaquim (pseudonym), former 32 Battalion soldier, Centurion, 11-07-2019. Afrikaans: *die drom*.

26 Interview with Ian Ines (pseudonym), former 32 Battalion soldier, Centurion, 10-07-2019.

27 DODDC, 32 Bn, Box 9, LOG/OPS/3/16/13/4, Vol. 1, Portugese / Ang'e, Veelvuldige oortredings. Afrikaans: *tot hulle bly lê*.

defence occasionally cross-examined the prosecution's witnesses, they only called the accused himself as a witness in their defence. He explained that he wanted to marry the victim and, although he had been denied permission by the village elders, including the prosecution's first witness, had not forced himself on the victim. According to the accused, she had neither given, nor denied, permission for him to have sex with her. He added that he had offered her the sum of R2 before he left. At this point, the court adjourned to discuss the evidence. Three of the four members were convinced that it was a case of rape, but the fourth contended that the case against the accused had not been proved conclusively. The alleged victim was called back to the court-martial and asked two follow-up questions regarding her role in the alleged rape. After she had denied giving the accused any reason to think that she might be amenable to his sexual advances, all four members of the court-martial agreed that the defendant was guilty of rape. He was sentenced to death by firing squad, though the court explained that the decision had to be ratified by the unit's 'high command' before the sentence could be executed.[28] Since there is no follow-up documents linked to the matter in the DODDC, it seems unlikely that the sentence was ever carried out.

Nonetheless, this scenario raises several key points. The aim of highlighting these points is not to contend that the accused was wrongfully convicted, or to comment on the suitability of capital punishment for cases of rape, but rather to illuminate the nature of the court-martial itself. The first contentious point relates to jurisdiction. Courts martial form a key part of maintaining discipline in any army, but the soldiers that are being court-martialled are, inevitably, part of the army by which they are tried. While the former Angolan soldiers of Bravo Group did become part of the SADF, February 1976 had just seen the end of Bravo Group's participation in Operation Savannah, and Breytenbach's struggles to get official recognition for his unit was still well under way. The Angolans did not yet have proper SADF force numbers and were identified by serial numbers given to them when they became part of the unit. The SADF only agreed to start paying salaries to Bravo Group's Angolan soldiers in March 1976, a month after the court-martial took place.[29] The obvious question that arises is: did the SADF members of the court-martial have the authority to pass any kind of sentence, let alone capital punishment, on soldiers that were not part of their military institution, either as enlisted soldiers or as mercenaries?

Secondly, it seems that the witnesses called by the court-martial were biased. The accused was the only witness that could realistically be expected to be sympathetic to his own cause. The family members of the victim were hardly likely to provide evidence or testimony that would exonerate the acts of the accused, which they perceived as rape. Though it cannot be predicted what they would have said, it seems that, at least, the two colleagues of the accused should also have been called to give evidence, if only to provide a more balanced representation. They were, of course, not present in the evening

28 DODDC, File reference omitted by author. Afrikaans: *opperbevel.*
29 Nortje, *The Terrible Ones*, p.161.

when the rape took place, but they might have been able to shed light on the events that preceded it, when the accused first had contact with the victim.

The Afrikaans statement, recording the accused's plea of not guilty, is quite poignant and indicates a degree of incomprehension about the severity of the accusations against him. The record of the court-martial states that, 'After it was carefully explained to the accused what rape entails, and after the accused explained that the woman had given her permission for the act, the court assumes that the accused pleads not guilty.'[30]

In Afrikaans, the word *mooi*, in relation to an explanation, is often used to highlight incomprehension by the party that is being explained to. For example, one would typically explain an unknown concept *mooi* to a child. It is doubtful that the author of the court transcript deliberately used the term in this way, but it is quite possible that its colloquial meaning was, subconsciously, intended. This is supported by the fact that the accused did not actually enter any plea, possibly because he did not understand the proceedings and what was expected of him. If this were the case, it would be natural to assume that he did not grasp the gravity of the situation, either.

Furthermore, though the R2 that the accused offered to the girl seems like a paltry amount today, when viewed against the R5 per month that the SADF initially paid riflemen in Bravo Group,[31] it constitutes a significant portion of the accused's disposable income. The question arises whether he would be willing to pay almost half of his monthly salary for what, according to the interpretation of the court-martial, amounted to little more than a night with a prostitute. Perhaps there was more truth behind the accused's contention that he wanted to marry the girl and that the payment was a token of his intent. This, of course, is no excuse for rape, but it does put the actions and intentions of the accused in a different perspective, one that was never seen or considered by the court-martial.

A final aspect that deserves consideration is the severity of the sentence passed by the court-martial. The issue is not whether, or not, a conviction of rape should carry a capital sentence, but rather whether the outcome of the court-martial would have been the same if the accused had been a white member of the SADF. This question cannot be answered conclusively, but it seems highly unlikely that a National Serviceman, for example, would be sentenced to death in a court-martial lasting only an afternoon. Given the severity of the white South African public's reaction to any SADF casualties, executions in the army were sure to have produced significant backlash. This is something that the SADF was keen to avoid, and the possibility of a more lenient sentence for a white soldier or, at the very least, a much more comprehensive court-martial, seems exceedingly likely.

The next court-martial examining a case of rape, on 6 November 1976, was chaired by an SADF colonel. A Portuguese WO2 was the other member.[32] Significantly, the presence of an Angolan on the board indicates an attempt to establish the truth of the matter, rather than just

30 DODDC, File reference omitted by author. Afrikaans: *Nadat mooi aan beskuldigde verduidelik is wat verkragting behels, en nadat die beskuldigde verduidelik het dat die vrou wel toestemming tot die daad gegee het, aanvaar die hof dat die beskuldigde onskuldig pleit* [*sic*].

31 Nortje, *The Terrible Ones*, p.161.

32 DODDC, File reference omitted by author.

get the court-martial over with. In the political climate of South Africa in the 1970s, it would have been easy not to give the black Angolan accused the same treatment as white South Africans could have expected, but the constitution of the court-martial and the proceedings appear exceedingly fair to the accused. In fact, after considering the testimony of the plaintiff, the defendant and two witnesses, the court found that the accused was not guilty of rape and that the whole case boiled down to a 'lover's tiff'.[33] Of course, not all courts martial should have the same outcome; in some cases, the defendants are guilty and in others they are not, but a comparison of the transcripts of the two cases illustrated above, which took place about a year apart, indicates a decidedly more lenient approach in the second case. It is also possible that the plaintiff, and women who had ties with 32 Battalion in general, had heard about the outcome of the earlier court-martial and had been emboldened by it to use the SADF legal system as a means to an end. Nevertheless, the firm approach taken by 32 Battalion towards disciplinary matters bore fruit, and by July 1978 the base commander at Buffalo was able to report that, although the former Angolan troops 'make many mistakes with women and drink' and were not particularly obedient towards their own NCOs and warrant officers (WOs), they impressed him with their 'obedience and loyalty towards the white soldiers'.[34]

The severity of the sentence passed in the February 1976 case is further highlighted by events in 1987. In November, a former member of 32 Battalion, who had been discharged, applied for re-attestation. On examination of his application, it became apparent that he had been discharged because he was sentenced to five years' imprisonment after being convicted of rape in 1985. After serving about half the sentence, he was released and re-applied to 32 Battalion, where his application was favourably considered, though not without gleaning advice from the office of the Chief of the Army whether the member could be allowed to re-attest.[35] However, the very fact that the severity in which cases of rape was viewed had moved from carrying a capital sentence to not even carrying permanent discharge from the unit as penalty raises some serious question marks about the conduct of the court-martial in 1976.

Corporal punishment was quite common in 32 Battalion for lesser cases, and it seems that some of the white leader group were over-eager in their implementation of this policy. To curb excess corporal punishment, and to maintain morale in the unit, Deon Ferreira issued an instruction in October 1980 that 'an SP member will only be punished after he has been brought to order properly' and 'blacks should be hit by blacks to maintain the white-black relationship.'[36] Hilton Husson (pseudonym) and Ian Ines (pseu

33 DODDC, File reference omitted by author.
34 DODDC, 32 Bn, Box 41, 309/1/ALG, Vol. 1, Spesifieke Operasies Gesamentlik, Persoonlike verslag aan Bev 32 Bn deur Bev Buffalo Basis, par. 22. Afrikaans: *maak baie foute oor vroue en drank; gehoorsaamheid en lojaliteit teenoor die blanke soldate.*
35 DODDC, File reference omitted by author.
36 DODDC, 32 Bn Gp 2, Box 260, 522/1, Vol. 1, Konferensies, Kongresse, Seminare, Simposiums en Vergaderings: Konferensies, Notule van Bevelvoerderskonferensie gehou te 32 Bn Hoofkwartier op 12 Okt 1980, p.4. Afrikaans: *'n SP lid slegs gestraf sal word nadat hy op behoorlike orders gebring was; swartes deur swartes geslaan moet word en die wit-swart verhouding gesond te handhaaf.*

donym), former soldiers of 32 Battalion, remember this instruction: 'White guys never hit the soldiers. Black guys hit them. One of the [black] sergeants did it, or one of the sergeants major.'[37]

The first instruction makes good sense, to the extent that it is lamentable that the situation was allowed to deteriorate to a point where such an instruction became necessary, but the social implications of the latter instruction is probably much greater than first appearances would indicate. In order to maintain the 'white-black relationship', of course a vital aspect in a unit such as 32 Battalion, it is possible that Ferreira underestimated the importance of the black-black relationship. If it were not for the qualification that punishment should only follow proper procedures, his instruction would have been remarkable akin to the circumstances that the Angolans were used to before they joined 32 Battalion, where the black commanders had all the power and could lord it over their soldiers in any way they saw fit. However, Ferreira seems to have been fair in his assessment of problems within his unit, and did not use the easy excuse of placing all blame at his black troops' door. In fact, he stressed that promises made to the black troops – by white leaders – had to be kept, and insisted that white soldiers addressed black NCOs by their rank. Finally, and most significantly, Ferreira claimed that 'weak control by whites caused many problems',[38] effectively placing the responsibility and accountability on his white leader group, rather than deflecting blame towards the black contingent.

While deployed, leaders – both black and white – did not have immediate recourse to the disciplinary structures of the SADF. Therefore, corporal punishment was the accepted way of maintaining discipline in the field. During deployments, Ferreira's directives also became less clear-cut, and punishment was meted out by all of the leader group.

One white officer, in particular, earned the nickname 'One-One' for an incident that occurred during a deployment. The officer had warned two members of his platoon that they were getting out of line, and threatened to punch them if they did not improve their behaviour. One of them, however, had been Mohammad Ali's sparring partner for the 'Rumble in the jungle' and the pair decided to call what they might have thought was a bluff on the part of the officer. Hilton Husson (pseudonym) records what happened next: 'One shot, and the first one sat on his backside; next shot, and the next one sat on his backside. The rest of the platoon then ran away.[39]

37 Group discussion with former 32 Battalion soldiers, Centurion, 10-07-2019. Afrikaans: *Wit ouens het hulle nooit geslaan nie. Swart ouens het hulle geslaan. Een van die sersante het dit gedoen, of sa'majore.*

38 DODDC, 32 Bn Gp 2, Box 260, 522/1, Vol. 1, Konferensies, Kongresse, Seminare, Simposiums en Vergaderings: Konferensies, Notule van Basiskonferensie gehou te 32 Bn Buffalo op 28 Maart 1980, pp.6–7. Afrikaans: *swak beheer deur blankes veroorsaak baie probleme.*

39 Interview with Hilton Husson (pseudonym), former 32 Battalion soldier, Centurion, 10-07-2019. Afrikaans: *One shot, toe sit [die eerste een] op sy gat; volgende shot, toe sit [die volgende een] op sy gat, toe hardloop die res [van die peloton] weg.*

Education

When the school at Pica Pau was established for the children of 32 Battalion's soldiers, in April 1977,[40] their initial organisation would not have been familiar to South African teachers. In South Africa, children spent 12 years in basic education (with an optional exit point after 10 years). Depending on the province, a child started primary school in either Grade 1 and Grade 2, or sub-A and sub-B, at around six years old. After the first two years of basic education, subsequent years were known as Standard 1 to Standard 5 in primary school, followed by Standard 6 to Standard 10 (also known colloquially as 'matric') in high school. The minimum legal requirement was the completion of Standard 8, when the student should have been 16 years old. This, incidentally, is why SADF force numbers start with the year in which the soldier turned 16: they would have been eligible for national service if they did not continue with high school.

Rather than organise the children in standard groups, like in South African schools, the teachers at Pica Pau school decided to divide the children according to their ability and English proficiency, irrespective of their age. This meant that the school only had four levels, called A1, A2, B and C, and two kindergarten classes, which were age-dependant. Levels A1 and A2 were for students who could not read, write or understand English. Students in level B had a reasonable command of English and the most advanced students, those in level C, were taught at a level roughly equivalent to South Africa's Standard 3 in English and Standard 5 in mathematics.[41]

Of the seven teachers available in September 1977 – which equated to a healthy average of less than 15 students per teacher – three were totally unqualified.[42] In fact, a SADF member at the school who was put in charge of training the three Portuguese-speaking teachers, Lance Corporal E.T. Rayment, remarked that

> they are on completely different levels & thus each one has to be taught individually. Edalina had no idea of English whatsoever so I had to start with basic, down to earth, English. Paula is of about a Std. 4, 5 level. She can read & understand fairly complicated English but lacks practice in speaking English in conversation form. Her written sentences are usually fairly accurate but words intend [*sic*: tend] to be jumbled sometimes. Carlos now has a basic idea of English & understands simple speech, although it is spoken grammatically incorrectly … I am teaching him mostly from a Std. II Grammar book.[43]

40 Nortje, *The Terrible Ones,* p.258.
41 DODDC, 32 Bn, Box 41, 309/1/A5, Vol. 1, Buffalo Skool, Buffalo skool, Rapport: Cmdt Nel; Van: Onderwysers Pica Pau.
42 DODDC, 32 Bn, Box 41, 309/1/A5, Vol. 1, Buffalo Skool, Buffalo skool, Verslagtydperk: September 1977.
43 DODDC, 32 Bn, Box 41, 309/1/A5, Vol. 1, Buffalo Skool, Report: 11th July – 5th August.

The shortage of trained, qualified teachers left 32 Battalion with no choice but to employ unqualified teachers, particularly since student numbers rose dramatically, from 104 in September 1977 to 603 in January 1985.[44] This brought its own set of challenges. The daughter of the unit's Angolan weapon smith taught at Pica Pau school from the beginning, but when she fell pregnant to a married South African Citizen Force engineer, the social furore dictated that she had to resign. The qualified teachers that were available to the unit, however, did sterling work at the school. Former FNLA member, Mark Kanganjo, was promoted to staff sergeant (he would later become one of 32 Battalion's first black officers) and appointed as the first principal of the school, as he was a teacher before the Angolan Civil War.[45] Given the circumstances and the resources at the disposal of Kanganjo and his staff, the results that they were able to achieve are remarkable, as reflected by a proud teacher's report in June 1978: 'I am both satisfied and very excited because in about 6 months I have seen considerable progress in almost all subjects and I feel that this has been a mirror of my work.'[46]

Table 5.1: Inventory of basic school supplies: October 1977[47]

Quantity	Item
300	Workbooks (Scribblers)
38	Teaching Aid Sheets
70	Colouring Books
23	Tudor Exercise Books
68	Sketch Books
54	Small Exercise Books
13	Hardcover Exercise Books
51 boxes	Crayons
24 tins	Powdered Paint
8 sets	Watercolour Paint
372	Paintbrushes
240	Pencils
150	Rulers
40	Pens
63	Erasers
10	Scissors
244	Slate Pencils
126	Slates
20 boxes	Chalk
5	Chalkboard Erasers

44 DODDC, 32 Bn Gp 2, Box 262, 522/4, Vol. 1, Konf, Kong, Semnaar, Simposiums + Vergaderings: Vergaderings, Maandverslag: Buffalo Basis vir Januarie 1985, p.3.
45 Nortje, *The Terrible Ones*, p.258.
46 DODDC, 32 Bn, Box 41, 309/1/A5, Vol. 1, Buffalo Skool, Buffalo School Report.
47 DODDC, 32 Bn, Box 41, 309/1/A5, Vol. 1, Buffalo Skool, Buffalo skool Inventaris.

Of course, the majority of the students at the school spoke Portuguese as a first or second language, meaning that the teachers would have been able to communicate with them effectively, probably even more so than the better educated South Africans. However, the fact that the textbooks that were available at the school were almost exclusively in English and Afrikaans would have made teaching an immense challenge for the Portuguese-speaking teachers. They were, admittedly, employed in the lower grades, but it could not have been easy for someone who spoke English at a 'Std. 4;5 level' to teach someone else, regardless of the student's competence, in that language. However, this did not stop the school from maintaining its learner-numbers during its early existence and, as it became apparent that attending the school was beneficial to the children, increase those numbers significantly later in the war, as apparent from the number of learners in 1985.

The list of equipment at the school at Pica Pau in 1977 (Table 5.1) indicates that it was reasonably well-equipped in respect of basic equipment for lower grades – which was, of course, the level of education for the majority of learners. Much of the equipment was also reusable, such as the slates and slate pencils. This was a crucial factor in a school where access to supplies was infrequent, at best, and impossible, at worst.

However, more advanced supplies were severely lacking. The school had to make do with one dictionary and five attendance registers.[48] Particularly given the level of education of some of the teachers themselves, how it was even possible teach effectively with a single Portuguese-Afrikaans dictionary is mind boggling. Additionally, the shortage of registers would have made record keeping very challenging, particularly in an organisation such as the SADF, where records played a very important role. Nonetheless, the teachers improvised their own methods and, for example, the monthly reports to the OC follow a set format, which was developed at the school and served its purpose well enough.[49] These reports shed light on a significant aspect of teaching at Buffalo: education was not limited to children and there was an attempt to elevate the level of adult education too. In July 1978, Second Lieutenant J. L. Koekemoer reported that 'We also had a group of women (± 8) from the Kimbo coming for English lessons every day. These lessons are still being continued daily after school from 15h00 to 16h00'[50], while in August that year, he commented that 'The adult classes are still being attended well in the afternoons.'[51]

Although the school received additional textbooks in 1978, including some books in Portuguese, these were not necessarily relevant to the level of education that was provided, and Second Lieutenant Koekemoer noted that, 'Unfortunately these books, which are intended for the senior classes, cannot be used at the moment.'[52]

48 DODDC, 32 Bn, Box 41, 309/1/A5, Vol. 1, Buffalo Skool, Buffalo skool Inventaris: Beheerde Items.
49 Cf. DODDC, 32 Bn, Box 41, 309/1/A5, Vol. 1.
50 DODDC, 32 Bn, Box 41, 309/1/A5, Vol. 1, Buffalo Skool, Buffalo School Report, July 1978. Parenthesis original.
51 DODDC, 32 Bn, Box 41, 309/1/A5, Vol. 1, Buffalo Skool, Buffalo School Report, August 1978.
52 DODDC, 32 Bn, Box 41, 309/1/A5, Vol. 1, Buffalo Skool, Buffalo School Report, August 1978.

While the number of textbooks at the Pica Pau school is relatively high, their content negates the numbers (Table 5.2). At the level of the majority of the learners, very few textbooks were available and, even at higher levels, the textbooks are primarily of English as a subject. The 77 textbooks available to Standard 4 learners, for example, are made up of only four different titles, severely limiting teachers' abilities. Of course, the prevalence of English-orientated textbooks was not a completely negative situation as getting the Portuguese-speaking learners to a competent level of English was one of the main priorities of the school, but the relative sparsity of other textbook would have made teaching those subjects very difficult. While some of the other shortages at the school could have been addressed by improvised and makeshift measures, even the most skilled teacher – of which there were not many at Buffalo – would have difficulty in producing a comprehensive textbook from memory and in isolation.

In April 1982, education at the Pica Pau school was finally formalised, when SWA National Education took over the curriculum. From this point on, the school was administered to the same standards as any other school in Namibia. Table 5.3 indicates the growth of the school from the informal years to the point where National Education took over, and shows that both learner and teacher numbers, as well as the level of education available to learners had increased.

The SADF, in the form of 32 Battalion, was still instrumental in ensuring the success of the school, though, particularly since education at the school was free. The SADF sponsored activities like scouts,[53] and Fabia Fernando (pseudonym), a teacher at Pica Pau school, also remembers:

> For a sport weekend at Katima Mulilo, we drove in a ... Kwêvoël; ... the defence force provided the transport ... for the children to take part in this sport day ... We held a matric farewell, so we obviously needed money ... someone must have provided it and it wasn't the school, because nobody paid school fees ... We had gymnastics, we danced and we had Miss Pica Pau ... We arranged this from the school, but ... we had to find a building where these things could take place.[54]

53 Telephonic interview with Liam Lawindo (pseudonym), son of former 32 Battalion soldier; Kimbo and Pomfret resident, Centurion, 28-07-2019.

54 Telephonic interview with Fabia Fernando (pseudonym), former teacher at Pica Pau school, Centurion, 02-07-2019. A. Kwêvoël is a military, mine-protected truck. Afrikaans: *[Vir] 'n sportnaweek op Katima [Mulilo] het ons met 'n ... Kwêvoël ... gery; die weermag het die vervoer verskaf ... dat die kinders kon gaan deelneem aan hierdie sportdag ... Ons het 'n matriekafskeid gehou, so obviously was daar geld nodig ... iemand moes dit gee en dit was nie die skool nie, want niemand het skoolgeld betaal nie ... Ons het gimnastiek [gehad], ons het gedans en ons het Miss Pica Pau gehad ... Ons het dit gereël uit die skool uit, maar ... ons moes 'n gebou gekry het waar hierdie ding plaasgevind het.*

Table 5.2: Textbooks: October 1977[55]

Quantity	Title
1	*Europe and Africa*
1	*Active Geography Form III*
1	*Die Wêreld Gister en Vandag* [The World Yesterday and Today]
1	*Nuwe Moderne Landbou* [New Modern Agriculture]
1	*Natuurwetenskap Std. 3* [Natural Sciences Std. 3]
1	*Natuurwetenskap Std. 5* [Natural Sciences Std. 5]
1	*Moderne Natuurwetenskap Std. 5* [Modern Natural Sciences Std. 5]
1	*Algemene Wetenskap Std. 3* [Science Std. 3]
1	*Algemene Wetenskap Std. 5* [Science Std. 5]
1	*Rekeningkunde vir SA Skole Std. 3* [Accounting for SA Schools Std. 3]
5	*Die ABC van Rekeningkunde* [The ABC of Accounting]
2	*Rekeningkunde vir Almal Std. 3* [Accounting for Everyone Std. 3]
3	*Modern Basic Mathematics Std. 1*
1	*Primêre Wiskunde Std. 2* [Primary Mathematics Std. 2]
1	*Guided Mathematics Std. 7*
1	*Varia se Wiskunde Std. 1* [Varia's Mathematics Std. 1]
1	*Varia se Wiskunde Std. 2* [Varia's Mathematics Std. 2]
1	*Varia se Wiskunde Std. 3* [Varia's Mathematics Std. 3]
1	*Varia se Wiskunde Std. 4* [Varia's Mathematics Std. 4]
1	*English Made Easy Std. II*
1	*English Made Easy Std. III*
3	*English Made Easy Std. IV*
1	*English Reader Sub B*
1	*English Reader Std. I*
1	*English Reader Std. III*
1	*English Reader Std. IV*
51	*Junior English Std. II*
41	*Junior English Std. III*
60	*Junior English Std. IV*
12	*Modern Graded English Std. 4*
8	*Bilingual Letter Writer*
1	*LO vir Meisies* [PE for Girls]
1	*LO vir Seuns* [PE for Boys]

55 DODDC, 32 Bn, Box 41, 309/1/A5, Vol. 1, Buffalo Skool, Buffalo skool Inventaris: Handboeke.

Table 5.3: Buffalo School numbers after National Education (SWA) took over administration in April 1982

Month	Teachers	Pre-primary	Junior Primary	Senior Primary	High School	Total (excl. PP)	Students per Teacher	% Junior Primary	% High School
June 1982*			182	70	15	267		68.16	5.62
August 1982†			182	70	15	267		68.16	5.62
December 1982‡			162	65	15	242		66.94	6.20
June 1983§			258	81	28	367		70.30	7.63
December 1983|			227	73	26	326		69.63	7.98
January 1984¶	19	124	315	103	29	447	23.5	70.47	6.49
April 1984**	23	109	312	96	33	441	19.2	70.75	7.48
June 1984††	26		271	95	23	389	15.0	69.67	5.91
August 1984‡‡	26	126				400	15.4		
December 1984§§			278	86	26	390		71.28	6.67
February 1985||	25	58	402	110	34	546	21.8	73.63	6.23

* DODDC, 32 Bn Gp 2, Box 77, 309/1 B-skool, Vol. 3, Buffalo Skool (Pica Pau), Tweede kwartaalverslag: April tot Junie 1982.

† DODDC, 32 Bn Gp 2, Box 77, 309/1 B-skool, Vol. 3, Buffalo Skool (Pica Pau), Letter from principal to OC, 23 August 1982.

‡ DODDC, 32 Bn Gp 2, Box 77, 309/1 B-skool, Vol. 3, Buffalo Skool (Pica Pau), Jaarverslag: 1982.

§ DODDC, 32 Bn Gp 2, Box 77, 309/1 B-skool, Vol. 3, Buffalo Skool (Pica Pau), Kwartaalverslag: April – Junie.

| DODDC, 32 Bn Gp 2, Box 77, 309/1 B-skool, Vol. 3, Buffalo Skool (Pica Pau), Kwartaalverslag vir November / Desember.

¶ DODDC, 32 Bn Gp 2, Box 77, 309/1 B-skool, Vol. 3, Buffalo Skool (Pica Pau), Maandverslag vir Januarie 1984.

** DODDC, 32 Bn Gp 2, Box 77, 309/1 B-skool, Vol. 3, Buffalo Skool (Pica Pau), Eerste Termynverslag van 1984.

†† DODDC, 32 Bn Gp 2, Box 77, 309/1 B-skool, Vol. 3, Buffalo Skool (Pica Pau), Termynverslag: Tweede Termyn (Junie 1984).

‡‡ DODDC, 32 Bn Gp 2, Box 77, 309/1 B-skool, Vol. 3, Buffalo Skool (Pica Pau), Maandverslag: Augustus 1984.

§§ DODDC, 32 Bn Gp 2, Box 77, 309/1 B-skool, Vol. 3, Buffalo Skool (Pica Pau), Maandverslag: November (Laaste kwartaal).

|| DODDC, 32 Bn Gp 2, Box 77, 309/1 B-skool, Vol. 3, Buffalo Skool (Pica Pau), Maandverslag: Januarie 1985.

A more structured curriculum, and greater control over what the curriculum entailed, also provided opportunities for extracurricular activities. Fabia Fernando (pseudonym) compares Pica Pau to a typical white South African school of the time, though she adds the caveat that it would probably have been a slightly 'under-resourced' school in South Africa:

> On weekends ... we had camps with ... the children, where one held ... lectures ... did a bit of sport ... had a little concert ... We took the Standard 9s and matrics to Tsumeb and Otawi, because their ... Afrikaans set work was *Kringe in 'n Bos* ... which was performed in Otawi, or Tsumeb, and we drove there with them ... Outside of Tsumeb, we took them to the Hoba meteorite ... one made it something of an educational trip.[56]

For a school to progress from very basic education to providing Standard 10 education – on par with education standards in the rest of SWA; the Standard 10 learners wrote the standardised SWA final examination[57] – in just over five years is a feat that would be laudable today. Doing so with very limited resources in the 1970s and 1980s is, surely, one of the most underrated achievements of 32 Battalion.

Although facilities and staffing had improved almost beyond recognition, actually getting the children to attend classes continued to be a problem, to the extent that, in 1985, it was made a point of discussion at a meeting held between the Buffalo Base commander and women of the Kimbo. At the meeting, the importance of a decent education for the future of the children was stressed to the women present, and they were asked to disseminate the information within the Kimbo and help ensure better school attendance.[58] A former learner at Pica Pau school also recalls that the base was also patrolled by NCOs to ensure that learners did not skip classes. As with the soldiers, corporal punishment was swiftly administered to those who were caught doing so.[59]

Whether Pica Pau school influenced the teachers who taught there, and whether it attracted teachers of a specific calibre and mind-set is an open question. Nonetheless, far from being a stop-gap measure for professional teachers, it proved an excellent training

56 Telephonic interview with Fabia Fernando (pseudonym), former teacher at Pica Pau school, Centurion, 02-07-2019. Afrikaans: *Ons het naweke ... kampe met die kinders ... gehou ... waar 'n ou dan ... lesings gehou het ... bietjie sport gedoen het ... bietjie konsert gehou het ... Ons is met die standard 9's en die matrieks Otawi en Tsumeb toe, want hulle ... Afrikaanse voorgeskrewe boek was* Kringe in 'n Bos ... *Dit was opgevoer in Otawi, of in Tsumeb, en ons het ... soontoe gery met hulle ... Buite Tsumeb het ons hulle na die Hoba-meteoriet toe gevat ... 'n ou het dit so 'n bietjie van 'n opvoedkundige trip ... gemaak.*

57 Telephonic interview with Fabia Fernando (pseudonym), former teacher at Pica Pau school, Centurion, 02-07-2019.

58 DODDC, 32 Bn Gp 2, Box 156, 522/1, Konferensies, Minutes of meeting held on 8 August 1985 with Kimbo women at Buffalo Training Base.

59 Interview with Edwin Eduardo (pseudonym), son of former 32 Battalion soldier; Kimbo and Pomfret resident, Wonderboom, 24-06-2019.

ground, with many teachers going on to stellar careers in education. Fabia Fernando (pseudonym) claims that 'Most of them are still employed in education here in South Africa ... One of them is currently a head of department at Menlopark ... One is a headmaster at ... Coligny.'[60]

Medical

Although there was a relative lull in military activity between the clash at Ongulumbashe in 1966 and Operation Savannah in 1975, during which the SADF had the ideal opportunity to increase its medical capabilities, provided by the South African Medical Corps (SAMC), 1970 still saw SAMC's readiness, particularly regarding support during military operations as a 'cause for concern'.[61] This concern proved well-founded, and Operation Savannah started with only two medical officers, a pharmacist and four medical orderlies deployed with Alpha and Bravo Groups. This was, of course, when the involvement of regular SADF personnel was minimal and medical support increased when the SADF deployed to Angola in larger numbers. By 22 November, the SAMC had a forward hospital at Cela in Angola, where casualties could be stabilised locally before being transported to Rundu, if needed, for more comprehensive medical care. From Rundu, via Ondangwa or Grootfontein Air Force Bases, serious casualties could then be airlifted to 1 Military Hospital in Pretoria.[62] This set the tone for the SAMC's – which became SAMS in 1979 – standard operating procedure throughout the war: medical orderlies, part of every SADF section, would stabilise casualties in the field. On an as-needed basis, casualties could then be transported, usually by helicopter if it was considered safe enough, to one of the forward hospitals, located at larger bases like Omega, Oshakati, Rundu and Ondangwa.[63] From there, again if needed, casualties could be airlifted, to Grootfontein and ultimately to 1 Military Hospital.[64]

In addition to clinical medical services, the SADF also provided supplementary services, like psychologists, psychiatrists,[65] rehabilitation facilities, veterinary services, welfare officers, dentistry and recovery programmes for addicts,[66] although former

60 Telephonic interview with Fabia Fernando (pseudonym), former teacher at Pica Pau school, Centurion, 02-07-2019. Menlopark is one of the top secondary schools in Pretoria, if not in South Africa. Afrikaans: *Meeste van hulle is nou nog in die onderwys hier in Suid-Afrika... Een van hulle ... is op hierdie stadium 'n departementshoof by Menlopark ... Een is 'n skoolhoof in ... Coligny.*
61 Military Information Bureau, SADF, *Militêre geneeskunde in Suid-Afrika 1913–1983.* Pretoria: Government Printer, 1983, p.96. Afrikaans: *sorgwekkend.*
62 D. Naidoo (ed.), *The Fourth Dimension: The untold story of military health in South Africa.* Pretoria: South African Medical Health Service, 2009, p.132.
63 D. O. Stratford & H. M. Collins, *Military Nursing in South Africa, 1914–1994.* Pretoria: Chief of the National Defence Force, 1994, p.154.
64 Cf. S. Webb, *Ops Medic: A National Serviceman's Border War.* Alberton: Galago, 2008, pp.122–125.
65 Naidoo (ed.), *The Fourth Dimension,* pp.159–160.
66 Military Information Bureau, *Militêre geneeskunde,* pp.102–106.

soldiers do not all agree that this was the case. In terms of psychological support, Jan Joaquim, a former soldier of 32 Battalion, claims that 'we never had any access to psychologists or psychiatrists or anybody that could sit us down and go through it with us and help us get rid of it. Some guys went through it easy and some guys [had more difficulty].'[67]

Probably due to typical apartheid stereotypes, 32 Battalion was concerned about the prevalence of sexually transmitted diseases among their – predominantly black – troops. Writing about his national service in the early 1980s, Anthony Feinstein, a NSM doctor, echoes this idea when writing about this contact with 32 Battalion soldiers at the sickbay in Oshakati: 'In keeping with the politics, disease segregates too ... nearly all these [black] soldiers have venereal disease ... the gonococcus has found a home here in Owamboland, the chaos of war offering the perfect environment.'[68]

In an attempt to identify the extent of the perceived problem, all troops about to be deployed were examined by the medical officer in April 1977. He found that approximately 10 percent of the troops suffered from venereal disease (VD) and treated them accordingly.[69] His success was limited, however, by the fact that VD was only treated among the soldiers, not the civilians and, if anything, the prevalence of VD increased. Feinstein recalls that 'treating the men without the women ensures this is one battle the apartheid army cannot win.'[70] Fortunately for residents of the Kimbo, the medical officer, while limiting his VD treatments to soldiers only, also attempted to address the most pressing issues among the civilians. To this end, family planning was instituted with 'reasonable success' and 'all females on contraception [were] examined.' Children also received 'DPT and polio inoculations'.[71] This might well have been the first time in their lives that these children had access to comprehensive medical care, since this was not a high priority in their homeland, Angola, and the infrastructure for rural medical support was negligible. What medical care did exist, came mostly curtesy of the Red Cross, who reflected in a special edition to their *Bulletin* on Angola in 1985–1986 that '...needs vary enormously from one *municipio* ... to another,' while pointing out that the more densely populated areas had superior medical supplies and equipment to more rural areas. [72]The attention given to family planning and the access that women had to contraceptives empowered them to make choices about their own lives. Nevertheless, the base commander at Buffalo, reflecting on the women in the Kimbo in July 1978, recorded that 'The morals of the average woman are low and that poses a big problem in

67 Interview with Jan Joaquim (pseudonym), former 32 Battalion soldier, Centurion, 11-07-2019.
68 A. Feinstein, *Battle Scarred: Hidden costs of the Border War*. Cape Town: Tafelberg, 2011, p.48.
69 DODDC, 32 Bn, Box 9, LOG/OPS/3/16/8, Vol. 1, Medies en gesondheid (verslae, aanvrae, ens.), Medical Report Buffalo April, p.1.
70 Feinstein, *Battle Scarred,* p.49.
71 DODDC, 32 Bn, Box 9, LOG/OPS/3/16/8, Vol. 1, Medies en gesondheid (verslae, aanvrae, ens.), Medical Report Buffalo April, p.2.
72 DODDC, Sektor 10 HK, Box 57, 204/3/AG, Komops Inligting oor Angola, International Committee of the Red Cross: *Bulletin; Special Edition: Angola 85–86.*

the presence of so many men. Child neglect and malnutrition take place and it is impossible for the medical personnel to provide constant supervision. The women still require a lot of educating.'[73]

Despite the efforts of the SADF medical personnel, child-fatalities at Buffalo were a cause for concern. For the period 21 April to 17 July 1978, 14 children died in the Kimbo. Although there was a permanent nurse posted there, the fact that she was from Angolan origin meant that, in the words of the base commander, the Kimbo residents regarded her as 'just one of us' and disregarded her advice about the treatment of their children.[74]

From very early in the existence of 32 Battalion, the realisation dawned that the dependents of the soldiers would require as much support as the soldiers themselves, and the unit did not stint in providing this support. When a sixteen-year-old girl was injured in a landmine explosion in the Kimbo in November 1977, she received medical attention equivalent to that which a SADF soldier would have received, including a 'casevac', or casualty evacuation, from the Kimbo to the hospital in Rundu.[75] Of course, why there was a mine in the Kimbo to start with is as significant as the medical attention that the girl received, and 32 Battalion launched an investigation into the matter, though the only outcome of the investigation was some rumours that a black soldier suspected that someone was visiting his wife while he was away, and had planted the mine as an ambush before he deployed.[76]

Former Angolan soldiers of 32 Battalion continued to be important to the unit's officers, even after their military value had expired. An example of this can be found in an illiterate Portuguese soldier who had been blinded in 1979 while serving with 32 Battalion. Although the unit did not retain him, he was given a job making baskets at 'Ga-Rankuwa' (of which he was quite proud) and visited regularly by a 32 Battalion delegate. When problems arose with his military salary / pension, a portion of which he was still receiving despite not serving in the unit anymore, the Chief Clerk of 32 Battalion was tasked with resolving the issue.[77] Another example is a Portuguese-speaking rifleman who had become disabled in the line of duty. Not only were his wife and child flown to 1 Military Hospital in Pretoria to be with him during the last part of his recovery in 1980, but on his return to Buffalo, his house in the Kimbo was adapted,

73 DODDC, 32 Bn, Box 41, 309/1/ALG, Vol. 1, Spesifieke Operasies Gesamentlik, Persoonlike verslag aan Bev 32 Bn deur Bev Buffalo Basis, par. 23. Afrikaans: *Die gemiddelde vrou se sedes is laag en dis is 'n groot probleem in die teenwoordigheid van die oorvloed mans. Kinderverwaarlosing en ondervoeding vind plaas en dit is onmoontlik vir die mediese personeel om deurentyd toesig te hou. Die vroue het nog baie opvoeding nodig.*

74 DODDC, 32 Bn, Box 41, 309/1/ALG, Vol. 1, Spesifieke Operasies Gesamentlik, Persoonlike verslag aan Bev 32 Bn deur Bev Buffalo Basis, par. 4. Afrikaans: *maar net een van ons.*

75 DODDC, 32 Bn, Box 56, 309/1, Vol. 5, Kontakte, Message OPS/944/NOV 77 from HQ 101 TF to C Army.

76 Nortje, *The Terrible Ones*, p.266.

77 DODDC, 32 Bn Gp 2, Box 28, 104/12/1/1/SP, Instandhouding van personeel: Welsynsdienste: Gevallewerk: Individuele persone, Letter to Cmdt. Nel.

with 32 Battalion's funds, to accommodate his disability. In addition, his wish that he be employed in a non-combatant capacity at the unit was entertained.[78]

By 1981, 32 Battalion had required a reputation as a unit that had more contact with the enemy than most other, regular SADF, units. Despite this, 32 Battalion did not only want the brightest and fittest men. They were willing to accommodate the SADF structures, which were loath to give exemption to National Service, and recorded 11 members with a G4K3 medical classification on their strength on 3 August 1981.[79]

In August 1985, a committee was established at Buffalo to investigate whether any cases of drug or alcohol abuse or addiction could be found in 32 Battalion. The committee came to the dubious conclusion that there were no such cases, but pointed out that the morale of both black and white troops should be closely monitored, as depression could lead to substance abuse.[80] Given that, a year earlier, 32 Battalion had been identified as the main culprit regarding 'tempting a barman' by asking them to bend the rules and provide them with more alcohol than their entitlement,[81] the findings of the committee are suspect, at least. Also, in 1980, 32 Battalion's command structures were aware of about 25 black members who regularly crossed the border into Botswana, 'mainly because of liquor, cannabis and women'.[82] Steps were taken to identify these people, and it is plausible that the problem was addressed to a certain extent, but to argue that the problem had completely been rooted out, and that there was no longer any substance related problems at 32 Battalion in 1985 seems a stretch of the imagination. However, since the incidents with the barmen were only applicable to officers, it is possible that the committee was more interested in preserving the peace in the Kimbo than with addressing substance abuse issues within its white ranks. Additionally, the SADF in general, and frontline combat units like 32 Battalion in particular, had a culture of addressing emotional and psychological issues 'in-house', usually with the assistance of alcohol. Feinstein paints an evocative picture of the situation at Oshakati:

> Alcohol is consumed by the gallon – I have never seen drinking on a scale like this before… Wherever I look I see hefty men seeking oblivion. The floodgates are opened when the sun goes down, when bottles are uncorked, caps are snapped loose

78 DODDC, 32 Bn Gp 2, Box 28, 104/12/1/1/SP, Instandhouding van personeel: Welsynsdienste: Gevallewerk: Individuele persone, Letter from Welfare Officer 1 Military Hospital to OC 32 Bn.

79 DODDC, 32 Bn Gp 2, Box 28, 104/12/1/1, Klagtes.

80 DODDC, 32 Bn Gp 2, Box 156, 522/1, Konferensies, Minutes of Drug Committee meeting held on 1 August 1985 at Buffalo Training Base.

81 DODD, 32 Bn Gp 2, Box 155, 522/1 (PRO), Vol. 1, Konferensies: Konferensies, Kongresse, Seminare, Simposium, Vergaderings, Notule van die Algemene Jaarvergadering van die Offisiereklub gehou te Rundu op 10H1700B Februarie 1984. Afrikaans: *'n kroegman in die versoeking stel.*

82 DODDC, 32 Bn Gp 2, Box 260, 522/1, Vol. 1, Konferensies, Kongresse, Seminare, Simposiums en Vergaderings: Konferensies, Notule van Bevelvoerderskonferense gehou te 32 Bn Hoofkwartier op 26 Jul 1980, p.4. Afrikaans: *hoofsaaklik agv drank, dagga en vrouens.*

> and heads are thrown back in relish. The bar of the Oshakati sports club is a picture of perfectly silent, mind-numbing misery.[83]

This is echoed by David da Silva (pseudonym), a former soldier of 32 Battalion.[84] Additionally, although alcohol was not sold to troops, they were issued with a generous ration every week, and often found ways to acquire more.[85] Johan Anderson, another former member of 32 Battalion, also recalls that heavy drinking was at the order of the day, particularly after big operations and/or suffering heavy casualties, like the unit did at Savate in 1980.[86] This would have created an appearance of normality in military units in Namibia and would have negated the need for units to appear 'soft' by continuously requesting psychiatric support from the SADF. Particularly in units that had a reputation to uphold, like 32 Battalion, maintaining the appearance that soldiers were not affected by what they were required to do was an important consideration.

By 1987, however, 32 Battalion had conceded that there was, in fact, a problem with drug use in the unit, particularly cannabis. This is not an altogether unexpected phenomenon, particularly in frontline units, and a survey in 1971 found that more than half of US troops used cannabis, although it only needed intervention in 4.2 percent of the cases.[87] At 32 Battalion, although the problem was prevalent throughout the unit, NSM were identified as particular culprits, and the unit instituted an elaborate programme to combat drug use. Members were given a period of amnesty, during which they could admit to using drugs and voluntarily submit to a rehabilitation programme, after which action would be taken against offender. The eight-point plan that 32 Battalion instituted relied on searching soldiers' baggage when they returned from leave, searching messes and personal equipment during inspections, education about the characteristics of cannabis, the legal aspects surrounding the use of cannabis, the social consequences of drug use, the physical consequences of drug use, spot checks on incoming parcels and addressing drug use during chaplain's periods.[88] Additionally, alcohol abuse was also recognised as a problem, and in 1988, nine members of 32 Battalion were considered alcoholics and received medical and social assistance specifically for alcohol abuse. Seven of the nine members responded positively to the treatment that the unit provided, and were considered rehabilitated and allowed to resume their normal duties. However, one

83 Feinstein, *Battle Scarred*, p.53.
84 Interview with David da Silva (pseudonym), former 32 Battalion soldier, Pretoria, 20-06-2019.
85 Telephonic interview with Gancho Gonzalez (pseudonym), former 32 Battalion soldier, Centurion, 04-07-2019.
86 Historical Papers, Missing Voices, A3079-B1-7-001, Johan Anderson, 12-11-2008, p.12.
87 M. W. Woodruff, *Unheralded Victory: The defeat of the Viet Cong and the North Vietnamese Army 1961–1973*. Arlington: Vandamere, 1999, pp.234–235.
88 DODD, 32 Bn Gp 2, Box 155, 522/1 (PRO), Vol. 1, Konferensies: Konferensies, Kongresse, Seminare, Simposium, Vergaderings, Notule van 32 Bataljon Eenheidskommitteevergadering gehou op 070800B April 1987 te 32 Bataljon Opleidingsbasis, Buffalo.

of the remaining two members did not respond to treatment at all, and were dismissed from the unit.[89]

By 1988, 32 Battalion was establishing 'a comprehensive social development programme', part of which was medical support to disabled members. Although 32 Battalion requested the assistance of medical experts for advice and training from the South African Medical Services, the facilities that were to be used to support the disabled members were constructed using the unit's own funds. This included a purpose-built facility for quadriplegics.[90] Once more, black members of the unit were not considered expendable, and considerable effort and resources was invested in supporting those who had been wounded in service of 32 Battalion and the SADF. The assistance that 32 Battalion provided to its wounded was in complete accordance with standard SADF procedures, with Policy Directive GS1/77/82 claiming that, 'rehabilitation is the combined and coordinated application of medical, social, educational and occupational measures to train or retrain the disabled individual to the highest level of his functional ability.'[91]

However, 32 Battalion provided much greater direct assistance to its members. The directive listed the responsibility of a particular unit towards disabled members as 'in addition to the reporting and documentation regarding injuries and compensation, also moral support and assistance with after-care services.'[92]

The fact that 32 Battalion constructed facilities to comply with the policy directive in-house, and did so at their own cost, rather than that of the SADF and, indirectly, the South African government is not only a positive reflection on the ethos of the unit, but also facilitated greater social cohesion, eliminating the need for soldiers to be removed from their families for rehabilitation. However, social convenience did not outweigh practical suitability, and at least one potential site for the rehabilitation centre was rejected as unsuitable.[93]

89 DODDC, 32 Bn Gp 2, Box 261, 522/1, Vol. 14, Konferensies, Notule van 32 Bataljon eenheidskomitee vergadering soos gehou op 071100B September 1988 te Konferensiekamer Buffalo, pp.1–2.

90 DODDC, 32 Bn Gp 2, Box 28, 104/12/5, Vol. 2, Instandhouding van Personeel: Welsynsdienste: Rehabilitasie van oorlogsgewondes, Mediese ondersteuning vir gestremde lede van 32 Bn. Afrikaans: *'n omvattende gemeenskapsontwikkelings program.*

91 DODDC, 32 Bn, Box 12, 101/7/1/4, Vol. 1, Ondersoek ivm implementering van hervestigingsbeleid van verminkte / oorlede lede van 32 Bn, Aanhangsel A by Beleidsdirektief No GS1/77/82: Hantering van die rehabilitasie en nasorg van SAW lede wat gestremd raak tydens die uitvoering van militêre diens, p.1. Afrikaans: *rehabilitasie is die gekombineerde en gekoördineerde toepassing van mediese, maatskaplike, opvoedkundige en beroepskundige maatreëls vir die opleiding of heropleiding van die gestremde individu tot op die hoogste vlak van sy funksionele vermoëns.*

92 DODDC, 32 Bn, Box 12, 101/7/1/4, Vol. 1, Ondersoek ivm implementering van hervestigingsbeleid van verminkte / oorlede lede van 32 Bn, Aanhangsel A by Beleidsdirektief No GS1/77/82, p.2. Afrikaans: *benewens die aanmelding en dokumentasie tov beserings en vergoeding, ook morele ondersteuning en hulp ivm nasorgdienste.*

93 DODDC, 32 Bn Gp 2, Box 261, 522/1, Vol. 14, Konferensies, Notule van 32 Bataljon eenheidskomitee vergadering soos gehou op 071100B September 1988 te Konferensiekamer Buffalo, p.1.

Financial

While the SADF personnel of 32 Battalion was paid through normal SADF channels, the foreign component presented a set of unique challenges, inter alia that they did not have South African (or Namibian) bank accounts that their salaries could be transferred to, that no salary scales existed for foreign troops – Pretoria would have found it difficult to pay blacks at the same level as whites, regardless of the occupation – and, perhaps most significantly, that they did not have the knowledge to effectively manage their finances and do effective financial planning.

After Breytenbach succeeded in securing salaries for the men of 32 Battalion (then Bravo Group) payments were initially made in cash, and the SADF demanded that proof of receipt had to be obtained by way of a signature. As many of 32 Battalion's Angolan soldiers were illiterate, thumbprints had to be taken, creating something a logistical logjam. Understandably, under normal circumstances, the army auditor also demanded a complete name list before any payments were made.[94] This was, however, a difficult task in the early, unorganised days of 32 Battalion and undoubtedly led to delayed and skipped payment of the already low salaries.

In September 1976, the 32 Battalion combined club recorded outstanding loans to 10 former Angolan members totalling R926,55.[95] This led to an awareness that, for the first time, the Angolan troops had a guaranteed income, but did not know how to manage this situation. In an attempt to shift the mentality from one of borrowing on future earnings to one of saving for future events, 32 Battalion instituted a savings scheme in December 1976. Since it was virtually impossible for troops stationed at the bases that the unit used to make use of normal banking channels, the administrative staff did the accounting in-house. This meant that only one bank account had to be opened for use of all the 32 Battalion soldiers, but at the same time it made deposits and withdrawals somewhat problematic. In an attempt to streamline the process as much as possible, 32 Battalion's policy was that deposits and withdrawals could only be done once a month, and even then deposits would only be paid out to the soldiers once someone from the unit had been able to visit the bank in Rundu where the account was kept. No banking fees were charged, and interest was paid at a rate of 4.5 percent p.a., accruable monthly. This was representative of the interest rates offered by banks and building societies at the time and was not, in any way, unfair towards or exploitative of the troops. Provision was also made to pay out funds of deceased members to relatives.[96]

While this system was somewhat crude and gaining access to funds in an emergency would have been difficult, the fact that soldiers were being educated about saving and encouraged to do so reflects the 32 Battalion command cadre's concern for the wellbeing

94 Nortje, *The Terrible Ones*, pp.161–162.
95 DODDC, 32 Bn, Box 9, LOG/OPS/3/16/9, Vol. 1, Menasies en inrigtings, Uitstaande bedrag gesamentlike klub: Rundu.
96 DODDC, 32 Bn, Box 9, LOG/OPS/3/16/9/1, Vol. 1, Spaar Fasiliteite, Constitution.

of the men under their command. In fact, a reasonable argument can be made that, if the greater SADF had made similar attempts at educating the young conscripts under their command about the benefits of saving, the current South African economy would have been in a better state. This positive attitude of 32 Battalion's officers is further apparent from the fact that the shop at Buffalo Base, that sold general merchandise to the civilian inhabitants of the Kimbo, operated on a gross profit margin of 15 percent,[97] at least until the administration of the shop was transferred from 32 Battalion to SADFI in 1982. Given that they had the monopoly on sales in the Kimbo, it would have been a simple matter to increase profits, and thereby funds available to the unit, at the cost of the civilians. This was not, however, the case and while it was necessary for the unit to generate its own source of income to supplement the support received from the SADF, the profit margin of the shop was by no means extravagant.

In 1981, according to a broker at Volkskas Insurance Brokers (VIB), the insurance company Sanlam became unwilling to continue providing life insurance to 'non-whites'. This led to significant confusion within the broader South Africa, and caused particular uncertainty in SADF and SWATF units that had non-white personnel.[98] Fortunately for these units, VIB found it 'absolutely unacceptable' that non-white members of the security forces were not allowed to have a choice in the way in which they chose to provide for their relatives and claimed that VIB 'wanted to continue to provide services to members of non-white battalions.'[99] To this end they offered an insurance package that served as both a life insurance policy, with additional benefits in case of accidental death, and an endowment policy. The average annual growth on this package was around 8 percent, with no increase in members' contributions.[100] This was offered in addition to the normal SADF Group Insurance, to which members of 32 Battalion were also entitled.[101]

It appears that, although the non-white SADF and SWATF members were a captive and potentially lucrative market for VIB, they did not view these units merely as cash cows, and made genuine efforts to pay out claims as efficiently and speedily as possible, to the extent of waiving normal requirements, such as post-mortem examinations in cases of accidental death, due to the unusual circumstances at the units.[102] However, when

97 DODDC, 32 Bn, Box 9, LOG/OPS/3/16/9, Vol. 1, Menasies en inrigtings, Profit and loss account of Woodpecker shop on 24.3.77.

98 DODDC, 32 Bn Gp 2, Box 61, 107/1/1, Vol. 2, Personeelbeskikking: Versekering / Assuransie: Groepversekering, Letter from A. Schiebler to Brig. W. C. Meyer, p.1. Afrikaans: *anderskleuriges*.

99 DODDC, 32 Bn Gp 2, Box 61, 107/1/1, Vol. 2, Personeelbeskikking: Versekering / Assuransie: Groepversekering, Letter from A Schiebler to Brig. W. C. Meyer, p.4. Volkskas was a mainstream bank in South Africa and later became part of the ABSA group. Afrikaans: *absoluut onaanvaarbaar*; *wil voortgaan om dienste ... aan lede van die AK Bataljons ... aan te bied.*

100 DODDC, 32 Bn Gp 2, Box 61, 107/1/1, Vol. 2, Personeelbeskikking: Versekering / Assuransie: Groepversekering, Insurance agreement.

101 Cf. DODDC, 32 Bn Gp 2, Box 61, 107/1/1/4, Vol. 2, Groeplewensversekering in die SAW, Groeplewensversekering vir militêre diens in die SA Weermag.

102 DODDC, 32 Bn Gp 2, Box 61, 107/1/1/4, Vol. 2, Groeplewensversekering in die SAW, Letter from A. Schiebler to WO1 CF Roza.

delays in finalising claims did occur, 32 Battalion was quick to support their members, as a letter from the OC 32 Battalion, Eddie Viljoen, to the Area Manager of VIB, dated 24 June 1983, attests. In the letter, Viljoen criticises the reasons that VIB gave for the delay in paying out life insurance claims, stating that 32 Battalion had provided all the necessary documentation and that VIB's request for additional information was unfounded and added to the emotional trauma of the families under his care.[103] Civilians who were dependant on 32 Battalion soldiers benefitted from the willingness of VIB to continue providing life insurance, as well as the support that they received from the 32 Battalion leadership. In an interesting phenomenon, provision made for blood relatives, rather than spouses, is much greater (see Table 5.4).

Life insurance policies were a relatively simple matter to resolve if a soldier passed away, since the beneficiary had to be nominated when the policy was accepted. The rest of the deceased's estate, however, was a different matter, and the former Angolan troops were not all familiar with the intricacies of wills and testaments. To address this, Eddie Viljoen made a point of ensuring that the last wills and testaments of all 32 Battalion members, both black and white, were up-to-date in 1983.[104] This was intended to reduce the chances of a deceased's estate being disputed, and to ensure that dependants could have access to the estate of the deceased in as short a time as possible.

Table 5.4: Summary of life insurance claims paid out March 1982 – August 1983[105]

Date of Death	Value of Policy	Beneficiary
12 March 1982	R7,632.48	Uncle
13 March 1982	R2,817.99	Brother
31 May 1982	R97.00	Brother
31 July 1982	R223.00	Wife
2 August 1982	R12,361.69	Cousin
10 February 1983	R171.61	Wife
3 April 1983	R953.37	Wife
3 April 1983	R7,785.20	Sister
3 April 1983	R12,529.05	Father
22 August 1983	R11,653.46	Brother

It also came to the attention of the SADF and SWATF that, when beneficiaries came into their inheritance, they frequently did not know how to make effective use of the relatively large amount of cash at their disposal. At an OC's conference in February 1985,

103 DODDC, 32 Bn Gp 2, Box 61, 107/1/1/4, Vol. 2, Groeplewensversekering in die SAW, Onafgehandelde versekeringseise.
104 DODDC, 32 Bn Gp 2, Box 262, 522/1/1, Vol. 2, Bevelvoerderskonferensies, Notule van 32 Bataljon Bevelvoerderskonferensie gehou te HK 32 Bn op 8 April 1983, p.2.
105 DODDC, 32 Bn Gp 2, Box 61, 107/1, Vol. 1, Personeelbeskikking: Lewensversekering, Afhandeling van boedel van gestorwe lede 32 Bataljon.

the answer suggested by the meeting was that funds should not be paid out directly to beneficiaries, but should rather be invested on their behalf by an organisation acting for the SADF and SWATF. The only resistance to this suggestion came from 32 Battalion who did not want control over their members' funds to pass out of the unit. Despite strong arguments about the advantages of having an umbrella organisation administrating the funds of all the black units, the representative of 32 Battalion held firm that the system that was in place at the unit was more advantageous. The system developed by 32 Battalion involved investing a portion of the inheritance in a long-term investment, but keeping part immediately accessible in a savings account.[106] This negated the need for beneficiaries to request their funds months in advance of needing it and, at face value, does seem to be a solution better suited to the unique socio-economic situation in which many black soldiers and dependents found themselves. The financial administration of 32 Battalion had come a long way, together with the socio-economic knowledge of the black members, from the days in 1981 when the mere fact that soldiers' monthly salaries were paid into bank accounts, rather than paid out in cash, had been a cause for concern within the unit.[107]

The contrast is even more apparent when compared to the 1980 suggestion that widows of soldiers who had passed away before 1 September 1979 – probably the date at which the SADF Group Insurance came into effect for 32 Battalion – should be encouraged to remarry, because this would solve their financial woes.[108] In a 2011 article for the *Journal of Refugee Studies*, Loren Landau and Marguerite Duponchel concluded that, more than 30 years later, it was still advantageous for female refugees in sub-Saharan Africa to be married.[109] This shows that suggesting that widows remarry might not have been as callous as it appears today, and was even sensible from a survival perspective. The complexity of relationships in the Kimbo indicates that the advice was, to an extent, taken to heart, if not necessarily through the legal marriage route. At least some of the informal relationships in the Kimbo were bound to have been between widows and soldiers. However, some widows were also probably expelled from the Kimbo in 1980, when 'squatters' were removed from the Kimbo and only soldiers, their wives and children were allowed to remain.

106 DODD, 32 Bn Gp 2, Box 155, 522/1 (PRO), Vol. 1, Konferensies: Konferensies, Kongresse, Seminare, Simposium, Vergaderings, Notule van 'n bevelvoerderskonferensie gehou te Bastion, SWA GM op 08 Feb 85 om 08h30.

107 DODDC, 32 Bn Gp 2, Box 260, 522/1, Vol. 1, Konferensies, Kongresse, Seminare, Simposiums en Vergaderings: Konferensies, Notule van Bevelvoerderskonferensie gehou te 32 Bn HK op 4 Des 81, p.2.

108 DODDC, 32 Bn Gp 2, Box 260, 522/1, Vol. 1, Konferensies, Kongresse, Seminare, Simposiums en Vergaderings: Konferensies, Notule van Basiskonferense gehou te 32 Bn Buffalo op 13 Mei 1980, p.3.

109 L. B. Landau & M. Duponchel, 'Law, Policies, or Social Position? Capabilities and the Determinants of Effective Protection in Four African Cities' in *Journal of Refugee Studies, 24 (1),* 2011, pp.6–13.

Wellbeing

Breytenbach's claim that the wellbeing of the black soldiers under his command, as well as that of their families, was important to him and the later Officers Commanding[110] is given credence by a request from the OC to the base commander at Buffalo on 27 January 1978. In this request, the base commander was asked to furnish 32 Battalion HQ with details of 'SP soldiers who, due to injuries, are not able to live a normal life and experienced a loss of income as a result, as well as SP soldiers who have passed way, leaving behind dependents with no refuge or source of income.'[111]

The purpose of this request was to implement a policy of relocation and/or rehabilitation of wounded or maimed 32 Battalion soldiers and their families. This goes a long way towards proving that, despite the 'sales pitch' – that it was more expedient for the SADF to sacrifice foreign, black soldiers than white South African lives in their fight against PLAN[112] – that Breytenbach had originally offered the SADF to get recognition for his unit, 32 Battalion was an anomaly in apartheid South Africa, where black and white seemed to genuinely care for one another. It also indicates that, from an early stage in the unit's existence, black soldiers knew that they could depend on their white leaders, which adds poignancy to the events at Pomfret after the war.

In 1980, 32 Battalion recognised that the duration of their patrols – typically six weeks – was placing a strain not only on the white personnel, but also on the blacks. To this end, two weeks' leave was granted to black troops returning from a patrol. While they were not allowed to leave the Kimbo during their leave period,[113] the fact that their leave actually exceeded that of their white counterparts, who were more rigorously bound by SADF rules and regulations, indicates a realisation that nobody, black or white, could continuously function under the trying conditions at 32 Battalion, which far exceeded SADF norms. This is also reflected in the base routine at Buffalo. While separate routines existed for white and black members, in reality they differed very little. The black troop had to rise half an hour before the whites, at 0500, rather than 0530, and had a daily inspection that the white troops did not. Morning tea and lunch were taken at the same time, and dinner was served to the black troops at 1730, when the whites had an order group. They only got their dinner an hour later. Lights out for

110 J. Breytenbach, *The Tempered Sword: Forged in Battle Revisited; Operation Savannah and the birth of 32 Bn*. Bushwarrior.com, 2011, pp.255–262.

111 DODDC, 32 Bn, Box 12, 101/7/1/4, Vol. 1, Ondersoek ivm implementering van hervestigingsbeleid van verminkte / oorlede lede van 32 Bn, Message from 32 Bn HQ to Base Commander, Buffalo, 27 January 1878. Afrikaans: *SP lede wat agv beserings nie in staat is om 'n normale lewe te voer nie en gevolglik inkomste moes verbeur, asook SP lede wat oorlede is met afhanklikes wat geen heenkome of inkomste het nie.*

112 Breytenbach, *The Tempered Sword, p.256.*

113 DODDC, 32 Bn Gp 2, Box 260, 522/1, Vol. 1, Konferensies, Kongresse, Seminare, Simposiums en Vergaderings: Konferensies, Notule van Basiskonferense gehou te 32 Bn Buffalo op 13 Mei 1980, p.3.

both groups was at 2200.[114] It can only be surmised what the difference in quality of the meals would, or would not, have been, but that is a common occurrence in military messes throughout the world. Officers' messes are inevitably better stocked and equipped than WO's messes, which in turn are superior to NCO's messes and so forth. The actual difference in the schedules of the two groups amount to very little, and is another example of how 32 Battalion did not treat or value their white members more highly than their black members, just because of their race or origins. A fact that is easily overlooked on these schedules is that, except for Sundays, when brunch was served, all the men of 32 Battalion received three meals per day. That might seem trivial but, keeping in mind where the most of these men came from, it was a vast improvement on their past circumstances. Rations at 32 Battalion were not only supplied regularly, but were also considered to be of a high standard.

Although it cannot be proved conclusively, it seems that 32 Battalion was not averse to bending the rules in order to protect its members and their families. On 4 February 1981, the Acting Assistant Magistrate of Rundu sent a letter to 32 Battalion, requesting that a certain Kavango woman, the wife of an Angolan 32 Battalion soldier, and her children be found and sent to Rundu, because they were 'urgently wanted by the mother ... for one and certain reason [*sic*].'[115] In reaction to this rather vague request, on 24 February 32 Battalion informed the Magistrate's Office that, 'this unit conducted a search for the ... woman and children but they couldn't be found.'[116] It is, of course possible that the woman and her children were not present at Buffalo, but the tone of the correspondence suggests that 32 Battalion was not particularly eager to place the people under their protection at the mercy of the civilian government in Rundu and that they considered it in the best interest of the woman, her children and her husband if she 'could not be found'.

As with any other SADF or SWATF unit, the families and loved ones of the white NSM that served with 32 Battalion were concerned about their wellbeing. Breytenbach and Ferreira, in particular, were frequent correspondents with families in South Africa, and their letters exhibit a sensitivity for their men and their families.[117] In addition, from 1985 married members of 32 Battalion were allowed to bring their children to social events, such as barbecues, provided that the parents supervise their children.[118]

114 DODDC, 32 Bn Gp 2, Box 260, 522/1, Vol. 1, Konferensies, Kongresse, Seminare, Simposiums en Vergaderings: Konferensies, Notule van Basiskonferensie gehou te 32 Bn Buffalo op 28 Maart 1980, pp.2–4.
115 DODDC, 32 Bn Gp 2, Box 28, 104/12/1/1/SP, Vol. 4, Instandhouding van Personeel: Welsynsdienste; Gevallewerk: Individuele Persone, Letter from Rundu Magistrate's Office to 32 Bn.
116 DODDC, 32 Bn Gp 2, Box 28, 104/12/1/1/SP, Vol. 4, Instandhouding van Personeel: Welsynsdienste; Gevallewerk: Individuele Persone, Letter from 32 Bn to Rundu Magistrate's Office.
117 Cf. DODDC, 32 Bn Gp 2, Box 28, 104/12/1/1.
118 DODD, 32 Bn Gp 2, Box 155, 522/1 (PRO), Vol. 1, Konferensies: Konferensies, Kongresse, Seminare, Simposium, Vergaderings, Minutes of Officers' Meeting held on 29 April 1985 at Buffalo Training Base.

The sensitivity to the plight of 32 Battalion's black troops also spilled over to a greater level of compassion for the white NSM of the unit than was apparent elsewhere in the SADF. In this vein, 32 Battalion was willing to entertain a request from one of their lieutenants (of which there was a chronic shortage) to be transferred back to South Africa to take care of his ailing mother and teenage sister early in 1987. The matter was investigated internally, with help from a preacher in the lieutenant's home town, thereby cutting out much of the red tape that accompanied such requests in regular SADF units.[119] Later in the same year, Sector 20 heeded 32 Battalion's petitions for a permanent social work officer at Buffalo, although they stipulated that the officer had to address the needs of 201 Battalion (formerly 31 Battalion) at Omega base as well.[120] Despite the imposed workload, the addition of a social worker to the unit could only have been invaluable in social circumstances as trying as those experienced by 32 Battalion.

However, 32 Battalion's loyalty seemingly only extended to their own, and as early as 1980, a decision was taken that 'all squatters in the Kimbo be relocated,' as the Kimbo was reserved for soldiers, their wives and children.[121] At face value, this decision makes sense. The unit already found itself in unknown territory, having to take care of not only soldiers, but also civilians. Having civilians that were not directly linked to 32 Battalion would put an unnecessary drain on their resources, and would diminish the efficiency with which they could take care of the men, women and children in their care. Gert Nel had made a concerted effort to introduce some stability in the Kimbo in 1978, when he held a mass marriage ceremony for some 350 couples.[122] This went some way towards formalising the domestic situation in the Kimbo, but over the following years, the situation returned to something resembling its earlier, haphazard state. In October 1988, when it started becoming apparent that 32 Battalion would not be able to remain at Buffalo in Namibia indefinitely, the unit was faced with the realisation that the loopholes of the war-days would soon start closing. They launched an investigation into the marital situation in the unit, in order to facilitate soldiers and their dependents claiming benefits from the SADF. During this investigation, they realised that there were three categories of relationships in the Kimbo: couples legally married with a marriage certificate, couples who lived together without any legal documentation, and couples that were legally married in Angola, but who did not have a certificate to that effect.[123] However, the SADF only recognised legally binding marriages, with the accompanying

119 DODDC, 32 Bn Gp 2, Box 28, 104/12/1/1, Message PERS/695/20 JUN 87 from NW Cmd to 32 Bn.
120 DODDC, 32 Bn Gp 2, Box 28, 104/12/1/1, Message MWO/022/MEI 87 from Med Dept Sector 20 to 201 Bn, 32 Bn.
121 DODDC, 32 Bn Gp 2, Box 260, 522/1, Vol. 1, Konferensies, Kongresse, Seminare, Simposiums en Vergaderings: Konferensies, Notule van Bevelvoerderskonferensie gehou te 32 Bataljon Hoofkwartier op 23 Feb 1980, p.3. Afrikaans: *alle plakkers in die Kimbo uitgeplaas word.*
122 Nortje, *The Terrible Ones*, pp.327–328.
123 DODDC, 32 Bn Gp 2, Box 261, 522/1, Vol. 14, Konferensies, Notule van 32 Bataljon eenheidskomitee vergadering soos gehou op 110830B Oktober 1988 te Konferensiekamer Buffalo, p.2.

certificates, much like the internal decision taken in 1980. Unlike 1980, though, this time the unit recognised this to be a problem, particularly regarding immigration and benefit entitlement, and arranged for a 'marriage team' to come to Buffalo to provide the necessary documentation to the families that needed it,[124] much like Nel had done some 10 years earlier. In the interim, they had their chaplain start to issue temporary affidavits to help families stay together and receive aid from the SADF.[125]

The contrast between the two situations is stark: in 1980, only legally married couples and their children were allowed to stay in the Kimbo, but it took a considerable time before a plan was made to accommodate those that were not legally married. In 1988, the problem had reappeared, but this time 32 Battalion was much more accommodating towards the members that were not legally married. This raises the question of how many people were unnecessarily turned away from the Kimbo in 1980, because of a technicality, as Nel's mass marriage plans had clearly deteriorated over time.

By 1988, social interaction between black and white members of 32 Battalion was such that the unit's chaplain recorded that 'the focal point of the whites had moved from the base to the lines.'[126] In addition to socialising in the 'lines', the area where unmarried soldiers lived, it was also quite common for white leaders to be invited to the Kimbo, e.g. for dinner with a member of their platoon and his family.[127] In other words, white troops were no longer spending their free time in the base, isolated from the black troop lines, but instead chose to spend their free time in the company of their black brothers-in-arms. This was the case to such an extent that 32 Battalion decided to convert the recreational hall in the base into offices, and construct a new hall in the troop lines as a matter of priority, where soldiers would have access to a canteen, television room, games, a reading room, coffee room and bathroom.[128]

It is important to view the events described in this section against the backdrop of apartheid South Africa. Without commenting extensively on the relationship, or lack thereof, between black and white at the time, it is sufficient to point out that it was strained, at best. Anthony Feinstein's recollection provides a microcosm: when a helicopter carrying bodies landed at Ondangwa, a SADF captain walked over, looked inside

124 DODDC, 32 Bn Gp 2, Box 261, 522/1, Vol. 14, Konferensies, Notule van 32 Bataljon eenheidskomitee vergadering soos gehou op 071100B September 1988 te Konferensiekamer Buffalo, p.1. Afrikaans: *huwelikspan*.

125 DODDC, 32 Bn Gp 2, Box 261, 522/1, Vol. 14, Konferensies, Notule van 32 Bataljon eenheidskomitee vergadering soos gehou op 110830B Oktober 1988 te Konferensiekamer Buffalo, p.1.

126 DODDC, 32 Bn Gp 2, Box 261, 522/1, Vol. 14, Konferensies, Notule van 32 Bataljon eenheidskomitee vergadering soos gehou op 110830B Oktober 1988 te Konferensiekamer Buffalo, p.3. Afrikaans: *die fokuspunt van die Blankes verskuif het van die basis na die lyne toe.*

127 Telephonic interview with Gancho Gonzalez (pseudonym), former 32 Battalion soldier, Centurion, 04-07-2019.

128 DODDC, 32 Bn Gp 2, Box 261, 522/1, Vol. 14, Konferensies, Notule van 32 Bataljon eenheidskomitee vergadering soos gehou op 110830B Oktober 1988 te Konferensiekamer Buffalo, p.3.

the body bags and concluded 'Oh, it is only blacks',[129] turned around and went to the bar for a beer, seemingly unaffected by the casualties that the SADF had just suffered. At 32 Battalion, however, racial lines became increasingly blurred, not only in terms of the somewhat paternalistic way in which white South Africans viewed blacks, but to the point where whites *chose* to spend their free time with their black brothers-in-arms, rather than in the company of one another. The level of compassion and care exhibited by whites towards blacks, and the loyalty of the troops in the unit are more examples of atypical apartheid South Africa behaviour.

Conclusion

A product of its time, 32 Battalion cannot be removed from its surroundings and, indeed, its birthplace: apartheid South Africa. For this reason, favouritism was bound to be prevalent in the unit. Nobody could argue that white and black members were treated absolutely equally. While some of the discrepancies can be put down to differences in ranks – there were only a few black NCOs and no black officers during the early years of the unit – that is not the exclusive cause. Most of the white leaders were sympathetic to their black troops, but it was inevitable that some were biased, too. Additionally, SADF structures were well-established along segregated lines, making any support to the black members outside of 32 Battalion particularly challenging. Nevertheless, the majority of the black soldiers and civilians saw a significant increase in quality of life, starting with things as basic as receiving regular food, through to education, medical attention and support, and financial planning. A reasonable argument can be made that none of this would have been possible if they had chosen to remain in Angola. The interaction between black and white in 32 Battalion, as well as the amount of time and resources expended towards providing for the black contingent, far outweighed the South African norm. The crucible that was 32 Battalion not only shaped the unit, but also provided invaluable guidelines for shaping a multiracial, democratic South Africa in years ahead.

129 Feinstein, *Battle Scarred*, p.62. Afrikaans: *Ag, dis net swartes.*

6

'The Quench': The Battalion in South Africa

The future of units like 32 Battalion was always going to be uncertain after the war. From 1976, they had been assured by SADF officers that 'there is a future for you'[1] and, as a result, they had served South Africa's interests with distinction and emerged from the forge of the Border War as a complete and effective blade but, as is often the case with military units that excel at their task, was something of a liability at the cessation of hostilities. As it became increasingly clear that the United Nations' Resolution 435 – South African and Cuban withdrawal from Angola and Namibia – was going to be implemented, the future of the SADF's 'irregular' units was discussed at a SWATF Chaplain's Conference in 1988. There Brigadier Van der Westhuizen noted that the SADF's Chief of Staff Personnel had indicated that, after the war, these units would be demilitarised, but would continue to be employed by the, presumably Namibian, 'Government' and would continue to receive remuneration. However, a handwritten note on the document, probably by Chaplain Sydney Middlemost of 32 Battalion, indicates quite clearly that this was not an acceptable compromise, stating in rather stern Afrikaans: 'No – 32 is going to the RSA.'[2] Chaplain Middlemost's prediction would prove accurate, but it would not necessarily be a beneficial move for the members of 32 Battalion.

The logistics of moving around 3,500 people from the north of Namibia to South Africa was a challenging, as was the entire SADF withdrawal from Namibia. This was complicated by the fact that, as word spread about the relocation, civilians turned up at Buffalo in ever increasing numbers, intending to join the exodus to South Africa. The daily strength return at Buffalo on 23 May was 2,786 soldiers and civilians;[3] on 24 May

1 Interview with Edwin Eduardo (pseudonym), son of former 32 Battalion soldier; Kimbo and Pomfret resident, Wonderboom, 24-06-2019.

2 DODDC, 32 Bn Gp 2, Box 261, 522/1, Vol. 1, Konferensies / Kongresse / Seminare / Simposiums / Vergaderings: Notules, Notule van SWAGM Kapelaansdiens-konferensie gehou te Bastion, HK SWAGM van 15–16 September 1988. Afrikaans: *Regering; Nee – 32 gee pad RSA toe.*

3 DODDC, 32 Bn Gp 3, Box 54, 309/1, Vol. 1, Spesifieke Operasies (Agree), Message PERS/044 from 32 Bn to 32 Bn Tak HK.

this rose to 3,169[4] and the number increased again to 3,502 on 25 May.[5] The number of SADF personnel remained roughly constant.

In April 1991, 32 Battalion changed to a battalion group, and the two subservient operational battalions were known as 321 and 322 Battalions.[6] '321 Battalion was parabats ... they were trained at Bloemfontein ... 322 Battalion was Mech [mechanised Infantry] who were at ... Lohatla.'[7]

The quench is the ultimate test of a forged weapon: however good the blade might seem, it is of no use if it does not survive the quench. The quench of 32 Battalion took place after the Border War, when they relocated to South Africa. Unfortunately for the unit, they had very little influence and control over their own quench; if they had, their history might have looked quite different.

Active Deployment

Township Operations

With the withdrawal of the SADF from Namibia in 1989, 32 Battalion was relocated to Pomfret in South Africa's North West Province. Edwin Eduardo (pseudonym), the son of a 32 Battalion soldier, thinks that the SADF's choice of Pomfret was not incidental:

> The only reason why they opted for Pomfret was because of the politics of the day. The country was still not stable – there was [*sic*] a lot of uncertainties – so what people in high positions thought would be ideal was to keep us as far as possible ... For me, the move was very strategic ... in the sense that they wanted to keep us as far away from other as possible.[8]

The unit's perennial leadership problem now suddenly evaporated. From very few white South Africans willing to join the unit during the Border War, the availability of white leaders now outstripped vacancies.[9] It seemed that white South Africa was more willing to join a racially integrated unit when it was not almost continuously

4 DODDC, 32 Bn Gp 3, Box 54, 309/1, Vol. 1, Spesifieke Operasies (Agree), Message PERS/050 from 32 Bn to 32 Bn Tak HK. Afrikaans: *321 Bataljon was parabats ... hulle het opleiding gekry in Bloemfontein ... 322 Bataljon was Meg [gemeganiseerde infanterie] wat by Lohatla ... was.*

5 DODDC, 32 Bn Gp 3, Box 54, 309/1, Vol. 1, Spesifieke Operasies (Agree), Message PERS/056 from 32 Bn HK to 32 Bn Tak HK.

6 P. Nortje, *The Terrible Ones: A complete history of 32 Battalion.* Cape Town: Zebra, 2012, p.1136.

7 Interview with Hilton Husson (pseudonym), former 32 Battalion soldier, Centurion, 10-07-2019.

8 Interview with Edwin Eduardo (pseudonym), son of former 32 Battalion soldier; Kimbo and Pomfret resident, Wonderboom, 24-06-2019.

9 Nortje, *The Terrible Ones,* p.1120.

deployed in a combat capacity. This new influx of white officers and NCOs created some tension within the ranks of 32 Battalion, with the black soldiers loath to accept untried white newcomers and the existing leader group also viewed them with suspicion. Relocating to South Africa had done little to diminish the unit's pride, and the wearing of the coveted 32 Battalion 'camo beret' continued to be viewed as a badge of honour. This is emphasised by the fact that Colonel Machiel[10] Delport, then OC 32 Battalion, had to give special permission for a senior NCO, with RSM status, who was apparently not permanently assigned to 32 Battalion, to wear the unit's beret at a parade.[11] Internal matters such as these did not, however, influence the operational readiness of the unit and, although the SADF planned to initially deploy them to the South African borders with Zimbabwe and Botswana, urban warfare training started soon after their arrival at Pomfret. 'In the unit, on the parade ground, they did … COIN-urban drills. At the back of the unit, we had a complete shooting range … and we had a training ground … This COIN-urban training and doctrine was taught to them there … before they deployed.'[12]

This training was not, however, exhaustive or comprehensive and, during deployments in May 1990, Northern Cape Command had to authorise 'internal' training, while on deployment, of soldiers that had not received the necessary training in the use of shotguns.[13] The soldiers of 32 Battalion would, undoubtedly, have known how to use shotguns, so the aim of this training could only have been how to use shotguns in an urban, civilian environment. The unit's relative lack of experience in such contexts highlights how valuable such training would have been, if done prior to deployment; it borders on cynicism to deploy a 'foreign' unit, with little or no prior experience of peacekeeping, without comprehensive retraining.

The SADF rightly recognised that rural COIN operations, such as those undertaken on South Africa's borders, would be a natural continuation of the northern Namibian COIN operations in which 32 Battalion excelled. These operations, combined with the fact that 32 Battalion was now effectively also protecting South Africa's own borders against illegal immigration, agreed with the SADF's perception that COIN warfare was 'a carefully co-ordinated system of actions, political, economic, administrative,

10 There is some confusion over Delport's first name. Nortje refers to him as 'Machiel', while Bretenbach call him 'Michau'. He was also known by his nickname, 'Mucho'.

11 DODDC, 32 Bn Gp 3, Box 54, 309/1, Vol. 1, Spesifieke Operasies (Agree), Message from 1 Op Bn to 32 Bn.

12 Interview with Charles Churra (pseudonym), former 32 Battalion soldier, Pretoria, 15-05-2019. Afrikaans: *Binne die eenheid, op die paradegrond, het hulle … TEIN-stedelike drills gedoen. Ons het aan die agterkant van die eenheid 'n volledige skietbaan gehad … en ons het 'n opleidingsterrein gehad… Hierdie TEIN-stedelike oefening en doktrine is daar met hulle geleer … voor hulle ontplooi is.*

13 DODDC, 32 Bn Gp 3, Box 54, 309/1, Vol. 1, Spesifieke Operasies (Agree), Message OPL/845/MEI 90 from Kmdmt NK to Gp 21 HK, Gp 22 HK, Gp 23 HK, 3 SAI Opl Eenh, 8 SAI Opl Eenh, 31 Bn, 32 Bn.

psychological, police and military.'[14] Despite the enmity of white farmers in the area, border operations were generally successful. In October 1989, Far North Command's SO1 Personnel, Commandant J. A. Kruger, together with 32 Battalion's second in command, Major T. van Staden, inspected the units deployed on South Africa's borders, under the command of 32 Battalion. His impressions were overwhelmingly positive; the following excerpt from his report is a microcosm of the whole: 'Here I would like to compliment Lt Andrè of 32 Battalion. He and his men presented impeccably. His TB [temporary base] was clean, neat and beyond reproach. One could see that they were truly proud to be soldiers and that they had comprehensive knowledge of their task. All the other members were clean, ready and awake.'[15]

However, urban deployments were a greater challenge. The SADF reasoned that the Portuguese-speaking, Angolan soldiers of 32 Battalion would be ideal for township duty, because they were black but did not share the political views of the majority of black South Africans. The men of 32 Battalion were, indeed, less politically motivated than the rest of South Africa, including the other SADF units and the SAP, and were successfully deployed – effectively as a police force – to curb unrest on a number of occasions between 1989 and 1992.[16] During initial deployments, the SADF was at pains to establish whether 32 Battalion was effective and efficient in their new role. For the most part, the feedback was positive and seemed to underscore the SADF thinking in their deployment of 32 Battalion on township duty. The Greytown Municipality, for example, reported that 'The majority of the inhabitants apparently welcome the presence of 32 Battalion, as it is the only effective way of controlling unrest in the area. My council did not receive any complaints about members of 32 Battalion not being impartial in the discharge of their duties.'[17]

But the fact that 32 Battalion was, to a large extent, used to operating by their own rules in a context somewhat isolated from society was bound to haunt them. According to guidelines at a 1988 Infantry Training Conference, encouraging SADF personnel to act decisively during urban deployments, even in the absence of SAP members, 'The SADF has ... exactly the same powers as the SAP [except]

14 C. A. Fraser, *Revolutionary Warfare: basic principles of counter-insurgency (being a revision of 'Lessons learnt from past revolutionary wars')*. 4 Survey and Printing Regiment, p.1.

15 DODDC, 32 Bn Gp 3, Box 100, 520/4, Vol. 1, Binnelandse bewegings, Besoek aan basisse in gebied SMG deur SO1 Pers vanaf 24 tot 27 Okt 89. Afrikaans: *Hier wil ek graag 'n kompliment gee vir Lt Andrè van 32 BN. Hy en sy manne kon deur 'n ring getrek word. Sy TB was onberispelik skoon en netjies. 'n Mens kon sien dat hulle waarlik trots is om soldate te wees en hulle ken hulle taak uit-en-uit. Al die ander lede was skoon, paraat en wakker.*

16 Cf. Nortje, *The Terrible Ones*, pp.1116–1161.

17 DODDC, 32 Bn Gp. 3, Box 54, 309/1, Spesifieke Operasies, Letter from Greytown Town Clerk to Maj. Fourie. Afrikaans: *Die meerderheid inwoners verwelkom blykbaar die teenwoordigheid van 32-Bataljon aangesien dit die enigste effektiewe manier is om die onrus in die woongebied te beheer. My raad het geen klagtes ontvang dat die lede van 32-Bataljon nie onpartydig is in die uitvoering van hul pligte nie.*

the investigation of crime.'[18] This removed a potential restraining mechanism from the SADF, which would have been particularly necessary for units like 32 Battalion after the war. As a result, several allegations were made about 32 Battalion, including murder, assault and rape,[19] though very few were ever prosecuted. For the most part, South African society seemed to echo the thoughts of the Greytown inhabitants, though on occasion enquiries about the actions of 32 Battalion were escalated to the ministerial level. It is understandable that South African politicians were concerned about the actions of an, essentially, foreign force within their borders and occasional ministerial enquiries were justifiable. To continue referring charges against 32 Battalion to higher echelons, after some of the initial enquiries had been successfully defended, seems excessive, however.[20] It is therefore perhaps not a pure coincidence that the final withdrawal of 32 Battalion from township duties, and therefore from a role of useful contribution to South African society, was due to an investigation into the Phola Park incident in April 1992, where charges of brutality were brought against 32 Battalion members.[21]

The incident was widely criticised by the South African media, frequently anonymously[22] and sometimes at the behest of the ANC.[23] Writing in 1989, three years before the Phola Park incident, Laurie Nathan describes the SADF's role in the townships using evocative terms like 'invasion', 'raid' and 'repression'.[24] While 32 Battalion took no part in shaping the social opposition to township deployments – they were still actively deployed in Namibia at the time – they were convenient scapegoats in the early 1990s. Although no criminal proceedings were initiated against 32 Battalion, the SADF decided to accept the advice of the Goldstone Commission, who investigated the Phola Park incident, and withdraw 32 Battalion from township duty.[25] Despite the recommendations of the Commission, it is likely that 32 Battalion acted in accordance with SADF guidelines at Phola Park. A Command Cadre's Conference of Northern Cape Command, held in July 1992, reiterated the command directive of the SADF regarding operations, which enabled commanders 'to act immediately in cases where lives and

18 DODDC, 32 Bn Gp 2, Box 262, 522/1/1, Vol. 7, Bevelvoerderskonferensies, Notule van 'n Infanterie opleidingskonferensie gehou te SA Leërkollege oor die tydperk 5–6 Julie 1988. Afrikaans: *Die SAW het … presies dieselfde magte as die SAP [behalwe] die ondersoek van misdaad.*
19 E. Janssen, 'Why was SADF in Phola Park?' in *Pretoria News*, 10 April 1992.
20 DODDC, 32 Bn Gp 3, Box 160, 509/1, Vol. 2, Ministeriele Navrae m.b.t. personeelaangeleenthede, Enquiry: shooting incident and alleged harassment: members 32 Bn.
21 Nortje, *The Terrible Ones*, pp.1149–1154.
22 Janssen, 'Why was SADF in Phola Park?; Anon., 'Phola Park: SADF to hold an inquiry' in *The Citizen*, 11 April 1992; Anon., 'Phola Park Raid' in *Sunday Times*, 12 April 1992; S. Nyaka, 'Reliving the nightmare of 32 Battalion raid' in *The Sunday Star*, 12 April 1992.
23 Anon., 'Mass assaults, rapes: SADF denies ANC claims' in *The Star*, 10 April 1992.
24 L. Nathan, 'Troops in the townships, 1984–1987' in J. Cock, & L. Nathan (eds), *War and Society; The militarisation of South Africa*. Cape Town: David Philip, 1989, pp.68–69.
25 Nortje, *The Terrible Ones*, p.1156.

property are at risk' and recommended that it is advisable to 'do too much, too soon' and deal with the aftermath later.[26]

Social

The SADF chose Pomfret as the sight of 32 Battalion's new home, because it was, in a sense, a ready-made community. The town had been an asbestos mining town before it had been abandoned, and all the facilities still existed, although in differing states of disrepair.[27] The relocation of 32 Battalion from Buffalo to Pomfret, while not quite a return to 1976, saw the resurgence of problems that had been experienced, and resolved, in Namibia. An example of this can be found in June 1991, when the water supply to the troops' lines became faulty, and they had to rely on a tanker to supply them with water.[28] In a document to the SAMS HQ on 27 November 1991, Captain P. H. Hartslief, writing on behalf of the OC, Colonel Machiel Delport, highlighted some of the social difficulties that 32 Battalion experienced at the time:[29]

- Out of 34 disabled persons at 32 Battalion, 28 were employed actively within the unit. The remaining six lived in a home that was constructed from the unit's own regimental fund, but this home was located 3km from the SADFI shop. As five of the six were wheelchair-bound, they experienced difficulties in getting access to the SADFI shop to purchase basic necessities.
- Two former members of 32 Battalion still lived in Pomfret (and presumably received a degree of support from the unit) but were no longer on SADF strength. This meant that their unserviceable wheelchairs could not be replaced through normal SAMS channels.
- While 32 Battalion was based in Namibia, none of the unit's foreign soldiers had contributed to a pension fund. They only started making monthly contributions in June 1989, which meant that there were members who would only receive their contributions back on retirement, as they had not contributed for a long enough period. Captain Hartslief pointed out that this would be 'totally insufficient' to cover even the most basic costs of living. He explained the difficulties in securing civilian employment in Pomfret after retirement and suggested that a retirement

26 DODDC, 32 Bn Gp 3, Box 101, 522/1, Vol. 5, Konferensies, Notule van bevelskader konferensie gehou te LAS/10 LA Regt oor tydperk 17 tot 18 Julie 1992. Afrikaans: *om onmiddelik op te tree in gevalle waar lewens en eiendom bedreig word*; *doen te veel te gou*.
27 Interview with Charles Churra (pseudonym), former 32 Battalion soldier, Pretoria, 15-05-2019.
28 DODDC, 32 Bn Gp 3, Box 19, 522/1, Vol. 4, Konferensies, Notule van die 32 Bn weeklikse konferensie gehou op 260845B Jun 91 in die sportsaal te Pomfret.
29 DODDC, 32 Bn Gp 3, Box 28, 104/12/4, Vol. 1, Maatskaplike werkdiens: Nasorg van oorlogbeseerdes, Finiansiële hulp aan oorlogsgestremdes, weduwees en weeskinders: 32 Bn. Afrikaans: *totaal ontoereikend*.

home be built in the town to provide subsidised housing for former 32 Battalion members with insufficient means, as well as for the widows of members who had passed away in Namibia and Angola. The estimated cost of the project was R2.5 million at the time, approximately R17 million in 2025 terms.[30]

- Members of 32 Battalion did not contribute to the SADF's medical continuation fund, which meant that their medical privileges did not transfer to their dependents on their deaths. While four of the 14 widows living in the base had remarried, the remaining 10 and their children had no recourse to SADF medical support. While 32 Battalion did not cease their support, contrary to SADF policy, they could not refer these women and children to other SADF units and facilities for more complex and comprehensive medical care, as they were not part of the SADF's administrative system. This meant that, inter alia, the service of an optometrist was not available to them. Hartslief therefore suggested that some form of a medical aid scheme be provided for the widows and their children.
- Members of 32 Battalion were seldom able to provide for their children's education, and Hartslief recommended that scholarships be awarded not only to orphans, but to all black students who completed high school.

Immigration

At the end of 1988, in a personnel plan for 1989, Major K. D. Koekemoer, 32 Battalion's Head Administrative Officer, identified acquiring permanent South African citizenship for long-serving members, and temporary citizenship for the 1987 and 1988 intakes, as a priority goal for the unit's administrative office.[31] However, six months later the unit would find itself based in South Africa, with much of the administration surrounding immigration and citizenship still incomplete. This would have considerable implications not only for soldiers of 32 Battalion, but also for their dependants, as life in South Africa would be much more strictly regulated than at Buffalo.

Two years after 32 Battalion's move to South Africa, the unit's command group took a strict approach to 'illegals', and those housing or supporting them, on the base. These 'illegals' were blamed for most of the unit's problems.[32] It is, of course, perfectly plausible that someone from outside the unit could, indeed, cause problems in the unit. However, strictly speaking many of the wives and dependents would also have been considered 'illegals', if all the necessary paperwork had not been completed. Additionally, it was considered illegal for 32 Battalion to 'house people without RSA citizenship.'[33] However, the unit also recognised that not all the applications of soldiers' dependents for South

30 Inflation rates from http://www.inflation.eu/inflation-rates/south-africa/historic-inflation/cpi-inflation-south-africa.aspx [Accessed 26-06-2018].

31 DODDC, 32 Bn Gp 3, Box 75, 501/4, Vol. 4, Bevel en Beheer: 32 Bn doelwitte, 32 Bataljon Personeelplan 1989.

32 DODDC, 32 Bn Gp 3, Box 19, 522/1, Vol. 4, Konferensies, Minutes of the 32 Battalion weekly conference held on 210900B May 1991 in the sports club at Pomfret.

33 DODDC, 32 Bn Gp 3, Box 101, 522/1, Vol. 3, Konferensies, Minutes of the 32 Battalion weekly conference held on 080900B May 1991 in the sports club at Pomfret.

African citizenship had been finalised, pointing out that they could not be registered as dependents if they were not citizens.[34] To a certain extent, though, the problem was of 32 Battalion's own making, as they did not provide much assistance to their members in going through the legalities of a marriage in South Africa. In contrast with Gert Nel's mass marriage ceremony in 1978 in September 1990, there was a five-year waiting time for marriages among the black members of the unit,[35] probably due to the more complicated administrative system in South Africa. This combination of factors had dire implications for legitimate dependants who had not yet received South African citizenship, a process which was, by no means, simple. In December 1991, 32 Battalion's command group was informed that 'a woman from Namibia who marries a soldier of the unit can obtain RSA citizenship after two years.'[36] While a 'woman from Namibia' could potentially be an Angolan woman who had lived at Buffalo with 32 Battalion, the ambiguous language that does not include Angolan women could potentially be problematic. More poignantly, though: before the two-year waiting period had elapsed, 32 Battalion had ceased to exist.

Education

At the end of 1988, when planning for the relocation of 32 Battalion had already started, Pica Pau school recorded a total of 866 learners, an increase of 230 from the previous year. The requirement for teachers grew concurrently, and eight new teachers were requested, five of whom had to be conversant in Portuguese.[37] The number of subjects taught at the school had also expanded considerably, and the school boasted students of all primary and secondary school levels (cf. Table 6.1).

Although Pica Pau school had been under the administration of SWA National Education since 1982, an inventory of textbooks at the new school in Pomfret still indicated severe shortages. The school made use of a total of 14 different textbooks (including a Bible) for all standards / grades, but identified a shortage of an additional 19 different textbooks, indicating that the school had less than half of the necessary books at their disposal.[38]

34 DODDC, 32 Bn Gp 3, Box 101, 522/1, Vol. 3, Konferensies, Notule van die 32 Bataljon weeklikse konferensie wat gehou is op 240845B Apr 91 in die sportsaal te Pomfret.

35 DODDC, 32 Bn Gp 3, Box 125, 104/12/14/6, Vol. 1, Welwilendheidsgebare in die SAW, Notule van 32 Bn MGOK en MAK vergadering geou op 121100B Sep 90 in die konferensiekamer te Pomfret.

36 DODDC, 32 Bn Gp 3, Box 121, 104/10/14/6, Vol. 2, Instandhouding van Pers: Geneeskundige dienste: Hopitalisasie: Dwelmverslaafdes, Notule van MGOK vergadering soos gehou op 101100B Desember in die konferensiekamer. Afrikaans: *'n vrou van Namibia [sic] wat met 'n soldaat van die eenheid in die huwelik tree, kan na twee jaar RSA burgerskap verkry.*

37 DODDC, 32 Bn Gp 3, Box 55, 310/1, Vol. 1, Spesiale Operasies SA Leër: Pica Pau Skool, Information regarding Pica Pau school.

38 DODDC, 32 Bn Gp 3, Box 54, 309/1, Vol. 1, Spesifieke Operasies (Agree), Message from 32 Bn to NW Kmdmt.

Table 6.1: Subjects taught at Pica Pau school, 1989[39]

Subject	Standard								
	2	3	4	5	6	7	8	9	10
English	√	√	√	√	√	√	√	√	√
Portuguese	√	√	√	√	√	√			
Hygiene	√	√	√						
General Science	√	√	√	√	√	√			
Bible	√	√	√	√					
Afrikaans	√	√	√	√	√	√	√	√	√
History	√	√	√	√	√	√	√	√	√
Geography	√	√	√	√	√	√	√	√	√
Mathematics	√	√	√	√	√	√	√	√	√
Basic Techniques				√					
Accounting					√	√			
Needlework					√	√			
Agricultural Science					√	√			
Biology							√	√	√
Physical Science							√	√	
Business Economics									√

In 1991, the decision was taken to establish an independent Portuguese primary school at Pomfret.[40] The implications thereof, not only in terms of educating the children of 32 Battalion soldiers, but in preserving the heritage of the Portuguese-speaking contingent, is immense. The decision was, however, quickly repealed and the school's language of tuition changed to English.[41] While it made sense to educate children, now living in South Africa, in the lingua franca of the country, education in Portuguese need not have neglected equipping learners with sufficient English skills, and would have promoted a sense of continuity for the greater unit. However, while social aspects were not neglected at Buffalo, the demands on a peace-time unit in South Africa were significantly less, and there was enough time to address extracurricular activities at the new school. The sub-A and sub-B (Grades 1 and 2) traditional dance routine at Pica Pau school proved very popular, and 20 learners from the school were invited to perform at the opening of 'the new building of [the Department of] Education and Training' at Potchefstroom on 9 and 10 August 1990.[42] The school also held a talent evening on

39 DODDC, 32 Bn Gp 3, Box 55, 310/1, Vol. 1, Spesiale Operasies SA Leër: Pica Pau Skool, Subjects taught at Pica Pau school exclusive of Sub A, B and Std 1.
40 DODDC, 32 Bn Gp 3, Box 19, 522/1, Vol. 4, Konferensies, Notule van die 32 Bn weeklikse konferensie gehou op 120845B Jun 91 in die sportsaal te Pomfret.
41 DODDC, 32 Bn Gp 3, Box 19, 522/1, Vol. 4, Konferensies, Notule van die 32 Bn weeklikse konferensie gehou op 190845B Jun 91 in die sportsaal te Pomfret.
42 DODDC, 32 Bn Gp 3, Box 55, 310/1, Vol. 1, Spesiale Operasies SA Leër: Pica Pau Skool, Vervoer te Potchefstroom op 9 + 10 Augustus '90 vir 23 persone. Afrikaans: *die nuwe gebou van [die departement van] onderwys en opleiding*.

16 and 17 August 1991,[43] and learners from the school were invited to take part in the National Arts Festival in Pretoria during August and September 1991.[44] Possibly due to the potential shown at these events, 32 Battalion authorised ballet and music classes, at the Sport Club and primary school respectively, in 1992, further increasing the cultural exposure of unit members and their families.[45]

In April 1992, Army Headquarters identified a 'a critical shortage of teachers for the Adult Education Programme' at both 31 and 32 Battalions. To rectify the situation, an agreement was reached with Goudstad Education College, whereby the top students could complete their final-year practical modules at the two units, thereby increasing the available teaching staff.[46] Non-military teachers were also provided by the Department of Education. Charles Churra (pseudonym), a former soldier of 32 Battalion, recalls that, 'The Department of Education sent teachers there ... there were Education Department teachers in the school and the Department ... paid them.'[47]

In September 1992, the Foreign Military Attaché Association concluded a Memorandum of Agreement and Understanding (MOAU) with the SADF, according to which scholarships would be awarded to certain adult members of the SADF. The purpose of the MOAU was to promote high education standards in the SADF, and it appears to have been targeted specifically at 'non-traditional' SADF units, whose manpower differed from the typical white male units. The aim of the MOAU was to enable qualifying candidates to obtain a matriculation certificate. The MOAU contained a list of units that qualified for the scholarship, and stated that one applicant from each unit would be successful. However, despite the shortcomings in Adult Education at 32 Battalion, identified earlier that year, they were not on the list of units mentioned, although the document was distributed to them.[48] While it is futile to speculate why 32 Battalion was not included in the programme, their subsequent disbanding in 1993 raises questions regarding who had knowledge of the imminent disbanding, and whether this could have been communicated to members of the unit more expeditiously.

43 DODDC, 32 Bn Gp 3, Box 19, 522/1, Vol. 4, Konferensies, Minutes of the 32 Battalion weekly conference held on 030845B Jul 91 in the sports club at Pomfret, p.3.

44 DODDC, 32 Bn Gp 3, Box 55, 311/2/3, Vol. 2, Staatsdepartemente: Onderwys en Opleiding, Vervoer van leerlinge.

45 DODDC, 32 Bn Gp 3, Box 55, 311/2/3, Vol. 2, Staatsdepartemente: Onderwys en Opleiding, Toestemming vir ballet- en musiekklasse.

46 DODDC, 32 Bn Gp 3, Box 55, 311/2/3, Vol. 2, Staatsdepartemente: Onderwys en Opleiding, Magtiging: Goudstad Onderwyskollege Proefonderwys te 31 Bn en 32 Bn. Afrikaans: *kritieke tekort aan onderwysers vir die Volwasse Onderwysprogram.*

47 Interview with Charles Churra (pseudonym), former 32 Battalion soldier, Pretoria, 15-05-2019. Afrikaans: *Die Departement van Onderwys het onderwysers gestuur soontoe... daar was Departement van Onderwys onderwysers gewees in die skool en die Departement het hulle ... betaal.*

48 DODDC, 32 Bn Gp 3, Box 55, 311/2/3, Vol. 2, Staatsdepartemente: Onderwys en Opleiding, Memorandum of Agreement and Understanding between the Foreign Military Attache Association and the South African Defence Force concerning the Foreign Military Attache Association Scholarship Programme.

Medical

Possibly as a result of the way in which 32 Battalion was administrated in Namibia, where everything that the unit needed was provided by the SADF, families of 32 Battalion members experienced difficulties when visiting hospitalised relatives at 1 Military Hospital in Pretoria. While this was not exclusively the case, some of the family members neglected to make the necessary arrangements for accommodation in Pretoria, and expected the staff of 1 Military Hospital to resolve the situation, as the staff of 32 Battalion had done for the last 15 years.[49]

In line with the Northern Medical Command's far-sighted decision in 1990 that its unit should receive greater education about HIV/AIDS to reduce the spread of the virus,[50] 32 Battalion launched a fairly extensive campaign to inform its members, and their families, of the dangers and characteristics of the virus. HIV increases the effects of a widespread disease in southern Africa, tuberculosis (TB), and complicates treatment regimes. In a vicious circle, 'TB promotes the acceleration of HIV replication, and progressive HIV suppresses the immune system, making the individual more vulnerable to TB.'[51] The earlier a diagnosis is made, the more effective treatment for both illnesses can be, if administered and maintained correctly. HIV only became a widespread problem in South Africa in the early 1990s,[52] and Northern Medical Command's early recognition of the problem, as well as 32 Battalion's embracing of their decision, are laudable, though ultimately probably driven by their own interest in maintaining an effective combat force.

By July 1992, 32 Battalion was able to conclude that the programme had achieved good results, with education provided to most soldiers, to all wives of soldiers and at the local schools.[53] However, the SADF's policy regarding the provision of antiretroviral medication (in the form of azidothymidine, or AZT) held considerable implications for members of 32 Battalion: the criteria for the provision of AZT to SADF members contained much technical information about how the medication functions and when it is efficient and concluded that, after this had been explained to the person with HIV, he or she had to make an 'informed decision' (underlined in the policy document) about whether to commence a regime of antiretroviral medication or not.[54] In the light of the level of education of the average member, and family member, of 32 Battalion, it is unlikely that they

49 DODDC, 32 Bn Gp 3, Box 19, 522/1, Vol. 4, Notule van rehabilitasiepasiënte-vergadering tussen NTvl Kmdmt en 1 Mil Hosp gehou op 26 September 1991.

50 DODDC, 32 Bn Gp 3, Box 28, 32BN/MBH/B/104/11/6/9, Vol. 1, VIGS: Hantering in spanverband; Aanmeldbare siektes, Noord Med K/B/104/11/6/9: Seksuele oordraagbare siektes: VIGS-virus.

51 U.G. Lalloo & S. Pillay, 'Managing tuberculosis and HIV in sub-Sahara Africa' in *Current HIV/AIDS reports, 5,* 2008, p.132.

52 M. Balter, 'On World Aids Day, a shadow looms over Southern Africa' in *Science, 282 (5395),* 1998, p.1790.

53 DODDC, 32 Bn Gp 3, Box 28, 104/11/6/9, Vol. 3, Gesondheidsdienste: Aanmeldbare siektes, Mediese dienste Pomfret: VIGS.

54 DODDC, 32 Bn Gp 3, Box 28, 104/11/6/9, Vol. 3, Gesondheidsdienste: Aanmeldbare siektes, Kriteria vir AZT toediening. Afrikaans: *ingeligte keuse* (underlined in original).

would even have completely grasped how the medication worked, let alone be in a position to make an informed decision about a medication regime. It would then have fallen to the SADF medical personnel to guide their decisions, at times to the conclusion that taking AZT would not be effective. This, however, would have been difficult to understand, and would probably have contributed to a feeling of abandonment among the unit.

Additionally, from 31 March 1991, the SADF required all applicants to be screened for HIV. Those who tested positive were considered unsuitable for employment in the SADF, either in Permanent Force or National Service capacity. Serving members in the PF were allowed to continue with their service, albeit in a much-diminished role and only for fear of legal repercussions.[55] Once more, this decision had significant implications for 32 Battalion. In 1991, the transfer of personnel from SADF auxiliaries to PF members had not been completed.[56] This meant that, regardless of how long a soldier had served with the unit, if he tested positive for HIV during the administrative process, he would be refused service in the SADF. A soldier who had performed the same length of service in a regular SADF unit would, however, be allowed to continue with his service and enjoy all the privileges thereof. Particularly in light of the fact that many of the soldiers of 32 Battalion fell into one of the 'High Risk' categories identified by the SADF, 'Individuals with a history of STDs',[57] the likelihood of this event occurring is high.

Relocating to South Africa did have certain advantages, among them the construction of modern medical facilities on the unit's doorstep. An example of this can be found in the laboratory that was constructed in Pomfret in 1991[58], where basic medical tests could be carried out. This negated the need to send specimens to larger hospitals, like 1 Military Hospital in Pretoria or 3 Military Hospital in Bloemfontein, and reduced the time it took to receive test results, in turn increasing treatment efficiency. At the same time, however, the SADF insisted that the dependents of soldiers had to be in possession of identity cards before they would be allowed medical treatment at SADF sickbays or hospitals. These cards were issued at 'command level'.[59] From an administrative perspective, this is a sensible policy but, although the men, women and children of 32 Battalion had been living in South Africa for two years by then, they would still have been used to a much more relaxed approach to military administration. Having requests for medical treatment refused for want of an identification card would have been an alien experience to them, and would not have promoted the idea that the SADF still cared

55 DODDC, 32 Bn Gp 3, Box 28, 104/11/6/9, Vol. 2, Instandhouding van Personeel: Gesondheidsdienste / Gesondheidsverslae en opgawes: Aanmeldbare siektes, Human Immunodeficiency Virus (HIV) and service in the SADF, pp.3–6.

56 Nortje, *The Terrible Ones*, p.1110.

57 DODDC, 32 Bn Gp 3, Box 28, 104/11/6/9, Vol. 2, Instandhouding van Personeel: Gesondheidsdienste / Gesondheidsverslae en opgawes: Aanmeldbare siektes, Human Immunodeficiency Virus (HIV) and service in the SADF, p.2.

58 DODDC, 32 Bn Gp 3, Box 19, 522/1, Vol. 4, Konferensies, Notule van die sentrale mediese kommandement bevel en staf vergadering gehou om 09:00 op 20 Augustus 1991 in die konferensiekamer te sentrale mediese kommandement, p.4.

59 DODDC, 32 Bn Gp 3, Box 19, 522/1, Vol. 4, Konferensies, Notule van die 32 Bn weeklikse konferensie gehou op 190845B Jun 91 in die sportsaal te Pomfret. Afrikaans: *kmdmt vlak*.

about the unit after the war. Additionally, acquiring such cards from the Northern Cape Command would have been time-consuming and not necessarily guaranteed, if questions arose about nationality and citizenship. Nonetheless, medical facilities at Pomfret was, at least, adequate for the needs of a comparatively small community:

> There was a clinic in the Portuguese community, but also a hospital ... A fully equipped hospital, with a theatre ... The military fully staffed that hospital; there was always at least two to three doctors and ... nursing staff ... It was a military hospital. Patients that could not be treated there, where airlifted to 1 Military Hospital. Not by road, always by air.[60]

Social

Removed from the isolation of Buffalo, members of 32 Battalion had much greater exposure and access to the advantages, but also the vices, of society. Inter alia, there was much easier access to alcohol than had been the case in Namibia, where all legal sales of alcohol at Buffalo was controlled by 32 Battalion. Upon visiting 1 Military Hospital in Pretoria, though, five members of 32 Battalion, including a sergeant and two corporals, were arrested for drunkenness by the Military Police of Northern Transvaal Command for 'behaviour detrimental to military discipline (drunkenness)'.[61] This is further illustrated by a meeting held between 'Bophuthatswana officials' and 'Pomfret officials' on 14 February 1991. At the meeting it was agreed that the primary reason for assaults (by members of 32 Battalion in Bophuthatswana) was 'excessive drinking at shebeens and other sports'.[62] While the meeting was held in a good spirit, with both parties complimenting each other on their conduct, a complaint from the Bophuthatswana Police (BP), addressed to the South African Secretary of Foreign Affairs, on 21 May 1991 indicates that the matter had not entirely been resolved. In the complaint, the Commissioner of the BP, Major General P. J. Seleke, alleged that 'a certain woman' had been 'undressed, assaulted and even dropped ... into the swimming pool' at the Tseoge Sun Lounge in Bophuthatswana by seven members of 32 Battalion. In the ensuing ruckus between the soldiers and the BP, the latter was forced to use batons and teargas to restore order, and damage to the Tseoge Sun Lounge occurred.[63] The sequence of events described above is a clear indication that 32 Battalion's

60 Interview with Charles Churra (pseudonym), former 32 Battalion soldier, Pretoria, 15-05-2019. Afrikaans: *Daar was 'n kliniek in die Portuguese gemeenskap, maar ook 'n hospitaal... 'n Volledig ingerigte hospitaal, met 'n teater... Die militêr [sic] het daardie hospitaal ten volle gestaf; daar was ten minste altyd twee na drie dokters ... [en] verpleegstaf... Dit was 'n militêre hospitaal. Pasiënte wat hulle nie daar kon behandel nie, is per vliegtuig vervoer na 1 Militêre Hospitaal toe. Nie per pad nie, altyd per vliegtuig.*

61 DODDC, 32 Bn Gp 3, Box 43, 106/20/2, Vol. 1, Polisiedienste: Arrestasies en aanhoudings, Arrestasie en aanhoudings. Parentheis original. Afrikaans: *gedrag tot nadeel van militêre dissipline (dronkenskap).*

62 DODDC, 32 Bn Gp 3, Box 55, 311/1, Vol. 1, Hulpverlening en samewerking met lande, Meeting between Bophuthatswana officials and Pomfret Officials (Battalion 32). Bophuthatswana was one of the tribal homelands which had a degree of autonomous rule.

63 DODDC, 32 Bn Gp 3, Box 55, 311/1, Vol. 1, Hulpverlening en samewerking met lande, Alleged offences: Members of the SADF: Pomfred.

soldiers had not yet come to terms with the greater degree of freedom that they enjoyed in South Africa (and the adjacent tribal homelands). While alcohol abuse was by no means absent at Buffalo, it seems that the frequency and severity increased once the unit moved to Pomfret. It is, of course, possible that cases of alcohol abuse were more visible in South Africa than it had been in the Caprivi, and that matters now had to be addressed publicly, rather than internally. However, it is equally possible that the Angolan and Namibian soldiers of 32 Battalion had not quite come to terms with their new lot.

Disbanding

As part of the ongoing peace negotiations between the ANC and NP, Pik Botha, Nelson Mandela and others visited the UN in New York in July 1992. During this visit, the decision was taken that 32 Battalion, as well as 31 Battalion, were to be disbanded. In all likelihood, this decision was taken in contravention of the SADF's SA Army Order (SAAO) GS 3/25, which not only pointed out that the decision to disband a SADF unit had to go through the Chief of the SADF and the Minister of Defence,[64] but also laid down stringent criteria for the disbanding of a unit:

- Reasons for the need to disband the unit had to be provided
- The influence on other, existing, units had to be evaluated
- The way in which the function of the unit would be managed after disbanding had to be explained
- The way in which manpower, equipment and facilities would be managed or distributed after disbanding had to be outlined
- A date for disbanding had to be provided
- The financial implications of disbanding had to be illustrated.[65]

Unless planning for the disbanding of 32 Battalion had started much earlier, it is virtually impossible that all these conditions were adhered to, even if the decision makers were not at the UN in New York.

Nevertheless, the decision was pushed through rapidly and, although several communication problems hindered the swift relay of this decision to 32 Battalion – neither Chief of the Defence Force, General A. J. Liebenberg, nor Chief of the Army, Lieutenant General G. L. Meiring, could be reached and it fell to Major General Daan Hamman, Deputy Chief of the Army, to deliver the news – the message was telephonically delivered to 32 Battalion HQ on 14 July 1992. No date for disbandment was established at the

64 DODDC, 32 Bn Gp 3, Box 78, 502/1/B, Vol. 1, Organisasie-beheer: Stigting en ontbinding van hoofkwartiere en eenhede: Beleid, SALO GS 3/25.

65 DODDC, 32 Bn Gp 3, Box 78, 502/1/B, Vol. 1, Organisasie-beheer: Stigting en ontbinding van hoofkwartiere en eenhede: Beleid, Aanhangsel A by SA Leërorder GS 3/25.

time, despite SAAO GS 3/25, but it was made clear that the planning for disbandment had to commence as soon as possible.[66] However, as late as 1 March 1993, the Chief of the SADF gave the assurance that, although 32 Battalion was to be disbanded, the members of the unit would not be abandoned:

> Men and women who had the privilege of enjoying their military training at 32 Bn can confidently look forward to employing their loyalty, discipline and individual talents in the broader SADF … Although we are saying goodbye to the name of 32 Bn, we welcome the opportunity that now presents itself to the proud members of this unit to employ the trust that they have earned in the past in the service of the SA Defence Force in future.[67]

Table 6.2: Morale at 32 Battalion

Month	Factors negatively affecting morale
May '91[*]	Personnel administration, water supply
October '91[†]	Payment of salaries, Leisure-time utilisation equipment
December '91[‡]	Payment of salaries
January '92[§]	Witchdoctors, payment of salaries
February '92[|]	Water supply, support to grass widows
March '92[¶]	Water supply, leisure-time utilisation
August '92[**]	Rationalisation and reorganisation
January '93[††]	Uncertainty about the future

* DODDC, 32 Bn Gp 3, Box 77, 501/13, Vol. 1, Maandelikse terugvoer, Maandelikse terugvoer.
† DODDC, 32 Bn Gp. 3 Box 77, 501/13, Vol. 1, Maandelikse terugvoer, 32 Bataljon Maandelikse terugvoer: Oktober 1991.
‡ DODDC, 32 Bn Gp 3, Box 77, 501/13, Vol. 1, Maandelikse terugvoer, 32 Bataljon Maandelikse terugvoer: Desember 1991.
§ DODDC, 32 Bn Gp. 3, Box 77, 501/13, Vol. 1, Maandelikse terugvoer, 32 Bataljon Maandelikse terugvoer: Januarie 1991.
| DODDC, 32 Bn Gp. 3, Box 77, 501/13, Vol. 1, Maandelikse terugvoer, 32 Bataljon Maandelikse terugvoer: Februarie 1992.
¶ DODDC, 32 Bn Gp. 3, Box 77, 501/13, Vol. 1, Maandelikse terugvoer, 32 Bataljon Maandelikse terugvoer: Maart 1992.
** DODDC, 32 Bn Gp. 3, Box 77, 501/13, Vol. 1, Maandelikse terugvoer, 32 Bataljon Maandelikse terugvoer: Augustus 1992.
†† DODDC, 32 Bn Gp 3, Box 77, 501/13, Vol. 2, Maandelikse terugvoer, 32 Bataljon Maandelikse terugvoer: Januarie 1993.

66 Nortje, *The Terrible* Ones, pp.1156–1157.
67 DODDC, 32 Bn Gp 3, Box 78, 502/1, Vol. 1, Stigting en ontbinding van koofkwartiere en eenhede, Message for commemorative program: 32 Bn. Afrikaans: *Mans en vroue wat die voorreg gehad het om hulle militêre opleiding by 32 Bn te geniet kan met vertroue uitsien om hul toewyding, dissipline en individuele talente in die breër SAW uit te leef… Alhoewel ons vaarwel sê aan die naam van 32 Bn verwelkom ons die geleentheid wat nou gebied word aan die trotse lede van hierdie eenheid om die vertroue wat hulle in die verlede verdien het uit te leef tot diens van die SA Weermag in die toekoms.*

A comparison of the assessment of morale in 32 Battalion's monthly reports poignantly indicate how troops' concerns rapidly escalated from typical, run-of-the-mill concerns to anxiety about their future (Table 6.2), indicating at least a level of scepticism of promises made by the SADF command structures:

Efforts at Integration

Although many programmes and initiatives to smooth the transition of 32 Battalion to South Africa were planned and discussed, few of these were effectively implemented. During the planning phase, a large number of issues were considered. The overarching consideration was, in essence, what to do with the soldiers of 32 Battalion. To this extent, feasibility studies were done to determine whether the unit could be rationalised into other units. Significantly, though, when the issue of rationalisation was discussed with the Chief of the Army (or, at least, his office; documentation is unclear on the matter), it was explicitly stated that the community at Pomfret should not be considered as an entity.[68] This implied that the soldiers and, by extension, their families, could be rationalised piecemeal and placed as individuals throughout units of the South African Army. Considering that the Pomfret community was the only familiar aspect of South African life to these Angolan/Namibian/South Africans, the potential social disruption of this decision cannot be overstated. Regardless of the outcome of rationalisation attempts, the mind-set of the SADF towards 32 Battalion, exemplified by this statement, shows to what lengths the high level SADF command was prepared to go in order to ensure their survival in a democratic South Africa.

A 32 Battalion soldier is quoted as saying

> They disbanded 32 Battalion, but by the solutions made by the politicians, we would be integrated. So we started to debate. How will this integration be? We have our own habits and customs, most people do not speak English or Afrikaans, and don't speak Sotho, or Zulu or Xhosa. How are we going to adapt and live with these people? They said, 'No, we will do what is possible; there are places you will be deployed.' [69]

Despite the laboured language, this statement contains the essence of the fears and concerns of members of 32 Battalion during the period leading up to disbandment. In an attempt to address these concerns, a task team convened by the Chief of the Army's Senior Staff Officer Force Design[70] prepared a questionnaire to send to all the geographical commands within South Africa.

68 DODDC, 32 Bn Gp 3, Box 158, 502/1/1 (32 Bn), Vol. 1, Stigting en Ontbinding van Hoofkwartiere en Eenhede – 32 Bn, Aanvullende Instruksie tot Beplanningsinstruksie 26/92: Ondersoek na die ontbiding van 32 Bn.

69 Quoted in Nortje, *The Terrible Ones*, p.1161.

70 DODDC, 32 Bn Gp 3, Box 158, 502/1/1 (32 Bn), Vol. 1, Stigting en Ontbinding van Hoofkwartiere en Eenhede – 32 Bn, Fax nos. 265–273.

Questionnaires were sent out to all the SADF Commands to determine their ability to rationalise the soldiers and civilians of 32 Battalion within specific units identified by the task team. While not all of the commands responded, the salient points of the available replies of the various commands are outlined below.

Although highlighting the fact that the Eastern Transvaal Command would predominantly only be able to accommodate single soldiers from 32 Battalion, mainly due to a housing shortage and the absence of schools, Major General J. P. M. Möller, General Officer Commanding Eastern Transvaal Command, was nonetheless generally positive about the ability to rationalise, at least, parts of 32 Battalion. He repeatedly emphasised the housing shortage, especially for married personnel, but also indicated how this could be overcome over a medium to long term. Major General Möller stated that Eastern Transvaal Command was able to accommodate at least 200 members of all ranks of 32 Battalion. At various times in the Eastern Transvaal Command reply, significant emphasis was placed on the need for members of 32 Battalion to have the correct attitude towards rationalisation, should they be transferred to Eastern Transvaal Command. At the same time the historical adaptability of 32 Battalion was highlighted, though it was pointed out that rationalisation would be their biggest challenge to date. Predictions regarding the acceptance of 32 Battalion members in the local communities were positive, though the caveat was added that the white community would probably accept them 'at a convenient distance'.[71]

Brigadier F. A. Botha (Officer Commanding Eastern Province Command), initially illustrated the ability of Eastern Province Command to provide accommodation for single members of 32 Battalion over short, medium and long term as well as providing a medium term plan for accommodating married members, although he pointed out that the Chief of the SADF had already accepted an 'option' for the integration of the Transkei Defence Force / Ciskei Defence Force (TDF/CDF)[72] and that vacancies within Eastern Province Command could be filled from these defence forces. Unfortunately for 32 Battalion, by 1993 the SADF was aware that a change in South Africa's government was likely to take place in the near future, and that this would have significant implications for the SADF. The integration of armed forces of liberation movements, as well as the defence forces of the tribal homelands, like the TDF/CDF, was decidedly less negotiable than that of a perceived apartheid-unit like 32 Battalion. Brigadier Botha further stated that members of the TDF were unequivocal in their rejection of the rationalisation of 32 Battalion to Eastern Province Command. Although, unfortunately, he did not provide explicit reasons it is clear that the wishes of the TDF were considered more important than those of 32 Battalion. It should also be noted that the accommodation solutions at Eastern Province Command would only be feasible if 32 Battalion

71 DODDC, 32 Bn Gp 3, Box 158, 502/1/1 (32 Bn), Vol. 1, Stigting en Ontbinding van Hoofkwartiere en Eenhede – 32 Bn, Fax serial no. OPS/285/10 Aug 92: Rasionalisering: 32 Bn. Afrikaans: *op 'n gerieflike afstand.*

72 Transkei and Ciskei were both tribal homelands under the apartheid regime, and enjoyed a degree of self-government.

were divided between various units and stationed in various towns. Probably for this reason, it was stated that it would be impossible to rationalise 32 Battalion as a unit. Rationalisation as various sub-units was considered feasible, but fraught with difficulty.[73]

In a very comprehensive response, Colonel S. Schreuder, Officer Commanding Orange Free State Command, made it very clear that members of 32 Battalion would be completely acceptable within Orange Free State Command, which was also geographically closer to Pomfret that the preceding two commands. He pointed out, however, that accommodation for married members would be severely limited and, were they to become homeowners in some way, tensions were likely to arise with their white neighbours. It is unclear why ownership of houses in predominantly black areas, where such tensions would be less likely to occur, was not considered. The availability of churches and schools was not considered problematic. Colonel Schreuder added the caveat that the HQs of the various groups within Orange Free State Command had not been finalised and that any personnel requirements were therefore only to be considered preliminary. In an annexe to Colonel Schreuder's response, Colonel L. Rudman, Officer Commanding 44 Parachute Brigade, was somewhat more ambiguous and considered the integration of members of 32 Battalion into 44 Parachute Brigade a 'definite possibility'. He also pointed out the difficulty in providing sufficient accommodation for married members. On balance, though, Colonel Rudman seemed eager to accept certain elements of 32 Battalion, specifically mentioning former members of 32 Battalion's Reconnaissance Wing as well as a number of other officers and senior NCOs by name. The two units had several common threads in their histories, not least a common founding OC, Jan Breytenbach. Additionally, 44 Parachute Brigade had provided training for members of 32 Battalion. Rudman's eagerness was therefore not purely based on a desire to assist 32 Battalion; he might well have recognised the opportunity of recruiting experienced, capable soldiers, known to him and his men, to his unit.[74]

In the Northern Cape Command, Colonel J. Liebenberg, Officer Commanding 8 South African Infantry Brigade, stated that no accommodation was available for married soldiers. However, accommodation for single soldiers was ample. Notably, Colonel Liebenberg did not foresee any problems with the soldiers of 32 Battalion's integration into the local community as far as the white population was concerned, but pointed out that the black population's political leanings were very much pro-ANC. This was identified as a major obstacle to the successful integration of 32 Battalion into Northern Cape Command. Although a small Catholic Church was present in the area, no English schools would be accessible. Significantly, Northern Cape Command was able to accommodate a full-time battalion (six rifle companies) 'easily'. The suggestion was made that this battalion could be retrained as a mechanised infantry battalion, though it was also

73 DODDC, 32 Bn Gp 3, Box 158, 502/1/1 (32 Bn), Vol. 1, Stigting en Ontbinding van Hoofkwartiere en Eenhede – 32 Bn, Fax serial no. OPS/14081/Aug 92: Rasionalisasie van 32 Bn. Afrikaans: *opsie*.

74 DODDC, 32 Bn Gp 3, Box 158, 502/1/1 (32 Bn), Vol. 1, Stigting en Ontbinding van Hoofkwartiere en Eenhede – 32 Bn, Rasionalisasie van 32 Bn. Afrikaans: *besliste moontlikheid*.

pointed out that soldiers would have to be single. It was also stated explicitly that the recommendations of Northern Cape Command were based on preliminary studies only and that later studies might prove different.[75]

In a letter to Colonel Delport, OC 32 Battalion, dated 20 August 1992, the Officer Commanding Northern Cape Command, Colonel D.G. Roux, proposed a short-term plan regarding the rationalisation of 32 Battalion. As OC of the command where 32 Battalion had resided for the previous four years, he would have been well-acquainted with the unit and specifically identified the Portuguese soldiers, their wives and children as individuals affected by rationalisation and went further to identify key areas of concern among these groups as

- Fear of unemployment
- Uncertainty about soldiers' future within the SADF
- Intimidation and retribution by 'radical elements'
- Alienation of members of the community rationalised to other parts of South Africa
- Housing
- Social Development[76]

Perhaps because of the vague guidelines given by Colonel Roux (which was primarily centred around information and education sessions) and despite the enquiries to all the SADF Commands as to their ability to rationalise soldiers of the unit[77], the 32 Battalion monthly report for March 1993 seems to indicate that little headway had been made in reassuring the Pomfret community of a secure future. It states that

- Soldiers' wives are very negative about their future prospects
- The disbandment of 32 Battalion caused a large number of marital problems and multiple divorce proceedings had been started. Some of the soldiers had also started sending their wives back to Namibia and Angola in order to avoid the costs of getting divorced[78]

On 11 February 1993, Delport held a workshop with the OCs of various units to which 32 Battalion personnel had been provisionally assigned. Troops from 32 Battalion would be disseminated in the following quantities:

75 DODDC, 32 Bn Gp 3, Box 158, 502/1/1 (32 Bn), Vol. 1, Stigting en Ontbinding van Hoofkwartiere en Eenhede – 32 Bn, Fax serial no. 135 : Toekomstige Aanwending: 32 Bn. Afrikaans: *met gemak*.

76 DODDC, 32 Bn Gp 3, Box 158, 502/1/1 (32 Bn), Vol. 1, Stigting en Ontbinding van Hoofkwartiere en Eenhede – 32 Bn, Voorlopige Bevkomplan: 32 Bn Rasionalisering.

77 DODDC, 32 Bn Gp 3, Box 158, 502/1/1 (32 Bn), Vol. 1, Stigting en Ontbinding van Hoofkwartiere en Eenhede – 32 Bn, Fax nos. 265–273.

78 DODDC, 32 Bn Gp 3, Box 160, 509/1, Vol. 2, Ministeriële Navrae m.b.t. Personeelaangeleenthede, 32 Bataljon Maandelikse Terugvoer: Maart 1993.

- 44 Parachute Brigade: all parachute elements; one company of five platoons and 20 pathfinders
- 61 Mechanised Battalion: one mechanised company, one support company and one reconnaissance platoon
- 111 Battalion: two infantry companies
- 7 South African Infantry Battalion: one infantry company

Clearly, this does not constitute the whole of 32 Battalion, and even for those troops who fell into the categories mentioned above, the future was far from certain, as their families had to remain at Pomfret for the remainder of 1993, and would only be transferred to the new units 'when accommodation becomes available'.[79]

It appears that the SADF would have been able to accommodate all the single soldiers of 32 Battalion with ease, in some cases without the need for dissemination. Married soldiers (and specifically the ability to provide accommodation for them and their families) were a concern throughout, though. Several short-term suggestions were made, mainly relating to temporary housing or the refurbishing of existing but deteriorating housing. Despite this, Northern Cape Command and Orange Free State Command seemed quite eager to accommodate, at least, certain elements of 32 Battalion.

It is quite significant that the biggest problem with social integration was not, as would be expected in light of the tempestuous political climate at the time, the relationship that soldiers of 32 Battalion would have with the local white population. This was either regarded as a non-issue or downplayed to a large extent. However, integration of 32 Battalion within the local black communities was identified as a potentially volatile aspect throughout the various commands' replies. This seems to illustrate the isolation in which the 32 Battalion community found itself after relocation: they would be accepted by the white population (who, it proved, were not in a strong position to assist with their integration in the lead up to the first democratic elections) but rejected by the black population, who proved to have the majority voice in South Africa and, as such, were the ones in a position to improve the plight of the individuals associated with the unit.

Furthermore, as illustrated most clearly by the reply of Northern Cape Command, given that the questionnaires were sent to the various commands on the afternoon of 4 August 1992 – seven months before the unit was disbanded – and a deadline of 9 August 1992 was set[80], this task was probably undertaken too late and insufficient time given to the various commands to do a thorough analysis. Nonetheless, even in the short time accorded to them, all the available commands' responses indicate a willingness to assist with the rationalisation of 32 Battalion.

79 DODDC, 32 Bn Gp 3, Box 78, 502/1, Vol. 1, Stigting en ontbinding van hoofkwartiere en eenhede, Notule van 'n werksessie met eenheidsbevelvoerders aan wie 32 Bataljon lede toegewys is by 32 Bataljon om 111100B Feb 93. Afrikaans: *wanneer daar akkomodasie beskikbaar is.*

80 DODDC, 32 Bn Gp 3, Box 158, 502/1/1 (32 Bn), Vol. 1, Stigting en Ontbinding van Hoofkwartiere en Eenhede – 32 Bn, Fax nos. 265–273.

Post-disbandment efforts

Though the official disbandment parade of 32 Battalion took place on 26 March 1993, arrangements for the disbanding of the unit were not yet complete. The former 32 Battalion was still to be based at Pomfret until the end of 1993, though no longer as an active unit, while transfers were affected for members who were so destined.[81] The piecemeal transfer of 32 Battalion started when troops started leaving Pomfret for other units on 30 March 1993, predominantly for 61 Mechanised Battalion, based at Lohatla, 7 SAI, a traditional Shangaan battalion stationed at Phalaborwa, 44 Parachute Brigade in Bloemfontein and 111 Battalion, a traditional Swazi unit at Camden (near Ermelo).[82] The troops still on strength at Pomfret were to become the nucleus of the reactivated 2 SAI.[83] This was not accomplished without its own set of problems, as will be illustrated. Regarding troops that were transferred from Pomfret – as had been indicated by the various commands' responses to the questionnaire sent out by before disbandment – housing was a problem for married soldiers. At 7 SAI, married troops were housed at Hebron, about 10km from Phalaborwa. Even when taking into account that Hebron was the base camp of 5 Recce, which included some former 32 Battalion soldiers as well as other Portuguese troops – these had transferred there before 32 Battalion had been disbanded – this relocation appears to be a fair compromise. However, not only did the former 32 Battalion soldiers and their wives have trouble adjusting to the customs and culture of 5 Recce, but 5 Recce itself had insufficient accommodation for the families of its soldiers. By June 1993, the rest of the married soldiers' families had also received permission to join them in Phalaborwa. They were allocated flats in a military block in Phalaborwa where about 160 military personnel from other units were also housed. Though no documented evidence could be found, presumably this created similar adaption problems as before. Only the soldiers that transferred to 111 Battalion experienced few housing issues; 111 Battalion had its own town where married couples and families could stay.[84] Nonetheless, as late as 11 March 1993, two weeks before the disbandment parade, concern about the housing situation at 111 Battalion was expressed at a rationalisation coordination conference.[85]

By 25 May 1993, it had become clear that the reactivation of 2 SAI would not be accomplished without some problem areas. 'In order to make the disbanding of 32 Battalion and the reactivation of 2 SAI more acceptable', Army Staff Intelligence (Command Communication Directorate) was tasked with coordinating a low-profile

81 Nortje, *The Terrible Ones*, p.1163.
82 DODDC, 32 Bn Gp 3, Box 78, 502/1, Vol. 1, Stigting en ontbinding van hoofkwartiere en eenhede, Notule van 'n werkessie met eenheidsbevelvoerders aan wie 32 Bataljon lede toegewys is by 32 Bataljon om 111100B Feb 93.
83 Nortje, *The Terrible Ones*, p.1169.
84 Nortje, *The Terrible Ones*, p.1170.
85 DODDC, 32 Bn Gp 3, Box 158, 502/1/1 (32 Bn), Vol. 1, Stigting en Ontbinding van Hoofkwartiere en Eenhede – 32 Bn, Notule van die Koörd Konf tov die rasionalisasie van 31 SAI en 32 Bn wat gehou is op 11 Maart 1993 om 08:00 te Vasbyt Lokaal, Leër HK.

media plan to announce the reactivation of 2 SAI and to support Northern Cape Command in convincing the local population of the value that the reactivation of 2 SAI would add to the local economy as well as to illustrate the multi-ethnic composition of 2 SAI.[86] It appears that the Chief of the Army anticipated some resistance from the local community to the reactivation of 2 SAI and tried to pre-empt this situation by implementing these measures. The fact that the multi-ethnic composition of 2 SAI is specifically mentioned is significant in light of the Convention for a Democratic South Africa (Codesa) negotiations, where one of the key issues was the way in which the various armed organisations (of multi-ethnic origins) were to be integrated. Although the National Peacekeeping Force – brainchild of Codesa and the first test of the way in which integrated, multi-ethnic units could be utilised – was stillborn,[87] lessons had apparently been learnt and these were now being implemented pro-actively.

As part of this strategy, 'orientation programmes' were planned by the SADF. On 30 April 1993, somewhat belatedly considering that the official disbanding of 32 Battalion had taken place and transfers of personnel was well under way, Army HQ held a workshop to assess the effect of these programmes. It was noted that, since no final decision had been taken about the housing and schooling issues at the various receiving units, only 111 Battalion was able to launch an effective orientation programme. The workshop identified that housing and education were, indeed, the biggest concerns among 32 Battalion members and their families, followed by concerns about the availability of churches, public transport and infrastructure at receiving units.[88] This indicates that, despite the plans to involve the 32 Battalion community throughout the rationalisation process, sufficient up-to-date and accurate information had not filtered down from the SADF decision makers to the community.

In addition to the orientation programmes at the various receiver units, a specific programme was developed for 'those left behind [at Pomfret].' This programme focused on language development, self-development and specialised education. The language development phase was done under the auspice of the Chief of Staff Personnel's Language Services Directorate by eight instructors provided by 32 Battalion as well as some Portuguese women from the community that could speak Afrikaans. The target date for the finalisation of the language training was set at 30 November 1993.[89] This

86 DODDC, 32 Bn Gp 3, Box 158, 502/1/1 (32 Bn), Vol. 1, Stigting en Ontbinding van Hoofkwartiere en Eenhede – 32 Bn, Magsontwikkeling Implementeringsinstruksie 18/93. Afrikaans: *Ten einde die finale ontbinding van 32 Battalion en die heraktivering van 2 SAI meer aanvaarbaar te maak.*

87 I. van der Waag, *A Military History of Modern South Africa*. Cape Town: Jonathan Ball, 2015, p.289.

88 DODDC, 32 Bn Gp 3, Box 158, 502/1/1 (32 Bn), Vol. 1, Stigting en Ontbinding van Hoofkwartiere en Eenhede – 32 Bn, Gemeenskapsvoorbereidings werksessie tov 32 Bn. Afrikaans: *inburgeringsprogramme.*

89 DODDC, 32 Bn Gp 3, Box 158, 502/1/1 (32 Bn), Vol. 1, Stigting en Ontbinding van Hoofkwartiere en Eenhede – 32 Bn, Gemeenskapsvoorbereidings werksessie tov 32 Bn. Afrikaans: *agtergeblewenes.* This term is generally used as a catch-all when referring to poor,

seems like a very short time to learn a new language, though the participation of local women as instructors probably indicates a degree of continuation envisaged by the planners. The self-development phase was initially undertaken by the Senior Staff Officer tasked with Command Communication at Northern Cape Command, but instructors from 32 Battalion took over once it became clear that language was an insurmountable barrier between the instructors of Northern Cape Command and the trainees. The initial target group of this phase was civilian women, but it was envisaged that the 32 Battalion soldiers who had transferred to the support company of 61 Mechanised Battalion at the Army Battle School at Lohatla would also attend at a later date.[90] The content of the self-development phase is illuminating; attention was given to Man in Creation, politics and ideologies, education and training, communication, values and ethics, establishing goals, budgeting and economic development, economics, problem-solving and the realities of life in South Africa. At the Pica Pau High School, that the majority of the children attended, a continuation of this phase addressed topics such as relationships, abortion, rape, discrimination, differences between political parties and discipline. The local clinic was the venue for information sessions on the need for relocation of certain troops, hygiene at home, the way in which the Post Office worked, public transport and alcohol abuse.[91]

The choice of topics chosen for discussion during the self-development phase are indicative of the problems faced by the larger South Africa at the time. Indeed, economic development, rape (and other crimes) education and discrimination remain contentious issues to this day. Other topics, such as the various political information sessions, hygiene issues and logistical aspects of everyday life highlight just how different Pomfret was from the environment and culture that 32 Battalion had been used to prior to moving to South Africa. The final phase of the programme, specialised education, which focused on the multi-ethnic composition of receiver units as well as basic cultural differences between different racial and ethnic groups in South Africa, the structure of the SADF and basics of the South African legal system[92] further emphasise the socio-cultural rifts between pre-1975 Angola, 1970s and 1980s Namibia and post-1990 South Africa. The degree of adaption required by a community to move between these chrono-social constructs is staggering.

On 8 June 1993, a coordination conference was at Army HQ to discuss the rationalisation of 31 SAI (formerly 31 Battalion) and 32 Battalion. At this conference, it was pointed out that the difference in remuneration between Portuguese soldiers and soldiers

disadvantaged communities. However, a literal use could also refer to 'those left behind', which is probably the intent in this context.

90 DODDC, 32 Bn Gp 3, Box 158, 502/1/1 (32 Bn), Vol. 1, Stigting en Ontbinding van Hoofkwartiere en Eenhede – 32 Bn, Gemeenskapsvoorbereidings werksessie tov 32 Bn.

91 DODDC, 32 Bn Gp 3, Box 158, 502/1/1 (32 Bn), Vol. 1, Stigting en Ontbinding van Hoofkwartiere en Eenhede – 32 Bn, Gemeenskapsvoorbereidings werksessie tov 32 Bn.

92 DODDC, 32 Bn Gp 3, Box 158, 502/1/1 (32 Bn), Vol. 1, Stigting en Ontbinding van Hoofkwartiere en Eenhede – 32 Bn, Gemeenskapsvoorbereidings werksessie tov 32 Bn.

in other non-traditional units was causing a drop in the morale of Portuguese troops.[93] Additionally, the Chief of the Army made several decisions regarding 31 SAI and 32 Battalion on 16 June 1993. Again, the prevailing tone of these decisions seems to be quite nonchalant. Although the Chief of the Army was aware of the negative influence 'certain disparities' (presumably including the unequal remuneration tabled at the coordination conference) had on the morale of personnel, it was pointed out that action had been taken in this regard, but would take time before the problem would be solved. In the meantime, the Chief of the Army suggested that the problem be managed.[94] This was probably done according to a 1 June 1993 document from his office, in which four main 'causes for concern' were identified regarding the disbanding of 31 and 32 Battalions.[95] The office firstly noted that all members of these battalions were classified as PD-members (the suffix to their force numbers), which was used for temporary members who were not South African citizens. He pointed out that, as soon as the administrative process to change their force number suffixes to PB had been completed, their employment status would no longer be problematic. How and, more importantly, how soon, this was to be done was not, however, stipulated. Secondly, although members of the units had contributed towards the SADF pension scheme from 1989, many of their pension numbers did not appear on their payslips, creating doubt whether their contributions had been recorded and would be recognised. Thirdly, the PD-suffix apparently carried a negative connotation and, in decision that could only further complicate administrative matters, the Chief of the Army noted that the suffix could eventually – presumably after it had been changed to PB – be changed again, this time to PE. How exactly this would remove the stigma associated with a PD-suffix remains unclear. The final, and perhaps most significant, matter of concern to 31 and 32 Battalion members surrounded retirement packages. Although many of the soldiers had been with these units since 1975, a total of almost 20 years, the Chief of the Army pointed out that retirement packages could only be negotiated according to their contributions to the SADF retirement scheme. As they had only started contributing in 1989, this amount would be negligible. Even after 32 Battalion had officially been disbanded, however, the Chief of the Army stated that 'The assurance is given that the SA army will not turn its back on these members and will continuously liaise with members through coordination forums to resolve uncertainties and problems.'[96]

93 DODDC, 32 Bn Gp 3, Box 158, 502/1/1 (32 Bn), Vol. 1, Stigting en Ontbinding van Hoofkwartiere en Eenhede – 32 Bn, Notule van die Koörd Konf tov die rasionalisasie van 31 SAI en 32 Bn wat gehou is op 8 Junie 1993 om 08:00 te Vasbyt Lokaal, Leër HK.

94 DODDC, 32 Bn Gp 3, Box 158, 502/1/1 (32 Bn), Vol. 1, Stigting en Ontbinding van Hoofkwartiere en Eenhede – 32 Bn, Opmerkings deur die voorsitter. Afrikaans: *sekere dispariteite*.

95 DODDC, 32 Bn Gp 3, Box 78, 502/1/1, Vol. 1, Stigting en ontbinding van hoofkwartiere en eenhede: SA Leer, Knelpunte: Ontbinding van 31/32 Bn. Afrikaans: *knelpunte*.

96 DODDC, 32 Bn Gp 3, Box 78, 502/1/1, Vol. 1, Stigting en ontbinding van hoofkwartiere en eenhede: SA Leer, Knelpunte: Ontbinding van 31/32 Bn. Afrikaans: *Die versekering*

Conclusion

The disbanding of 32 Battalion was clearly a rushed attempt to implement a decision taken in haste to promote the agendas of politicians leading up to democratic elections in South Africa. It would appear that 32 Battalion was an embarrassment of sorts for both the government of the time and the apparent successor government; neither was prepared for the political consequences of having a unit on strength that had been successful in an increasingly unpopular war. To rid themselves of an inconvenient reminder of the past, little thought was given at a political level as to the consequences of disbanding the unit. Senior SADF officers did, however, attempt to provide for the unit before the new dispensation, sure to view 32 Battalion unfavourably, took over. These efforts to make the disbanding of the unit as painless as possible were ultimately unsuccessful and 32 Battalion did not survive the quench. Given the attitude of the SADF Command and the apparent political apathy, efforts would ultimately prove unsuccessful at preserving the integrity of the 32 Battalion community and the blade was cast aside. Nonetheless, the effort that the white members of the unit and greater SADF went to – many of them admittedly only when they were still active in the SADF – to try and secure a future for the black members indicates not only the ingrained non-racial culture prevalent within 32 Battalion, but also the ability members of the unit had to influence other SADF members towards a more inclusive approach to military thinking. On the eve of democracy and the integration of various defence forces into the SANDF, the uncertainty about how integration would affect South Africa seems to have been a non-issue for the men and women of 32 Battalion. As many of the former members claim in their memoirs, race does not appear to have played a large role within the unit. While the greater South Africa was struggling with bringing an end to apartheid – and, notably, the SADF command, who had not done a great deal about the welfare of those left at Pomfret, played a significant part in this – 32 Battalion had overcome many of the obstacles that were still, and continue, to face South Africa.

word gegee dat die SA Leër nie sy rug op die lede sal keer nie en dmv koördineringsforum [*sic*] *voortdurend met die lede sal skakel ten einde onduidelikhede of probleme op te klaar.*

Conclusion

The latter part of the twentieth century saw a long and drawn out battle between NATO and WP countries. The main power brokers of these two groups, the USA and the USSR, never fought one another, yet the Cold War did include several wars and conflicts, encouraged and supported by the two superpowers, in other parts of the world. In southern Africa, Soviet and American surrogates were engaged for an extended period of time, vying for supremacy in their own right while at the same time serving the purpose of their respective sponsors. Portugal's withdrawal from her African colonies left a power vacuum that, particularly in Angola, resulted in a protracted civil war, drawing support from countries all over the globe at one point or another.

South Africa had a vested interest in the Angolan Civil War, because the Angolan liberation movements that received support from the USSR were, by extension, sympathetic to South African liberation movements with a similar base of support. It therefore served South Africa's interests to see a sympathetic government installed in Angola. To this end, Pretoria supported both the FNLA and UNITA in the conflict to become the dominant force in Angola, though the latter proved significantly more successful. The FNLA, because they were unsuccessful in their bid to gain political ascendancy in Angola, provided a significant contribution to the South African war effort: the FNLA troops that were stationed in the south of Angola in the lead up to independence in 1975 became 31 and 32 Battalions of the SADF.

After the MPLA assumed power in Angola, Pretoria continued with her fight against the South African and Namibian liberation movements, both now supported and given refuge by the Angolan government. The SADF now deployed the former FNLA troops of 31 and 32 Battalions continuously and successfully against these liberation forces and, indeed, against Angolan and Cuban armed forces. By using troops that were not from South Africa, they minimised South African casualties and the concurrent public backlash and it suited the apartheid mind-set of the time to sacrifice black lives in the conflict rather than diminish the pool of precious white manpower in South Africa.

Of course, the Angolan troops who joined the SADF had, to a certain extent, a choice in the matter. Although their choices were limited – they had been abandoned by their Angolan leaders and were facing an uncertain future in Angola – some chose not to serve in the SADF and preferred to find out what life as refugees would hold. Others joined the SADF in units like 32 Battalion, but soon realised that discipline in the SADF far exceeded the norms that they had been used to in the FNLA and soon left their units, either formally or by simply going AWOL. Those that chose to stay with 32 Battalion were able to provide a measure of security to their families, but had to face the prospect of fighting against their Angolan countrymen in an attempt to prolong a policy – apartheid – that was inherently orientated against them.

This situation had all the hallmarks of a spectacular failure, yet the men of 32 Battalion were able to turn the odds in their favour and they became a highly successful unit. While some of the white leaders of 32 Battalion might not have agreed with the NP government's policies, including apartheid and conscription to, essentially, defend that policy, they were nonetheless accustomed to living in a segregated society. At 32 Battalion, apart from the normal military division along lines of rank, segregation was minimal. Despite this, though, many white South Africans who served with 32 Battalion requested to remain there, or return on subsequent camps, after their term of service expired. The supposed inherent differences between black and white, so assiduously perpetrated by the National Party, apparently became insignificant on the fighting front, and particularly in the heat of battle. In fact, the South Africans did not merely tolerate the presence of their black comrades; a strong and lasting bond, based on mutual respect, developed between the two groups. Whatever the motivations of the black members of 32 Battalion might have been to join the unit in the first place, they soon realised that they could depend on their white leaders to provide, if not a luxurious standard of living, at least the basic necessities of life. In return, the white members of the unit understood that, despite coming from a totally different mould than the typical SADF soldier, the black soldiers of 32 Battalion were just as formidable as their white counterparts.

In a microcosm of present-day South African society, 32 Battalion proved that a 'rainbow unit', if not a rainbow nation, was possible and, in the process, demonstrated the efficiency that such a symbiosis could produce: in battle, 32 Battalion had few equals in the SADF, and probably in southern Africa.

The combat capabilities of 32 Battalion evolved from the ill-disciplined, poorly-trained men that Jan Breytenbach had found at Mpupa in 1975 and hastily organised into Bravo Group, in time for Operation Savannah, into a highly efficient and adaptable unit, structured along regular SADF-lines. The unit emerged from a culture of adaptability, when they had to make use of whatever dated equipment the SADF provided, along with what they could scrounge during Operation Savannah. Nonetheless, they proved that they had the potential to become a significant part of the SADF's combat forces. The culture of innovation and improvisation that was necessary for success during Operation Savannah remained part of the unit's DNA, and was well-suited to the SADF's culture of decentralised command. The continued evolution of 32 Battalion allowed them to assume the role of a counterinsurgency force, dominating areas in the south of Angola and denying South Africa's opponents routes of infiltration in Namibia, as well as that of a conventional unit, complete with support elements, capable of functioning effectively in combination with other SADF units. Additionally, 32 Battalion was at the forefront of developing and testing new weapons and tactics for the SADF. They recognised the importance of thorough reconnaissance before this became prevalent in the greater

SADF and developed their own reconnaissance wing to fulfil this role. Towards the end of the war, they were also often asked to field-test new weapons systems for the SADF, including advanced systems like the Ratel-ZT3 missile system.

Although 32 Battalion experienced some difficulties in gaining official recognition from the SADF, once they had achieved that, a reasonably dependable line of supply was soon established. This line, however, focused primarily on combat materiel, rather than necessities of life. When problems surrounding lines of supply and communication arose, these were addressed much sooner if they related to the combat expediency of the unit than when they concerned the wellbeing of the soldiers. Nonetheless, 32 Battalion was able to rely on the same level of medical support as other SADF units, at least as far as casualties and emergencies went. Over the course of time, supplementary services like dentists, optometrists and social workers also provided their services to the unit. However, the SADF's primary view of 32 Battalion continued to be that of a frontline combat unit, and lines and levels of supply reflected that. It often took direct intervention from 32 Battalion's OC to ensure that supplies that were not essential to combat reached the unit in good time.

The nature and origins of 32 Battalion dictated that they differed significantly from regular SADF units. The SADF relied, for the most part, on NSM for their pool of manpower, anchored by a small number of PF members. While the PF contingent had a comparatively large degree of social freedom – they were able to take their families with when they were stationed abroad, for example – NSM had to leave their social existence behind when they reported for duty. This meant that very few SADF units had large complements of civilians attached to the unit and the SADF was consequently not geared towards accommodating large numbers of family members. In the case of 32 Battalion, however, most of the black soldiers brought their families with them when they joined the unit. This presented a significant challenge to the SADF: they had to establish how to supply a large civilian attachment to one of their units and, to complicate matters for South Africa's apartheid government, these civilians were black. Predictably, then, the SADF did not assign a high priority to the supply and support of 32 Battalion's civilians, and it took significant agitation from various senior members of the unit to ensure that the civilians were provided with basic necessities. Nonetheless, conditions at 32 Battalion's Buffalo Base were probably still better than those in Angola and, over time, civilians did come to enjoy significant benefits from their association with 32 Battalion and the SADF, relating to education, medical care, financial security and the protection of the SADF's legal system.

The attitude towards the civilians, and soldiers, of 32 Battalion highlights a significant dichotomy among South Africans who were involved with 32 Battalion. On the one hand, the officers and NCOs of the unit were sympathetic to the plight of their black brothers-in-arms. They frequently went to great lengths to ensure the wellbeing of black members, and their families, and often remained in touch with the unit after their terms of service had ended. Indeed, many returned to the unit on subsequent National Service 'camps' to continue their association with their black comrades. At the other end of the spectrum, South African politicians seemed much less concerned about the wellbeing of 32 Battalion and focused primarily on how they could most effectively utilise the unit while minimising international embarrassment. This was probably true for regular SADF units, too, but the nature of 32 Battalion's composition necessitated a greater level of sensitivity that was not forthcoming from political circles. Senior SADF officers fell somewhere in between these extremes: while they were more sensitive to the nature and needs of 32 Battalion than politicians, they did not have the same level of empathy as men who had served with the unit, alongside the black troops. These three points of view would have a significant impact on 32 Battalion after the Border War, when they relocated to South Africa.

Relocation to Pomfret in South Africa presented a significant social disruption for 32 Battalion. The lingua franca of the unit was Portuguese, and while most soldiers were conversant in English or Afrikaans, many civilians were not. Portuguese, by contrast, is not widely spoken in South Africa. Additionally, 32 Battalion's combat focus shifted from aggressive patrols and offensive operations to peacekeeping operations in South African townships. While they achieved admirable results, soldiers who had known nothing but a life of combat, first in Angola and then in Namibia, were not ideal peacekeepers. The unit faced the challenge of not being acceptable to either the white or black South African population. They were either 'too black' or, for the black South African population, they had fought with the SADF against black liberation movements. This made for an untenable situation and allegations of criminal offences, whether real or imaginary, were soon brought against the unit. This resulted in them being withdrawn from active deployments and, ultimately disbanded. The men, women and children who had chosen to side with South Africa could not return to an Angola run by their former enemies or to a newly-independent Namibia, also governed by those that 32 Battalion had fought during the Border War. The only alternative was to stay in a country of which they had little knowledge.

In the lead up to democratic elections in South Africa in 1994, 32 Battalion was part of the SADF's rationalisation and integration process, whereby armed forces of the former struggle movements became part of the SADF. At the same time, the SADF had to decrease in size significantly, since it was no longer required either to wage a war against the liberation movements that were now becoming a part of it or, theoretically, as a township peacekeeping force. The percentage of South Africa's GDP spent on the defence budget was also unacceptable. As a result, 32 Battalion was sacrificed on the altar of supposed progress for South Africa, even though they had, to a larger extent than many other SADF units, shown just how effective a multiracial, multicultural unit could be. Once again, 32 Battalion's own white officers made concerted efforts to secure a future for the black troops, but they were unsuccessful, apart from a few troops that integrated into other SADF units. The plight of the remaining members, and civilians, at Pomfret was ignored by South African politicians, both black and white.

The creation of 32 Battalion, as a useful addition to the SADF's combat capability, and their eventual abandonment at Pomfret invites comparisons with armies throughout the world and, indeed, throughout history, as far back as the Greek city-states. In the Roman Empire, soldiers serving as auxiliaries could gain Roman citizenship, and the attendant benefits, through their military service. This theme has continued to the present day, and many countries still accept foreigners into their armies, ultimately giving those soldiers citizenship of the country for which they fought. The situation was no different with 32 Battalion, although it was significantly less formalised. The Angolan soldiers of the unit served the SADF, in some cases for nearly 30 years, in order to secure a better future for them and their families. While many of them did receive South African citizenship, though not without crossing several administrative hurdles along the way, the benefits of citizenship were not as great as they would have expected. The healthcare that they received in the SADF was, largely not continued, their pension contributions were not used efficiently, they still found it very difficult to acquire property and the infrastructure at Pomfret was lacking, at best.

In a somewhat ironic twist of history, a deciding factor in gaining self-government from colonial powers was frequently the ability to take responsibility for the country's internal defence. Colonial powers were loath to grant self-government to countries that could not prove that they would be able to defend themselves against foreign aggression. The soldiers of 32 Battalion epitomised the ability to provide internal defence, of whichever country they chose to, or were forced to, support, yet they were probably, out of all the participants in the Border War, the furthest from self-sufficiency, and personal and financial freedom.

The thread that binds the book is the relationship between the military and social sides of 32 Battalion. Just as the soldiers could not be removed from their families, so military and society could not be separated. This is reminiscent of campaigning armies over the course of the last millennium. Although 'camp followers', particularly with European armies on campaign, were not attached to the armies in as formal a sense as 32 Battalion's civilians, they still essentially formed part of those armies, if only by deriving indirect support from them. In the case of 32 Battalion, the SADF directly supported the civilians involved with the unit. Nonetheless, the unit developed its own network of kinship. Historically, female camp followers of campaigning armies formed some form of attachment to the male soldiers, either formally through marriage or informally as prostitutes. If the camp follower's husband or 'patron' in the army passed away, the woman often had no choice but to find another soldier through which to continue her association with the unit, or be stranded in a foreign country. Children born to the camp followers were inevitably absorbed by the unit, initially as drummer boys and such, and as soldiers when they grew older. A similar situation existed and was encouraged, in 32 Battalion. Only civilians with direct links to the unit could stay in the SADF controlled civilian areas, and no informal settlements were tolerated. This meant that women had to continue their association with the unit if their husbands passed away. The SADF did not only accept this principle, they actively encouraged it to promote a sense of social stability. Similarly, children born on 32 Battalion bases, although provided with an education by the unit, grew up in a strictly military milieu.

This book used the motto of 32 Battalion – *Proelio Procusi*, or Forged in Battle – as a metaphorical lens through which the history of the unit was examined. Extending the metaphor of a forge, each chapter examined a particular aspect of the forging of a blade.

This made it apparent that, though battle played a significant role in forging the identity of the unit, society played as least as great a role. This includes the extent to which civilians attached to 32 Battalion were embraced by the SADF, the interaction between black and white members of the unit and, ultimately, the circumstances in which the former members of 32 Battalion were forced to spend their lives after the war. The Battalion was forged in battle; many of the soldiers knew nothing but war until they came to South Africa in 1989. However, battle alone did not generate sufficient heat to shape the character of a unit that continues to stimulate public discourse and academic study to this day. To forge, and ultimately break, the blade that was 32 Battalion took the interaction of battle, society and politics and tested the mettle of everyone involved with the unit.

Bibliography

Archival Sources

Department of Defence Documentation Centre (DODDC)

1 Military Area (1 MG)

Box 82, G/OPS/3/3/BRAVO, Vol. 1
Box 82, G/OPS/3/3/BRAVO, Vol. 1, Bravo
Box 82, Troep Bew: Feb
Box 102, G/OPS/3/3/CARPENTER, Vol. 1, Operations (specific) Unconventional Operation Carpenter

1 Military Area Sector 20 (1 MG Sektor 20)

Box 78, 302/6/C63, Vol. 1, Projek Carpenter

32 Battalion, Group 1 (32 Bn)

Box 2, G/OPS/3/3, Vol. 1, Konferensies
Box 3, Q/WKS/1, Vol. 1, Warren Hutte
Box 7, G/INT/1/ALG, Algemeen
Box 7, G/OPS/3/3, Vol. 1, Insam
Box 7, G/OPS/3/3, Vol. 1, Konferensies
Box 7, G/OPS/3/3/LETTA, Vol. 1
Box 7, G/OPS/3/3 – LETTA, Vol. 1, Bravo Group
Box 7, G/OPS/3/3/LETTA, Vol. 1, Letta
Box 8, G/INT/3/2, Inrap: Nov 76
Box 8, G/INT/5/1, Inligting samevatting
Box 8, LOG/OPS/1/16, Vol. 1, Admin Orders en Instrs
Box 9, LOG/OPS/3/16/8, Vol. 1, Medies en gesondheid (Verslae, aanvrae, ens.)
Box 9, LOG/OPS/3/16/9, Vol. 1, Menasies en inrigtings
Box 9, LOG/OPS/3/16/9/1, Vol. 1, Spaar Fasiliteite
Box 9, LOG/OPS/3/16/13, Vol. 1, Personeel beleid (Vrywillige diens ens.).
Box 9, LOG/OPS/3/16/13/3, Vol. 1, Pers Welsyn (Dood, siekte van naasbestaandes, uitstel van opl)
Box 9, LOG/OPS/3/16/13/4, Vol. 1, Portugese / Ang'e

Box 9, LOG/OPS/3/16/13/4, Portugese / Angolese
Box 12, 101/7/1/4, Vol. 1, Ondersoek ivm implementering van hervestigingsbeleid van verminkte / oorlede lede van 32 Bn
Box 12, 205/4, Insam – Intsum
Box 14, G/OPS/3/3, Bevelsdirektiewe.
Box 14, G/OPS/3/3, Vol. 1, Budgie
Box 14, G/OPS/3/3, Vol. 1, Budgie – B Group
Box 14, G/OPS/3/3, Vol. 1, Focus
Box 14, G/OPS/3/3, Vol. 1, Porto Vlugtelinge
Box 41, 309/1/A5, Vol. 1, Buffalo Skool
Box 41, 309/1/ALG, Vol. 1, Spesifieke Operasies: Gesamentlik
Box 41, 309/1/EVAL, Vol. 1, Gesamentlike Ops: Eval van Anderskleuriges.
Box 41, 309/1/PROJ CARP, Projek Carpenter
Box 41, 309/1/5, Vol. 1, Lesse geleer gedurende Op Savannah
Box 41, 309/1/51 (Savannah), Vol. 1, Lesse geleer gedurende Op Savannah
Box 50, 107/2/3, Ontslag SP lede
Box 55, 522/1, Vol. 1, Konferensies: 101 TM
Box 55, 522/1/1MG, Vol. 1
Box 55, 522/1 (Bev), Vol. 1
Box 56, 309/1, Vol. 5, Kontakte
Box 72, HVS/206/36/4, Beplanningsraad

32 Battalion, Group 2 (32 Bn Gp 2)
Box 21, 104/10/12/13, Instandhouding van personeel: Geneeskundige dienste: Mediese ondersoek beleid
Box 28, 104/12/1/1
Box 28, 104/12/1/1, Vol. 1
Box 28, 104/12/1/1 (SP), Vol. 4, Instandhouding van personeel: Welsynsdienste: Gevallewerk: Individuele persone
Box 28, 104/12/1/1/SP, Instandhouding van personeel: Welsynsdienste: Gevallewerk: Individuele persone
Box 28, 104/12/1/1/SP, Vol. 4, Instandhouding van Personeel: Welsynsdienste; Gevallewerk: Individuele Persone
Box 28, 104/12/5, Vol. 2, Instandhouding van Personeel: Welsynsdienste: Rehabilitasie van oorlogsgewondes
Box 61, 107/1, Vol. 1, Personeelbeskikking: Lewensversekering
Box 61, 107/1/1, Vol. 2, Versekering / Assuransie: Groepsversekering
Box 61, 107/1/1/4, Vol. 2, Groeplewensversekering in die SAW
Box 77, 309/1 B-Skool, Vol. 3, Buffalo Skool (Pica Pau)
Box 155, 522/1, Konferensies
Box 155, 522/1 (PRO), Vol. 1, Konferensies: Konferensies, Kongresse, Seminare, Simposium, Vergaderings
Box 156, 522/1, Konferensies

Box 156, 522/1, Vol. 3, Konferensies, Kongresse, Seminare, Simposiums, Vergaderings: Konferensies
Box 156, 522/4, Vol. 1, Konferensies, Kongresse, Seminare, Simposiums en Vergaderings: Vergaderings
Box 260, 522/1, Vol. 1, Konferensies, Kongresse, Seminare, Simposiums en Vergaderings: Konferensies
Box 260, 522/1, Vol. 1, Konferensies, Kongresse, Seminare, Simposiums en Vergaderings: Konferensies
Box 261, 522/1, Vol. 1, Konferensies / Kongresse / Seminare / Simposiums / Vergaderings: Notules.
Box 261, 522/1, Vol. 4, Log Konferensie.
Box 261, 522/1, Vol. 9, Notule van weeklikse monitor
Box 261, 522/1, Vol. 14, Konferensies
Box 262, 522/1, Vol. 1, Konferensies
Box 262, 522/1/1, Vol. 2, Bevelvoerderskonferensies
Box 262, 522/1/1, Vol. 4, Konferensies, kongresse, seminare, simposiums & vergaderings: SD Leer Sektor 20
Box 262, 522/1/1, Vol. 7, Bevelvoerderskonferensies
Box 262, 522/1/BEV, Vol. 1, Konferensies
Box 262, 522/4, Vol. 1, Konf., Kong, Semnaar, Simposiums + Vergaderings: Vergaderings

32 Battalion, Group 2A (32 Bn Gp 2A)
Box 132, File 01, Ops Kakebeen Sitrap
Box 132, Inligting, Vol. 1, 32 Bn Sielkundige Fiksie

32 Battalion, Group 3 (32 Bn Gp 3)
Box 19, 522/1, Vol. 4
Box 19, 522/1, Vol. 4, Konferensies
Box 28, 104/11/6/9, Vol. 2, Instandhouding van Personeel: Gesondheidsdienste / Gesondheidsverslae en opgawes: Aanmeldbare siektes
Box 28, 104/11/6/9, Vol. 3, Gesondheidsdienste: Aanmeldbare siektes
Box 28, 104/12/4, Vol. 1, Maatskaplike werkdiens: Nasorg van oorlogbeseerdes
Box 28, 32BN/MBH/B/104/11/6/9, Vol. 1, VIGS: Hantering in spanverband; Aanmeldbare siektes
Box 43, 106/20/2, Vol. 1, Polisiedienste: Arrestasies en aanhoudings
Box 54, 309/1, Spesifieke Operasies
Box 54, 309/1, Vol. 1, Spesifieke Operasies (Agree)
Box 55, 310/1, Vol. 1, Spesiale Operasies SA Leër: Pica Pau Skool
Box 55, 311/1, Vol. 1, Hulpverlening en samewerking met lande
Box 55, 311/2/3, Vol. 2, Staatsdepartemente: Onderwys en Opleiding
Box 75, 501/4, Vol. 4, Bevel en Beheer: 32 Bn doelwitte
Box 77, 501/13, Vol. 1, Maandelikse terugvoer
Box 77, 501/13, Vol. 2, Maandelikse terugvoer

Box 78, 502/1, Vol. 1, Stigting en ontbinding van hoofkwartiere en eenhede
Box 78, 502/1/B, Vol. 1, Organisasie-beheer: Stigting en ontbinding van hoofkwartiere en eenhede: Beleid
Box 100, 520/4, Vol. 1, Binnelandse bewegings
Box 101, 522/1, Vol. 3, Konferensies
Box 101, 522/1, Vol. 5, Konferensies
Box 121, 104/10/14/6, Vol. 2, Instandhouding van Pers: Geneeskundige dienste: Hopitalisasie: Dwelmverslaafdes
Box 125, 104/12/14/6, Vol. 1, Welwilendheidsgebare in die SAW
Box 158, 502/1/1 (32 Bn), Vol. 1, Stigting en Ontbinding van Hoofkwartiere en Eenhede – 32 Bn
Box 160, 509/1, Vol. 2, Ministeriele Navrae m.b.t. personeelaangeleenthede
Chief of Staff Operations, Group 1 (HS Ops Gp 1)
Box 9, HS/11/3/14, Vol. 1, Waardering oor die moontlike gebruik / aanwending van Chipenda / FNLA tot voordeel van RSA
Box 9, HS/11/3/14, Vol. 3, Report no. 004/nov/75
Box 10, HS/11/3/14, Vol. 4, Interrogation of Cuban POWs at Silva Porto on 27–29 Nov 75

Sector 10 Headquarters (Sektor 10 HK)
Box 57, 204/3/AG, Komops Inligting oor Angola

Sector 20, Group 3 (Sektor 20 Gp 3)
Box 72, 309/1, Vol. 1, Algemeen

South West Africa Headquarters Territory Force, Subdivision Counterintelligence (SWA HK GM OATI)
Box 105, SEK/202/02732, Vol. 1, DTI

South West Africa Headquarters (Operations) (SWA HK Ops)
Box 7, 309/1, Vol. 1, 32 Bn
Box 19, G/OPS/3/3, Vol. 2, Hoër In

SWS 3
Box 52, 309/1, Vol. 1

Historical Papers Archive
Missing Voices
A3079, Interviews and documents, 2004–2012
A3079-B1-7-001, Johan Anderson, 12-11-2008
A3079-B1-11-001, Kevin Fitzgerald Tape 0/11, A3079/B.21
A3079-D4-001, John Keene interviewed by Mike Cadman 19-09-07
A3079-D6-001, National Serviceman (name withheld) 10-09-07

A3079-D8-001, Anton Oberholzer Ratel 20mm Gunner 17-01-08
A30179-D9-001, Dr Colin Forbes 4-11-07

Published Works

Alden, C., *Apartheid's Last Stand: The Rise and Fall of the South African Security State.* London: MacMillan, 1996

Andrew, C. & Mitrokhin, V., *The World was Going our Way: The KGB and the battle for the Third World.* New York: Perseus Books, 2005

Arnold, G., *Wars in the Third World since 1945.* London: Cassell Publishers Ltd., 1991

Baines, G., *South Africa's 'Border War': Contested narratives and conflicting memories.* London: Bloomsbury, 2014

Beaufre, A., *Strategy of action.* Translated by Barry, R. H., London: Faber & Faber, 1967

Beckett, I. F. W., *Modern Insurgencies and Counterinsurgencies: Guerrillas and their opponents since 1750.* London: Routledge, 2001

Birmingham, D., *Empire in Africa: Angola and its neighbors.* Athens: Ohio University Press, 2006

Black, J., *Rethinking Military History.* London: Routledge, 2004

Blake, C., *From Soldier to Civvy: Reflections on National Service.* Cape Town: Zebra, 2010

Bothma, L. J., *Die Buffel Struikel: 'n Storie van 32 Bataljon en sy mense.* Bloemfontein: L.J. Bothma, 2007

Bothma, L. J., *Vang 'n Boer: Die stryd tussen Boer en Ovambo.* Bloemfontein: L.J. Bothma, 2012

Bourke, J., *An Intimate History of Killing: Face-to-Face Killing in Twentieth-Century Warfare.* London: Granta Books, 1999

Breytenbach, J., *Eden's Exiles: One soldier's fight for paradise.* Pretoria: Protea, 2015

Breytenbach, J., *Forged in Battle.* Cape Town: Saayman & Weber, 1986

Breytenbach, J., *Forged in Battle, Second Edition.* Pretoria: Protea, 2014

Breytenbach, J., *The Buffalo Soldiers: The Story of South Africa's 32-Battalion 1975–1993.* Alberton: Galago, 2002.

Breytenbach, J., *The Tempered Sword: Forged in Battle Revisited; Operation Savannah and the birth of 32 Bn.* Bushwarrior.com, 2011

Breytenbach, J., *They Live by the Sword.* Alberton: Lemur, 1990

Bridgland, F., *The War for Africa: twelve months that transformed a continent.* Gibraltar: Ashanti, 1990

Camp, S. & Heitman, H., *Surviving the Ride: a pictorial history of South African-manufactured mine-protected vehicles.* Pinetown: 30° South, 2014

Cann, J. P., *Counterinsurgency in Africa: The Portuguese Way of War, 1931–1974.* Westport: Greenwood, 1997

Castro, F., *My Life.* Translated by Hurley, A., London: Penguin, 2007

Colburn, F. D., *The Vogue of Revolution in Poor Countries.* Princeton: University Press, 1994

Conway, D., *Stop the Call-up: Masculinities, Militarisation and the End Conscription Campaign; war resistance in apartheid South Africa*. Johannesburg: University of the Witwatersrand, 2012

De Andrade, M. & Ollivier, M., *The War in Angola: a socio-economic study*. Dar es Salaam: Tanzania Publishing House, 1975

De Klerk, F. W., *The Last Trek – a new beginning: The Autobiography*. London: MacMillan, 1999.

Du Preez, S., *Avontuur in Angola*. Pretoria: Van Schaik, 1989

Echenberg, M., *Colonial Conscripts: The 'Tirailleurs Senegalais' in French West Africa, 1857–1960*. Portsmouth, New Hampshire: Heinemann, 1991

Feinstein, A., *Battle Scarred: Hidden costs of the Border War*. Cape Town: Tafelberg, 2011

Frankel, P. H., *Pretoria's Praetorians: Civil-Military Relations in South Africa*. Cambridge: University Press, 1984

Galula, D., *Counterinsurgency Warfare: Theory and Practice*. London: Pall Mall Press, 1964

Geldenhuys, D., *Isolated States: A ComparativeAanalysis*. Johannesburg: Jonathan Ball, 1990

Geldenhuys, J., *A General's Story: From an Era of War and Peace*. Johannesburg: Jonathan Ball, 1995

Glatthaar, J., *The March to the Sea and Beyond: Sherman's Troops in the Savannah and Carolinas Campaigns*. Baton Rouge: Louisana State University Press, 1985

Gleijeses, P., *Conflicting Missions: Havana, Washington, Pretoria*. Alberton: Galago, 2003.

Grundy, K. W., *Soldiers without Politics; Blacks in the South African Armed Forces*. Los Angeles: University of California Press, 1983

Guimarães, F. A., *The Origins of the Angolan Civil War: Foreign Intervention and Domestic Political Conflict*. Basingstoke: MacMillan, 1998

Holmes, R., *Acts of War: The Behaviour of Men in Battle*. New York: Free Press, 1985

Hull, I. V., *Absolute Destruction: Military Culture and the Practices of War in Imperial Germany*. Ithaca: Cornell University Press, 2005

Keegan, J., *The Face of Battle*. New York: Penguin 1976

Keegan, T. J., *Facing the Storm: Portraits of Black Lives in Rural South Africa*. Cape Town: Philip, 1988

Liddell-Hart, B. H., *History of the Second World War*. London: Cassell, 1970

Liebenberg, I., Risquet, J. & Shubin, V. (eds), *A Far-Away War; Angola 1975–1989*. Stellenbosch: SUN MeDIA, 2015.

Macksey, K., *For Want of aNnail: The Impact on War of Logistics and Communications*. London: Brassey's, 1989

Maier, K., *Angola: Promises and lies*. Rivonia: William Waterman, 1996

Malan, M. A. de M., *My Life with the SA Defence Force*. Pretoria: Protea, 2006

Marwick, A., *Britain in the Century of Total War: war, peace and social change, 1900–1967*. Harmondsworth: Penguin, 1970

Marwick, A., *The New Nature of History: Knowledge, Evidence, Language.* Basingstoke: Palgrave, 2001

Miller, J., *An African Volk: The apartheid regime and its search for survival.* Oxford: Oxford University Press, 2016

Morillo, S. & Pavkovic, M. F., *What is Military History?* Cambridge: Polity, 2013

Moyd, M. R., *Violent Intermediaries: African Soldiers, Conquest, and Everyday Colonialism in German East Africa.* Athens, Ohio: University Press, 2014

Namakalu, O. O., *Armed Liberation Struggle: Some accounts of PLAN's combat operations.* Windhoek: Gamsberg MacMillan, 2004

Ngculu, J., *The Honour to Serve: Recollections of an Umkhonto soldier.* Cape Town: Philip, 2009

Nortje, P., *32 Battalion: The Inside Story of South Africa's Elite Fighting Unit.* Cape Town: Zebra, 2003

Nortje, P., *The Terrible Ones: A complete history of 32 Battalion.* Cape Town: Zebra, 2012

Orpen, N., *War in the Desert.* Cape Town: Purnell: 1971

Parker, G. (ed.), *Cambridge Illustrated History: Warfare.* Cambridge: Cambridge University Press, 1995

Parsons, T. H., *The African Rank-and-File: Social Implications of Colonial Military Service in the King's African Rifles, 1902–1964.* Portsmouth, New Hampshire: Heinemann, 1999

Parsons, T. H., *The Rule of Empires: Those Who Built Them, Those Who Endured Them, and Why They Always Fall.* Oxford: University Press, 2010

Pearce, J., *Political Identity and Conflict in central Angola, 1975–2002.* Cambridge: Cambridge University Press, 2015

Pretorius, F., *Life on Commando during the Anglo-Boer War, 1899–1902.* Cape Town: Human & Rousseau, 1999

Ricoeur, P., *Memory, History, Forgetting.* Translated by Blamey, K. & Pellauer, D., Chicago: University Press, 2004.

Rodman, P. W., *More Precious than Peace: The Cold War and the Struggle for the Third World.* New York: Charles Scribner's Sons, 1994

Roherty, J. M., *State security in South Africa: Civil-military relations under PW Botha.* New York: M. E. Sharpe, 1992

Scheepers, M., *Striking Inside Angola with 32 Battalion.* Solihull: Helion and Pinetown: 30° South, 2012

Scholtz, L., *Die SAW in die Grensoorlog: 1966–1989.* Cape Town: Tafelberg, 2013

Scholtz, L., *The SADF and Cuito Cuanavale: A tactical and strategic analysis.* Johannesburg: Delta, 2020

Scott, J. C., *Seeing like a State: How certain schemes to improve the human condition have failed.* New Haven: Yale University Press, 1999

Shubin, V., *The Hot 'Cold War': The USSR in Southern Africa.* London: Pluto, 2008

Simpson, T., *Umkhonto we Sizwe: The ANC's Armed Struggle.* Cape Town: Penguin, 2016

Steenkamp, W. L., *South Africa's Border War, 1966–1989.* Gibraltar: Ashanti, 1989.

Stiff, P., *The Covert War: Koevoet Operations in Namibia 1979–1989.* Alberton: Galago, 2004

Stiff, P., *The Silent War: South African Recce Operations 1969–1994.* Alberton: Galago, 1999.

Taylor, J., *A Whisper in the Reeds: 'The Terrible Ones': South Africa's 32 Battalion at war.* Solihull: Helion & Rugby: GG Books, 2013

Thompson, J. H., *An Unpopular War: From Afkak to Bosbefok: Voices of South African National Servicemen.* Cape Town: Zebra, 2006.

Turner, J. W., *Continent Ablaze: The Insurgency Wars in Africa 1960 to the Present.* Johannesburg: Jonathan Ball, 1998

Van Creveld, M., *Supplying War: Logistics from Wallenstein to Patton.* Cambridge: Cambridge University Press, 1977

Van der Waag, I., *A Military History of Modern South Africa.* Cape Town: Jonathan Ball, 2015

Van der Waals, W. S., *Portugal's War in Angola 1961–1974.* Pretoria: Protea, 2011

Van der Walt, N., *Bos toe!: 'n Storie oor die laaste fase van die Grensoorlog soos beleef deur 'n junior offisier van 32-Bataljon.* Swartkops: N. van der Walt, 2007

Verster, F., *Omega, oor en uit: Die storie van 'n opstandige troep.* Cape Town: Tafelberg, 2016

Webb, S., *Ops Medic: A National Serviceman's Border War.* Alberton: Galago, 2008

Weigert, S. L., *Angola: A Modern Military History, 1961–2002.* New York: Palgrave MacMillan, 2011

Westad, O. A., *The Global Cold War: Third World interventions and the making of our times.* Cambridge: Cambridge University Press, 2005

Woodruff, M. W., *Unheralded Victory: The defeat of the Viet Cong and the North Vietnamese Army 1961–1973.* Arlington: Vandamere, 1999

Book chapters and journal articles

Alexander, M., 'The Militarisation of South African White Society, 1948–1990' in *Scientia Militaria: South African Journal of Military Studies, 30 (2)*, 2000

Alexander, M., 'We Fear Naught but God' in *Scientia Militaria: South African Journal of Military Studies 30 (2)*, 2000

Balter, M., 'On World Aids Day, a shadow looms over Southern Africa' in *Science, 282 (5395)*, 1998

Becker, H., 'We Want Women to be Given an Equal Chance: Post-independence rural politics in northern Namibia' in Meintjies, S., et al (eds), *The Aftermath: Women in Post-Conflict Transformation*, London: Zed Books, 2001

Berat, L., 'Conscientious objection in South Africa: Governmental paranoia and the law of conscription' in *Vanderbilt Journal of Transnational Law* 22, 1989

Blanch, H. L. & Liebenberg, I., 'A view from Cuba: Internationalists against apartheid' in *Journal for Contemporary History 34 (1)*, 2009

Byrne, J. J., 'Africa's Cold War' in McMahon, R. J. (ed.), *The Cold War in the Third World.* Oxford: Oxford University Press, 2013

Callister, G., 'Patriotic Duty or Resented Imposition? Public reactions to military conscription in white South Africa, 1952–1972' in *Scientia Militaria: South African Journal of Military Studies, 35 (1),* 2007

Cameron, C. M., 'Race and Identity: The Culture of Combat in the Pacific War' in *The International History Review 27 (3),* 2005

Cawthra, G., 'The South African War Resistance Movement 1974–1994' in *Scientia Militaria: South African Journal of Military Studies, 43 (2),* 2015

Conway, D., 'Every coward's choice? Political objection to military service in apartheid South Africa as sexual citizenship' in *Citizenship Studies 8 (1),* 2004

Cornwell, R., 'The War for Independence' in Cilliers, J. & Dietrich, C. (eds), *Angola's War Economy; the role of oil and diamonds.* Pretoria: Institute for Security Studies, 2000

Daniel, J., 'Racism, the Cold War and South Africa's regional security strategies 1948–1990' in Onslow, S. (ed.), *Cold War in Southern Africa: white power, black liberation.* London: Routledge, 2009

De Beer, H. & Gamba, V., 'The Arms Dilemma: resources for arms or arms for resources?' in Cilliers, J. & Dietrich, C. (eds), *Angola's War Economy; the role of oil and diamonds.* Pretoria: Institute for Security Studies, 2000

Drewett, M., 'Battling over Borders: Narratives of Resistance to the South African Border War Voiced through Popular Music' in *Social Dynamics 29 (1),* 2003

Dutton, J. R., 'The Military Aspects of National Security' in Louw, M. H. H. (ed.), *National Security: A modern approach.* Pretoria: Institute for Strategic Studies, 1978

Echenberg, M. J., 'Paying the Blood Tax: Military Conscription in French West Africa, 1914–1929' in *Canadian Journal of African Studies 9 (2),* 1975

Enterline, A. J., Stull, E. & Magagnoli, J., 'Reversal of Fortune? Strategy Change and Counterinsurgency Success by Foreign Powers in the Twentieth Century' in *International Studies Perspectives 14,* 2013

Ferreira, R. & Liebenberg, I., 'The impact of war on Angola and South Africa: Two southern African case studies' in *Journal for Contemporary History 31 (3),* 2006

Foster, R. B., 'Foreword' in Beaufre, A., *Strategy for Tomorrow.* London: Macdonald and Jane's, 1974

Fourie, S. M., 'Van Mobilisering na Transformasie: Die era van Suid-Afrika se militêre hoogbloei met die Vaaldriehoekse samelewing (1974–1994) as konsentrasieveld' in *Scientia Militaria 30 (2),* 2000

Gomes Porto, J., Parsons, I. & Alden, C., 'From Soldiers to Citizens; the social, economic and political reintegration of UNITA ex-combatants' in *ISS Monograph Series No. 130,* 2007

Gossmann, A. M., 'Lost in Transition: The South African military and counterinsurgency' in *Small Wars and Insurgencies 19 (4),* 2008

Grundlingh, A., 'The King's Afrikaners? Enlistment and ethnic identity in the Union of South Africa's defence force during the Second World War, 1939–1945' in *Journal of African History, 40,* 1999

Kleynhans, E. & Gordon, W., 'Legislative disconnect or institutional gatekeeping? The DOD archive, classified military information, and contemporary military historical research in South Africa' in *Scientia Militaria, Vol. 48 (1)*, 2020

Lalloo, U. G. & Pillay, S., 'Managing Tuberculosis and HIV in sub-Sahara Africa' in *Current HIV/AIDS reports, 5*, 2008

Landau, L. B. & Duponchel, M., 'Law, Policies, or Social Position? Capabilities and the Determinants of Effective Protection in Four African Cities' in *Journal of Refugee Studies, 24 (1)*, 2011

Jacobs, C. J., 'Books on the Border War 1966–1990' in *Scientia Militaria: South African Journal of Military Studies 41 (2)*, 2013

Lynn, J. A., 'Discourse, Reality and the Culture of Combat' in *The International History Review 27 (3)*, 2005

Mayer, H. A., 'From Forts to Families: Following the Army into Western Pennsylvania' in *The Pennsylvania Magazine of History and Biography 130 (1)*, 2006

Morrell, R., 'The Times of Change: Men and Masculinity in South Africa' in Morrell, R. (ed.), *Changing men in southern Africa*. Pietermaritzburg: University of Natal Press, 2001

Murray, W., 'Does military culture matter?' in *Orbis: A Journal of World Affairs 43 (1)*, 1999.

Nathan, L., 'Marching to a Different Beat: the History of the End Conscription Campaign' in Cock, J., & Nathan, L. (eds), *War and Society; The Militarisation of South Africa*. Cape Town: David Philip, 1989

Nathan, L., 'Troops in the Townships, 1984–1987' in Cock, J. & Nathan, L. (eds), *War and Society; The militarisation of South Africa*. Cape Town: David Philip, 1989

Ndaba, B. & Smith, J., 'Steve Biko and the Rise of Black Consciousness' in Ndaba, B. et al, *The Black Consciousness Reader*. Johannesburg: Jacana, 2017

Ndaba, B. & Smith, J., 'The Soweto Massacre and the Growth of a new Black Consciousness' in Ndaba, B. et al, *The Black Consciousness Reader*. Johannesburg: Jacana, 2017

Onslow, S., 'Introduction' in Onslow, S. (ed.), *Cold War in Southern Africa: white power, black liberation*. London: Routledge, 2009

Onslow, S., 'The Cold War in Southern Africa: White power, black nationalism and external intervention' in Onslow, S. (ed.), *Cold War in Southern Africa: white power, black liberation*. London: Routledge, 2009

Robbins, S., 'Model Campaigns of Futility: The Portuguese in Africa, 1961–1974' in Fremont-Barnes, G. (ed.), *A History of Counterinsurgency, Volume 2: From Cyprus to Afghanistan, 1955 to the 21st Century*. Santa Barbara: Praeger, 2015

Robinson, D., 'Colonial Conscripts: The 'Tirailleurs Senegalais' in French West Africa, 1857–1960' in: *The American Historical Review, Vol. 99 (4)*, 1994

Roth, M., 'Eddie, Brian, Jack and let's phone Rusty: Is this the history of the Communist Party of South Africa (1921–1950)?' in *South African Historical Journal, 42 (1)*, 2000

Sandler, D., 'The psychological experiences of white conscripts in the black townships' in Cock, J., & Nathan, L. (eds), *War and Society; The Militarisation of South Africa*. Cape Town: David Philip, 1989

Satchwell, K., 'The power to defend: an analysis of various aspects of the Defence Act' in Cock, J., & Nathan, L. (eds), *War and Society; The Militarisation of South Africa*. Cape Town: David Philip, 1989

Van der Waag, I., 'A History of the South African Defence Force Institute (SADFI) 1916–1991' in *Scientia Militaria: South African Journal of Military Studies, 21 (4)*, 1991

Wessels, A., 'Half a Century of South African 'Border War' literature: A historiographical exploration' in *Journal for Contemporary History, 42 (2)*, 2017

Xaba, T., 'Masculinity and its Malcontents: The Confrontation between 'Struggle Masculinity' and 'Post-Struggle Masculinity' (1990–1997)' in Morrell, R. (ed.), *Changing Men in southern Africa*. Pietermaritzburg: University of Natal Press, 2001

Government publications

Fraser, C. A., *Revolutionary Warfare: basic principles of counter-insurgency (being a revision of 'Lessons learnt from past revolutionary wars')*. 4 Survey and Printing Regiment, pp.23–24

Military Information Bureau, SADF, *Militêre geneeskunde in Suid-Afrika 1913–1983*. Pretoria: Government Printer, 1983

Naidoo, D. (ed.), *The fourth dimension: The untold story of military health in South Africa*. Pretoria: South African Medical Health Service, 2009

Spies, F. J. du T., *Die Angolese Burgeroorlog*. Pretoria: Militêre Informasieburo, 1980

Spies, F. J. du T., *Operasie Savannah: Angola 1975–1989*. Pretoria: SADF, 1989

Stratford, D. O. & Collins, H. M., *Military Nursing in South Africa, 1914–1994*. Pretoria: Chief of the National Defence Force, 1994

United Nations Security Council resolution, S/RES/134, Question relating to the situation in the Union of South Africa, 1 April 1960

Acts

Defence Amendment Act, No. 85 of 1967

Defence Further Amendment Act, No. 83 of 1974

Defence Amendment Act, No. 34 of 1983

Theses and dissertations

Callister, G., *Compliance, Compulsion and Contest: aspects of military conscription in South Africa, 1952–1992*. Stellenbosch University: MA thesis, 2007

Interviews

Interview with Abel Agostin (pseudonym), former 32 Battalion soldier, Pretoria, 14-12-2018

Telephone interview with Brian Baloyi (pseudonym), son of former 32 Battalion soldier; Kimbo and Pomfret resident, Centurion, 17-03-2019

Interview with Charles Churra (pseudonym), former 32 Battalion soldier, Pretoria, 15-05-2019

Interview with David da Silva (pseudonym), former 32 Battalion soldier, Pretoria, 20-06-2019

Interview with Edwin Eduardo (pseudonym), son of former 32 Battalion soldier; Kimbo and Pomfret resident, Wonderboom, 24-06-2019

Telephone interview with Fabia Fernando (pseudonym), former teacher at Pica Pau school, Centurion, 02-07-2019

Telephone interview with Gancho Gonzalez (pseudonym), former 32 Battalion soldier, Centurion, 04-07-2019

Interview with Hilton Husson (pseudonym), former 32 Battalion soldier, Centurion, 10-07-2019

Interview with Ian Ines (pseudonym), former 32 Battalion soldier, Centurion, 10-07-2019

Group discussion with former 32 Battalion soldiers, Centurion, 10-07-2019

Interview with Jan Joaquim (pseudonym), former 32 Battalion soldier, Centurion, 11-07-2019.

Telephone interview with Kevin Kambinda (pseudonym), former 32 Battalion soldier, Centurion, 21-07-2019

Telephone interview with Liam Lawindo (pseudonym), son of former 32 Battalion soldier; Kimbo and Pomfret resident, Centurion, 28-07-2019.

Conference papers and discussions

Panel discussion, *7th War & Society in Africa Conference: The War for Southern Africa; a quinquagenerial reflection*. Stellenbosch, 2016

Newspaper articles

Anon., 'Mass assaults, rapes: SADF denies ANC claims' in *The Star*, 10 April 1992

Anon., 'Phola Park: SADF to hold an inquiry' in *The Citizen*, 11 April 1992

Anon., 'Phola Park Raid' in *Sunday Times*, 12 April 1992

Anon., 'South Africa's secret war of terror' in *The Guardian*, 29 January 1981

Editor, 'Wet erken godsdiensbeswaar teen diensplig' in *Die Hervormer*, September 1984

Janssen, E., 'Why was SADF in Phola Park?' in *Pretoria News*, 10 April 1992

Nyaka, S., 'Reliving the nightmare of 32 Battalion raid' in *The Sunday Star*, 12 April 1992

Steele, J., 'Defector describes SA raids into Angola' in *The Guardian*, 2 February 1980

Internet sources

http://www.inflation.eu/inflation-rates/portugal/historic-inflation/cpi-inflation-portugal.aspx [Accessed 2018-07-06]

http://www.inflation.eu/inflation-rates/south-africa/historic-inflation/cpi-inflation-south-africa.aspx [Accessed 2018-06-26]

http://www.military-today.com/artillery/valkiri.htm [Accessed 07.10.2018]